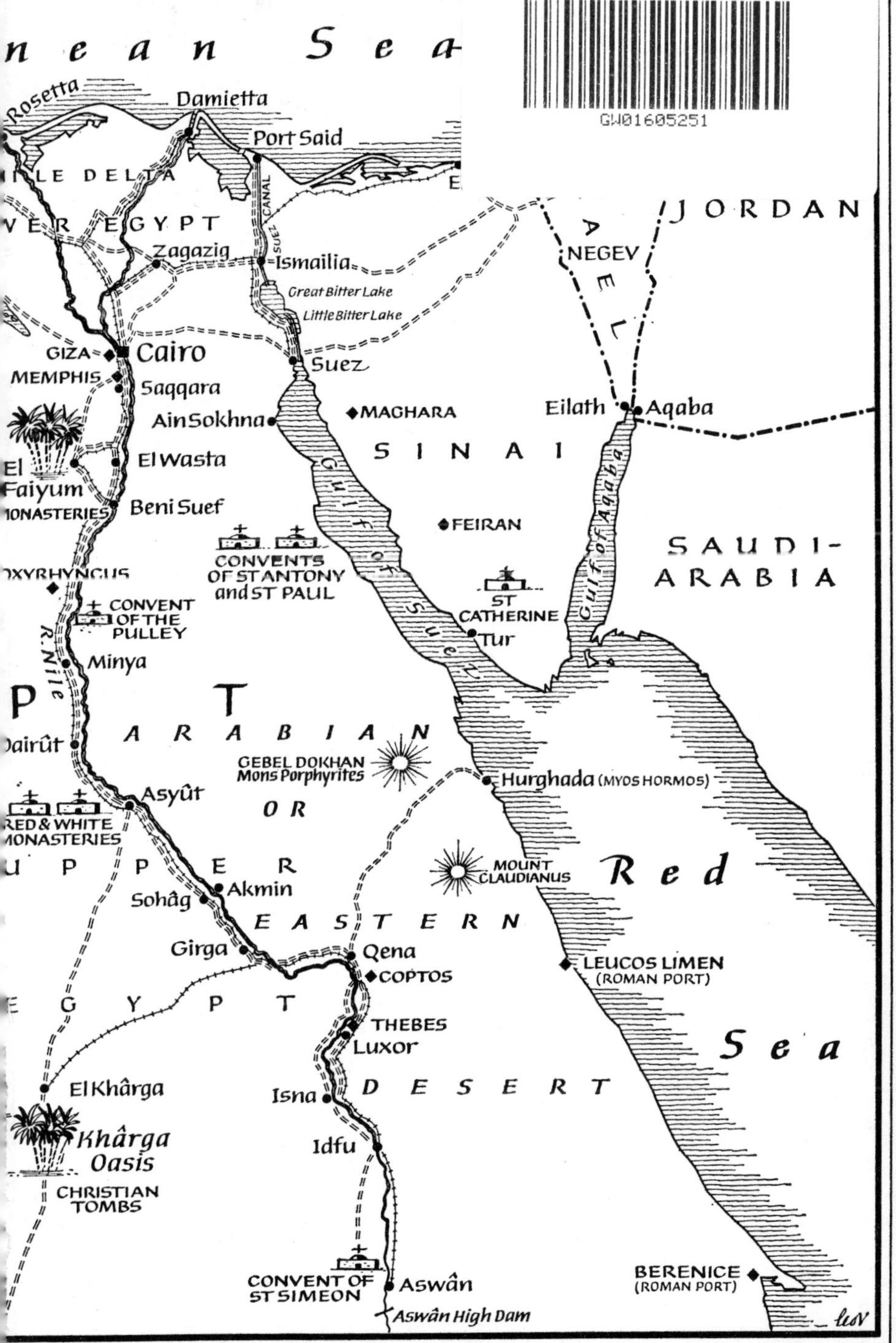

nean Sea
Rosetta
Damietta
Port Said
NILE DELTA
LOWER EGYPT
SUEZ CANAL
Zagazig
Ismailia
Great Bitter Lake
Little Bitter Lake
GIZA
Cairo
Suez
MEMPHIS
Saqqara
Ain Sokhna
MAGHARA
El Wasta
El Faiyum
MONASTERIES
Beni Suef
OXYRHYNCUS
CONVENTS OF ST ANTONY and ST PAUL
CONVENT OF THE PULLEY
R. Nile
Minya
Dairût
Asyût
RED & WHITE MONASTERIES
Akmin
Sohâg
Girga
Qena
COPTOS
THEBES
Luxor
Isna
Idfu
El Khârga
Khârga Oasis
CHRISTIAN TOMBS
CONVENT OF ST SIMEON
Aswân
Aswân High Dam
ARABIAN OR EASTERN DESERT
UPPER EGYPT
GEBEL DOKHAN
Mons Porphyrites
MOUNT CLAUDIANUS
Hurghada (MYOS HORMOS)
LEUCOS LIMEN (ROMAN PORT)
BERENICE (ROMAN PORT)
SINAI
FEIRAN
ST CATHERINE
Tur
Gulf of Suez
Gulf of Aqaba
Eilath
Aqaba
NEGEV
ISRAEL
JORDAN
SAUDI-ARABIA
Red Sea

DESERT PILGRIMAGE

BOOKS BY JAMES WELLARD

FICTION

Snake in the Grass
A Moment in Time
Journey to a High Mountain
Woman Returning
Deep Is the Night
Night in Babylon
Summer at the Castle
Action of the Tiger
Memoirs of a Cross-Eyed Man
Conversations with a Witch
The Affair in Arcady
A Sound of Trumpets
A Man and His Journey
You with the Roses—What are You Selling?
The Sun-Gazers

NON-FICTION

Understanding the English
General George S. Patton
The Ancient Way
The Great Sahara
Lost Worlds of Africa
Looking at Italy

St. Matthew and St. Mark from a seventeenth-century Ethiopian MS, reproduced by courtesy of the British Museum

JAMES WELLARD

Desert Pilgrimage

Journeys to the Egyptian and Sinai Deserts: completing the third of the trilogy of Saharan explorations

HUTCHINSON OF LONDON

HUTCHINSON & CO *(Publishers)* LTD
178–202 Great Portland Street, London W1

London Melbourne Sydney
Auckland Bombay Toronto
Johannesburg New York

First published 1970

This book has been set in Imprint, printed in Great Britain on Antique Wove paper by Anchor Press, and bound by Wm. Brendon, both of Tiptree, Essex

ISBN 0 09 101760 2

Contents

Illustrations

Preface

My two previous books *The Great Sahara* and *Lost Worlds of Africa* did not include an account of the Egyptian deserts, even though these regions are geophysically part of the Sahara which I set out to describe as an historical and cultural unity. On the other hand, neither the history nor the culture of Egypt is Saharan, nor does the story of its sand seas have much in common with the rest of the Great Desert. In fact, when we think of Egypt we think of the Nile, the Pharaonic civilisation, and the subsequent invasions and occupations. The Egyptian deserts, though comprising over four-fifths of the land mass, seem, in contrast, to have excited little interest.

Consequently, despite the vast literature on the subject of Egypt in general and of the Pharaohs in particular, the country's deserts have been neglected except by a handful of professional geographers and explorers. The probable reason for this is that these empty spaces remained among the last regions on earth to be systematically surveyed and charted. The location and very existence of the large and important oasis of Dakhla in the Western Desert, for instance, though frequently mentioned in Egyptian, Roman, and Arab records, was completely unknown until Sir Archibald Edmonstone reached it in 1819 and found there abundant evidence of ancient temples and tombs, both pagan and Christian.[1] Even 100 years later geographers were still compiling their maps of the desert 'from native information' and placing legendary cases according to estimates given in terms of caravan marches. About the same time, a group of British surveyors and archaeologists (including a young archaeology student called T. E. Lawrence) were exploring the deserts of the Sinai Peninsula where they discovered cities which had scarcely been seen by Europeans since the reign of the emperor Justinian. And the third desert with which we are concerned, the Arabian or Eastern Desert, was almost wholly ignored until well into the twentieth century, although it had been one of the busiest regions of Egypt during both the Pharaonic and Roman periods. In contrast, by 1910 most of the 3,500,000 square miles of the Sahara proper had been largely penetrated and surveyed. Timbuktu, the most mysterious city of Africa, if not of the world, during the eighteenth century, had been reached by the British explorer Major Laing in 1826. Yet no European had visited the equally mysterious Kufra Oases in the Libyan Desert until 1879, when the German Gerhard Rohlfs nearly lost his life there; and no other European reached Kufra until 1920, when Rosita Forbes made the journey from Benghazi via the oases of Jedebia, Aujela, and Jalo. Incidentally, Mrs. Forbes's book is still the best English account we have of Kufra, since Rohlfs's book, written in German and published in Leipzig in 1881, has never been translated.[2]

Yet Egypt itself has always been one of the world's most visited countries, for even the earliest travellers, like the Greek historian Herodotus, were irresistibly drawn to this cradle of civilisation. Herodotus, of course, had a 'modern' interest in the Egypt of the Pharaohs, whose monuments remained the principal attraction of that country throughout the classical period, as they remain today. But at the end of the Greco-Roman Age the interest in and knowledge of Pharaonic Egypt waned, and medieval travellers, for instance, restrict their accounts of pilgrimages to holy places like Sinai. Today the majority of tourists to Egypt are content to follow the age-old routes up and down the Nile, limiting their sightseeing to the famous temples and pyramids, which can now be reached with the minimum of effort and discomfort. Most of these travellers probably never realise that beyond the green belt of the river, both on the west towards Libya and on the east towards Arabia and north towards Palestine, lies an Egypt which has influenced the course of history far more than the Pharaohs.

One reason for this ignorance is that travel in the Egyptian deserts has only become convenient within the last twenty years or so. Before the Second World War some 370,000 square miles of Egypt were *terra incognita*, crossed only by camel caravans on their way to the 'lost' oases. Some idea of the bewilderment of the Englishman fifty years ago when he found himself in an Egyptian desert—though only a few miles from the Mediterranean Sea—will be found in the account of the crew of a British warship, H.M.S. *Tara*, torpedoed on the 5th November, 1915, by a German submarine eight miles off Solum on the Libyan coast. The ninety-two survivors were marched off into the desert as prisoners of the Senoussi, and from the reaction of these English sailors they might have been landed on the moon or transplanted 2,000 years back through time.[3] In a sense they were, because they were actually in country which belongs much more to ancient than it does to modern history. Greek colonists had built splendid cities along this coast, Roman legions had marched past on well-paved highways, and Christian pilgrims had tramped along trails to the cities, shrines, and monasteries in the desert where the crew of H.M.S. *Tara* were now so hopelessly lost. But understandably these British tars had not the slightest idea of all this history.

Even the professional historians and geographers did not know the whereabouts of a religious centre the size of the City of St. Menas, completely lost until the German archaeologist Monsignor Carl Maria Kaufmann finally located the site in 1905. And until Kaufmann had actually excavated the cathedral, churches, monastery, baths, inns, cemeteries, and kilns in which the famous Menas flasks were made, the very existence of a large Christian city was doubtful, so unexplored was the desert less than fifty miles from Alexandria. Even now St. Menas has its mysteries, for ancient writers refer to it as a 'little paradise' occupied by villas, farms, and gardens producing a good wine, many fruit trees, and the papyrus plant. The abundance of water is attested by the numerous cisterns and baths as well as by the sacred spring from which tens of thousands of pilgrims throughout the fourth and fifth centuries filled their clay flasks. Yet today no water of any sort is found in this region, even though there has been no particular change in the actual climate over the last 2,000 years.

The City of St. Menas was not found until 1905. Fifteen years later Rosita Forbes made her historic journey to Kufra, travelling 500 miles across a waterless desert by camel—a journey which can now be made in three hours by aeroplane. And it was not until 1925 that the monasteries of the Wadi Natrun were properly studied and surveyed by professional archaeologists.

Even in 1935, when mechanised transport capable of crossing desert terrain had been developed, explorers were still talking of 'lost oases', some of which they actually found, some of which they concluded existed only in the imagination of the Bedouin. Two of them, Gebabo and Tazerbo, were discovered in the 1879 expedition of Gerhard Rohlfs; one, Ribina, by Rosita Forbes and Hassanein Bey in 1921; and two more by Hassanein Bey in 1923. There remained two others, Arkenu and Ouenat, still awaiting discovery, and an oasis called Zerzura, 'abounding in palms, with springs, and some ruins of uncertain date', which has never been located; and a place called the 'Egyptian Oasis', seven to ten days from the Dakhla Oasis, consisting, according to Bedouin reports, of a large plantation of olive and palm trees and a big ruined town no longer inhabited. Such settlements with their reputation for containing buried treasure may not exist at all, except in the folklore of the tribes, but with the desert one can never tell. For that matter, we cannot affirm or deny the existence of several 'lost islands' to the west of Alexandria, mentioned by the geographer Strabo, but now apparently somewhere below the surface of the sea. The discovery of Strabo's Pedonia and Aenesipasta is presumably a job for underwater exploration.

Today, while there is scarcely any part of the Egyptian deserts which the traveller cannot reach in reasonable comfort, very few tourists feel the urge to go to all the trouble involved. There is more than enough to see from Cairo, Luxor, and Aswan during a fortnight's tour. Apart from the oasis of Fayyum, the

Red Sea resorts of Ein Sokhna and Hurghada, and the monastery of St. Catherine on the Sinai Peninsula, the desert does not seem worth the time and effort to visit, though we find the old and more leisurely travellers of the first half of the twentieth century setting off across the wastelands both to the west and east of the Nile as part of their Grand Tour. The absence of paved roads and motor cars obviously made their expeditions more adventurous, for in those days, and for that matter within living memory, the desert was still an untouched world, so that a traveller to the monasteries of the Wadi Natrun in the Western Desert could write of seeing gazelle, ostrich, wild boar, duck, and immense flocks of birds. Today he will be lucky if he sees a single bird.

For all these animals have gone; gone, even, the camels which transported the travellers and their campaign chests from the Nile to the desert outposts. The journey today is a far more prosaic affair: a ticket on a bus, a sandwich *en route*, a few hours along a concrete desert, and arrival at a rest station where one can hire a battered jeep in which to cross the sand to the high-walled citadels which were built 1,500 years ago to keep out an enemy who no longer exists. For though the Bedouin have not disappeared with the wild animals, their banditry has ended.

What, then, is the attraction of the desert and these desert places? It is, I think, that here one can catch a glimpse of history that is not given much, if any, space in the textbooks, since professional historians tend to derive their facts and opinions from more sophisticated sources of information—the writings of other scholars, the records of archives, the monuments of kings, and so forth. The desert, in contrast, and the men who have lived or travelled in it, remains secretive, or too obscure to bother about. Consequently the Roman camps built for the quarrymen on the slopes of Mons Porphyrites in the Eastern Desert, the ruins of the Christian monasteries in the Libyan Desert, the 'lost oases', and the wayside stations set up by Thomas Waghorn for his Overland Route to India are seldom mentioned in the formal histories of Egypt. Yet how much these monuments tell us about the other side of history, the side of those 'non-historical' events and people who influenced the course of our lives far more than we realise!

My journeys to the deserts were made under some difficulties as a result of the seemingly interminable dissensions of the Middle East, whence I was prevented from visiting several of the sites I particularly wanted to explore, notably in the Arabian Desert and Eastern Sinai, both under strict military surveillance. One of the curses of modern civilisation is an obsession with spying, the obsession which ensures that some regulation will hinder the footsteps of every traveller who wishes to wander from the main tourist routes. It is all right to go to see the temples of Karnak, nothing to spy on there; but the Roman porphyry quarries of the Djebel Dokhan are forbidden, though there is nothing *there* but the ruins of the miners' towns, temples, and the roads along which the great blocks of porphyry were carried to the Nile.

However, the civilian officials and others with whom I discussed my project and later worked were most co-operative and did all they could to help me at a difficult period in Israeli–Egyptian relations. I wish, therefore, to express my grateful thanks to Messrs. Mahboub and Alfarargi of the Egyptian Embassy, London; to Mr. Saad Saker and Dr. Shakr of the Department of Education, Cairo; to Miss Sophie George Zaki and Bishop Samuel of the Coptic Patriarchate in Cairo; to the Patriarch, Kirellos VI; to the Archpriest, the Rev. Timotheus el Moharraqi of Alexandria; and to all those monks, priests, and laymen who entertained me so kindly in the Coptic monasteries. Concurrently I record my sincere thanks to the Israeli officials and scholars, both in London and Jerusalem, who helped me during my journey to Israel and the Sinai Peninsula.

My research was done in the Reading Room of the British Museum which provided the many books I required, the most important of which are listed, with acknowledgments, in the bibliography at the end of this volume.

REFERENCES

1 Sir Archibald Edmonstone, *Journey to Two of the Oases of Upper Egypt* (1822).

2 *Reise Von Tripolis nach der Oase Kufra* (1881).

3 See Captain R. Gwatkin Williams, *In the Hands of the Senoussi* (1916), one of the most curious prisoner-of-war stories from the First World War.

1 From the Red Sea to the Nile

The total area of Egypt is some 386,000 square miles, of which over 90 per cent is desert. The desert to the west of the Nile, the Libyan, or Western, Desert, is one of the most arid regions on earth; the desert to the east, the Arabian, or Eastern, one of the most forbidding; and that of Sinai one of the most inhospitable.

The Nile Valley, in contrast, though only 750 miles long and never more than fourteen miles wide, has always been fertile enough to support an enormous population as far back as the dawn of history. It was here that the world's first great civilisation arose, whence it is inevitable that we identify Egypt with the Nile and not with its deserts. Consequently the deserts get little attention in the formal histories, even though they have played a more significant role in the development of Western culture than the river—a controversial statement perhaps, and one that the Egyptologists might not be prepared to admit. For, it can be asked, what have these enormous wastelands to do with the historical process as we know it?

True, certain rather obvious facts spring to mind concerning the part the desert has played in the early history of man. One has only to travel, for instance, in that region of the south-central Sahara called the Ténéré to find this out. The Ténéré is one of the most waterless deserts on earth, 10,000 square miles in area, where on the caravan route between Agadez and Bilma grows a single tree beside a well—the famous *Arbre du Ténéré*, dramatically marked on the maps as the name of a place, like London or Paris on the maps of Europe. One can cross this desert and find mollusc shells, arrow-heads, and fish-hooks by the basketful, proving that the Ténéré, 15,000 years or so ago, was an inland sea on whose shores our ancestors began that conquest of the earth of which we are so proud today.

So this much can be said of the deserts, including those of Egypt: there is something there other than sand, camels, and palm trees; they reveal certain secrets to those who have eyes to see; they even provide evidence that they were the nurseries of civilisation when most of Europe was covered with ice and snow. The men and animals who inhabited them have left their traces behind, even though whole races have disappeared—fishers, hunters, cattle-herders, agriculturists, and even the builders of cities; and with their disappearance, some fifteen millennia ago, the African deserts disappeared if not from history, then from the history books.

But this ignorance of the wastelands, and in particular of the Sahara and its contingent deserts, is a modern phenomenon. It was not true of the ancient world. Thus the Pharaohs, once they felt secure and strong enough in the Nile Valley, began to explore and reoccupy the deserts in their quest for raw materials and trade routes. As early as 2600 B.C. during the Fourth Dynasty the Egyptians had crossed into the Sinai Peninsula looking for iron ore, copper, and turquoise. Their turquoise mines, in fact, are still there, at Maghara, about 200 feet up in the sandstone cliffs. It was at this site that Flinders Petrie worked from December 10th, 1905, to January 11th, 1906, to save what was left of the ancient monuments which were being systematically destroyed by an English mining company.

> When we reached the Valley [he writes] we found that most of the monuments previously known had been destroyed or injured three years before. A company had been formed which had taken out of the hands of the Natives their ancient resource of turquoise hunting, in order to 'develop' it for the benefit of English shareholders. Everything gave way to the greed for dividends, with the result that the promoters lost their money, the natives lost their turquoises, and the world lost many of its most ancient monuments . . . Ignorant engineers destroyed what was, in the European

market of museums, worth far more than all the turquoises which they extracted.[1]

Flinders Petrie then lists the pharaonic inscriptions, scenes, tablets, and portraits which had been destroyed—'brutally bashed about with a hammer'—and he concludes:

> The Goths, who protected and preserved the monuments of Rome, were cultivated in comparison with the dividend-hunting Englishman.

The recorded history of Sinai, then, begins with the exploitation of the copper and turquoise mines whose original workings can still be seen inside the cliffs of Maghara and of Serabit. A comparable exploitation of precious minerals took place in the other Egyptian deserts from the Fourth Dynasty to the Arab invasion—that is, from 2600 B.C. to A.D. 641, so that during these three millennia the wastelands beyond the Nile were closely integrated into the military and commercial life of the old empires. In contrast, from the seventh to the nineteenth century of our era most of the Sahara, including the Egyptian extensions of it, was abandoned, except for the oases and the caravan routes used by the slave-traders. For well over a thousand years, in fact, the Great Desert was *terra incognita* to Europe, so that it is not surprising to read that Major James Rennell, the greatest of eighteenth-century geographers, 'has endeavoured to ascertain the sites [of the Egyptian oases] by calculation, but he allows that he goes upon mere conjecture'. This is no slight upon Rennell, however, since considerable areas of the Sahara are still unknown and uncharted to this day. Yet exploitation on the classical scale is beginning again due to the discovery of oil, which might be compared to the discovery of gold by the ancients; and it would not be rash to predict that the deserts in a few more decades will be as populated and productive as they were in Roman times—and for the same reasons: namely, for their mines, quarries, oil, and vast natural resources, including, one hopes, agriculture.

The problem that faced the administrators of the empires of Egypt and Rome as to how to exploit the desert was not one of machines or labour, as it is with us. Slavery answered both requirements, particularly in the working of the mines and quarries and the building of roads, forts, wells, and workmen's camps. The problem was crossing the sand seas without suitable means of transport, as Cambyses's generals had found in their disastrous attempt to march from Thebes to the oasis of Siwa; and the Romans, in their turn, found in their occasional excursions into the Sahara proper. The fact is that the camel had not been introduced into Africa by the beginning of our era, so that horses, donkeys, and oxen had to be used for transport, and while these animals were adequate for short journeys between wells, they severely restricted the operation of armies and caravans. Consequently all the grandiose military expeditions of the Egyptian, Persian, and Roman conquerors, if they were not doomed to failure, succeeded only at an enormous cost in men and animals, as many of the punitive expeditions of the British and French colonial armies during the nineteenth century barely succeeded in their missions. The Arab invaders of the seventh and eighth centuries, on the other hand, moving in small units of camel-cavalry, conquered the whole of North Africa and criss-crossed the whole of the Sahara Desert with comparatively few losses.

However, the Egyptian kings and Roman emperors who sent off expeditions across the deserts were not concerned with suffering or loss of life, in particular the lives of peasant conscripts who constituted the rank and file of the army and of the slaves who were always regarded as expendable. An inexhaustible supply of captives soon made possible the exploitation of the turquoise and copper mines of Sinai and the gold and emerald mines of the Eastern Desert, once the military had subdued the barbarian nomads who roamed these outlandish places. All that was now needed was the construction of roads, forts, and camps for the working of the mines and quarries—forts to guard the roads and wells, stables for post horses, stalls for cattle, and bare stone huts for the workmen. Yes, and a temple. The Egyptians, like the Romans, never took any chances of offending the gods.

The result was that the Eastern, or Arabian, Desert, during

the Pharaonic and Roman periods, was the most highly industrialised region of Egypt—a region of vast mining operations, main east-west highways, and important trade routes. The Eastern Desert, in any case, was the ancient land bridge between the East and the West, and it remained so until the Portuguese discovered the sea route to India via the Cape in 1487.

In ancient times there were three main roads that led from the Red Sea to the Nile. One ran from the port of Berenice to Coptos on the Nile, and its ten stations are mentioned in the Itinerary of Antoninus: Caenon Hydreuma, Cabalsi, Apollon, Phalacro, Aristonis, Jovis, Compasi, Aphrodito, Didyme, and Phoenicon. The ruins of some of these stations can still be seen—the broken walls of a fort, a few stone huts, a deep well, cisterns, and occasionally a small temple. The wells and cisterns are frequently cut into solid rock and were once covered by awnings supported on pillars of masonry.

This Berenice-Coptos highway was about 271 miles long, with a staging-post about every twenty-five miles, this being a good day's march in the desert. As usual, the Romans had worked out their distances according to strict military routine. The highway was known as the Emerald Road, as it passed close to the emerald mines which were first worked by the Pharaohs, then successively by Romans, Arabs, and Turks. The shafts run several hundred yards into the mountain on the side of which survives the miners' village with a little temple excavated out of the rock.

The second trans-desert road went from the ancient port of Leukos Limen, now silted up, again to Coptos, and this road was policed from eight stations about twelve miles equidistant from each other. It was used principally to bring granite from the mines near the Wadi Hammamet. The names of a score of Egyptian kings and conquerors are carved on the mountainside, recording their passage along this road, or events of their reign.

The third and most northerly of the three roads across the Eastern Desert runs from the abandoned port of Myos Hormos, also silted up with sand, but once the principal harbour of the Red Sea. This was the Porphyry Road which bypassed the enormous Roman quarries on Mons Porphyrites, or Djebel Dokhan as the mountain is called today.

The existence of these three Red Sea ports and the well-policed highways connecting them with the Nile is proof of the importance of the commerce between the Far East and the West, since nothing but valuable cargoes would have persuaded the old shipmasters to risk the dangerous reefs and shoals of the Red Sea coast, not to mention a prevailing north wind against which the shallow-draught vessels had to beat for hundreds of miles. And the ruins of Roman forts all along the three highways from the Red Sea to the Nile are additional evidence of the importance of the caravan trade across the desert. In other words, what with the network of roads, the forts and look-out stations, and the strategically placed wells, the Eastern Desert was a busy place up to the coming of the Arabs in A.D. 640. If there were any doubt about this, the tariff of taxes imposed on persons using the road during the Roman occupation is sufficient proof of the commerce between the Red Sea and the Nile. The tariff was found inscribed in a ruined guardhouse just behind old Coptos (modern Kobt) at the beginning of the highway. It reads:

BY ORDER OF THE GOVERNOR OF EGYPT

The dues which the operators of the Transport Service are authorised to levy are inscribed on this tablet by order of L. Antistius Asiaticus, Prefect of the Red Sea Highway.

For a Red Sea helmsman	*drachmas	8
,, ,, ,, ,, pilot	,,	10
,, an able seaman	,,	5
,, a shipyard hand	,,	5
,, a skilled shipwright	,,	8
,, a woman for prostitution	,,	108
,, a woman immigrant	,,	30
,, a wife of a soldier	,,	20

* The value of the drachma at this time was probably about an English shilling.

As well as being one of the most important highways of the ancient world, the Eastern Desert was intensively exploited for its minerals from the time of the First Dynasty (3200–2270 B.C.) until the fall of Egypt to the Arabs in A.D. 640. The most prized of these minerals was gold, found in such abundance that we find the King of a North Syrian state writing to Amenhotep III in 1550 B.C.

> Let my brother send gold in very large quantities, without measure, and let him send more gold to me than he did to my father; for in my brother's land gold is as common as dust.

King Solomon, too, may have worked his mines in this desert (if the Ophir of the Bible is located here). At all events, his emissaries brought back 420 talents, or over ten tons, of gold. It seems a great deal until one remembers that these gold mines filled the treasuries of the Persian, Greek, and Roman emperors, as well as those of the Pharaohs, for about 4,000 years. The mines have been worked off and on ever since, but they have not proved commercially profitable in recent years because of the problem of labour; the lack of water, supplied in olden times by convoys of carts and donkeys shuttling back and forth between the wells; and poor communications with both the Nile Valley and the Red Sea, despite the excellent road system built up by the Romans, then abandoned after the Arab invasion.

No industrial enterprise exemplifies the thoroughness and efficiency of the Romans more than their exploitation of the porphyry mines of the Eastern Desert. How did they, in fact, find the veins of the noble red stone (called porphyry on account of its purplish hue) on the ridge of a mountain 4,000 feet high amid a wilderness of fallen rocks? The answer must be that their armies were accompanied by geologists as well as geographers, as Napoleon's Egyptian Expedition was accompanied by a corps of men of science. Not that the Romans were interested in geology, except as a method for spotting valuable minerals, particularly marble, of which the imperial cities needed an inexhaustible supply. But the discovery of the Porphyry Mountain in the Eastern Desert led, within a few years, to the establishment of a colony of several thousand slave-labourers, all supplied from bases 100 miles away across a waterless wasteland. The extent of the Romans' activity is evidenced by the roads and paths which wind all over the mountain, including special slides for the blocks of porphyry, with pillars or cairns about every ten yards for easing the columns by ropes down a gradient of 1 in 2¼.

Because of its colour, porphyry, from the time of its discovery, was declared to be a monopoly of the emperors, and the quarries of Djebel Dokhan were worked only by and for the state. The early emperors seem to have guarded their monopoly most carefully, and even though their gangs of slaves quarried far more of the rock than was needed for the imperial palaces, the excess production was stored in warehouses in Rome and Alexandria for future use. Lapidaries and artists (Greek, of course) were employed to sculpt the stone into pillars, busts, and full-length statues, although the material is so hard that it is not really suitable for sculpture. In fact, it is not at all clear how the ancients worked the rock in view of their limited cutting tools. But work it they did, for a number of important statues from the Roman period are still extant, as well as many columns and wall linings in the Pantheon, the Temple of Venus, the Baths of Caracalla, the Palace of the Caesars, and the great Basilica of Constantine. It is said that there are at least 300 monolith porphyry pillars still preserved in the churches and cathedrals of Europe, nearly all of them dating from the Roman period, since the quarries of the Eastern Desert were lost altogether after the Arab invasion of Egypt in A.D. 639. Yet so much porphyry was quarried between A.D. 50 and A.D. 400 that thousands of tons of the rock sculpted into columns, pavements, sarcophagi, and stairways are found from the Atlantic to the Mediterranean. The plaques and pavement of the early royal tombs in Westminster Abbey are of porphyry, as is the baptismal font in St. Peter's. The latter piece, an oval thirteen feet long and six feet broad, was originally the lid of a sarcophagus, the whole of which must have weighed over twenty tons, cut from one solid block.

Tens of thousands of men must have died in the Red Sea deserts to produce these architectural adornments of pagan and Christian temples, killed by heat exhaustion in the summer and by exposure in the winter. It was taken for granted that men, women and children condemned to the quarries of the Porphyry Mountain would die within a few years, to be replaced by the endless supply of prisoners of war, slaves, and political suspects.

We get a glimpse of the conditions under which the miners and quarrymen worked from pagan and Christian writers of the Roman period—the latter being particularly concerned, since Christians were condemned in great numbers to this most dreaded form of servitude. The historian Diodorus of Sicily gave a description of the gold mines of the Eastern Desert. The miners wore a lamp tied to their forehead. The lamp was lit by crude petroleum, discovered as early as 2000 B.C. by the Egyptians in the Djebel Zeit (the Mons Petrolius of the Romans on the western shore of the Gulf of Suez) where the oil floats on the surface of lagoons or seeps into fissures in the rock. This petroleum, a thick dark-brown oil which burns well even in its crude form, was undoubtedly used in the miners' lamps, enabling them to work underground in the galleries. A long line of children carried the ore to the surface in bags slung over their backs; slaves pounded it in mortars with iron pestles; and the rubble was then fed into grinding mills worked by old men and women. The powdered ore was next washed on inclined tables, and the residue containing the gold was then crushed into powder and refined in crucibles.

In their day the Egyptians relied principally on local slave labour for working their gold and emerald mines, and for this purpose periodically rounded up the tribesmen who lived along the shores of the Red Sea. The Greek geographer Agatharchides describes these natives in 100 B.C. as possessing neither boats nor nets, though they lived principally on fish stranded on the shore. They also went about naked, dwelt in caves or under piles of seaweed. It seems to be an accurate description of a primitive people, typical of the scientific attitude of a Greek scholar, just as Pliny's description is typical of a Roman; for Pliny has these Ichthyophagi 'deprived, without exception, of their right testicle, savages who pull out their front teeth in order not to resemble donkeys'. Is the old Roman pulling our leg? On the other hand, his statement that these primitives 'possess no idea of good or evil and show a remarkable indifference to danger or pain' was no doubt correct and explains why, from the Egyptians' point of view, they made such excellent workers in the mines. Civilised men, on the other hand, hardly lasted long enough to make their transport across the Eastern Desert worth while.

For what these miners and quarrymen must have suffered no words can tell: in the winter they must have often frozen to death at night, and in the summer almost literally burnt to death by day. The rocks are so hot that they cannot be touched by the bare hand and a ring on the finger will blister the surrounding flesh. Walking brings a white lather to the lips and one is blinded by sweat pouring into the eyes. Yet both the Egyptians and the Romans kept their mines working throughout the entire year, using up in the process thousands of slaves, men, women, and children.

> Bound in fetters, they work continually, without being admitted any rest day or night . . . No care at all is taken of the bodies of these poor creatures, so that they have not a rag so much as to cover their nakedness. For though they are sick, maimed, or lame, no rest, no intermission in the least is allowed them . . . but all are driven to work with blows and cudgelling till at length, overborne with the intolerable weight of their misery, they drop down dead in the midst of their labours.[2]

The reason for this non-stop operation was the increasing demand for precious metals and ornamental stones—gold from the mines at Djebel Olaki, emeralds from Djebel Zabara, turquoises from the mountains west of Qoseir, red porphyry from the quarries at Dokhan, granite from Mount Claudianus, iron from a half a dozen valleys deep in the desert, and alabaster from elsewhere.

All of this vast industry required an organisation and administration which must have taxed the ingenuity of even the Romans. There were thousands of miners to be fed and watered, most of them working in the inaccessible mountain ranges. Enormous caravans of bullock-drawn carts, donkeys, and porters set out regularly to provision the mining camps and to bring back the gold, precious stones, and blocks of granite or porphyry. These caravans sometimes left a record of their expeditions on the rock faces, much as armies have done ever since. The names of chief architects, master builders, assistant artisans, scribes, treasurers, ship captains, and their families who were stationed at the quarries can still be read along the Wadi Hammamat. In 2400 B.C. the Pharaoh Imhotep sent his son Zati with 1,000 slave-labourers, 100 quarrymen, and 1,200 soldiers to obtain stone for his pyramid and despatched 50 oxen and 200 donkeys every day to provision the expedition. A thousand years later Rameses IV sent an expedition of 8,362 men, not including (as the inscription on the rock states) the 900 who perished from fatigue, hunger, disease, or exposure. Among the original 9,260 men were 200 Egyptian and 800 foreign slaves who worked under the direction of a chief artificer, three master quarrymen, and 130 stone-cutters. Such was the scale on which the Egyptians exploited the Eastern Desert.

The Romans, with their unsurpassed organisation, systematised the trans-desert trade as no one has done before or since. They had, as their ruins all over Africa and Europe testify, a lordly disdain for the difficulties of terrain. Hence the lack of water did not prevent them from setting up their forts and watch-towers at regular intervals across the Arabian Desert. If water could not be found by drilling wells it was brought in by supply trains and stored in reservoirs. But wells were dug with a determination which strikes one as almost fanatical. For the quarries on Djebel Dokhan a well fifteen feet in diameter and over sixty feet in depth was sunk through the solid porphyry rock. In fact, these Roman wells and reservoirs continued to be used all over North Africa for the next 1,600 years, and some of them are still in use today.

But perhaps the most interesting period in the history of the Egyptian deserts is the period of their Christianisation which lasted from the fourth to the seventh centuries, though there is very little material evidence left today to show that such a conversion actually took place. But it is certain that there was during this period a flourishing confederation of Christian communities which extended from the Western or Libyan Desert through the Eastern or Arabian Desert across the Gulf of Suez to the Sinai Peninsula and thence north and east to the confines of Asia proper. This commonwealth, which co-existed, as it were, side by side with the military-commercial empire of the Romans, began in the most desolate regions of the Egyptian deserts to which the first hermits had withdrawn during the persecutions of Diocletian. We know that in the Western Desert, for instance, religious communities quickly sprang up around the cells of Desert Fathers like Macarius, while in the Eastern Desert a comparable development occurred near the hermitage of St. Antony; and similarly all over Sinai and the Negev. The process was always the same: first the arrival of a hermit seeking solitude; then the coming of disciples who set up their hermitages nearby; then the visitation of pilgrims, some of whom stayed as admirers and converts of the original holy man; then the erection of a chapel, with refectory attached for the Sunday service and the *agape* to follow; then the development of hostels and other facilities for pilgrims; and eventually the emergence of a settled community centred around a monastery and its outlying hermitages.

In order to maintain such a community it became necessary to cultivate the surrounding countryside, even where it was desert. And this was done with extraordinary success, particularly in the Libyan Desert at a place called the City of St. Menas[3] and in southern Palestine in the arid region of the Negev. Thus, areas which today produce nothing but desert weeds were during the sixth and seventh centuries veritable Gardens of Eden, covered with fields of grain, orchards, olive groves, and vineyards. Sizable cities grew up around large monasteries, cities like Isbeita, Eboda, and Auja, first explored by the surveyors of the Palestine Exploration Fund not much more than fifty years ago. The whole area of the Negev, in fact, which until the Israeli redeveloped it supported only a few hundred Arab nomads and their flocks, was during the Christian period a land of monasteries, cathedrals, towns, villages, and farms, boasting a population of tens of thousands of industrious, prosperous, and God-fearing citizens. And all this was achieved without military conquest and the subjugation of the aboriginal population. It was achieved, too, without the use of forced labour such as the Egyptians and the Romans employed in their exploitation of the desert. It was, in short, the prototype of the Christian commonwealth which lingered on in Europe in the great monasteries and their estates and which has reappeared from time to time in the religious communities based on a communistic social and economic system. These latter-day communities, without exception, have collapsed or been destroyed by the hostility of conventional Christians who object to the introduction of religion into business; the early Christian settlements were more fortunate, since neither the state nor private business had any use for the deserts. The non-intervention of the usual exploiters, opportunists, and profiteers permitted the monastic communities to grow and extend their boundaries, allowing the monks, missionaries, and pilgrims to pass safely and easily from one centre to another. They now travelled west and south into the Sahara, south into Nubia and Ethiopia, and east as far as the coast of India. We read that the Syrian bishop Jacob Baradaeus, born about A.D. 490, wandered about throughout the Middle East between Persia and Egypt, on foot and garbed only in an old horse blanket, consecrating patriarchs, bishops, and priests to the number of a hundred thousand. The figure is, of course, exaggerated, but it implies, along with the extent of his travels, the strength in terms of population of this Christian commonwealth of the desert.

Why, then, did such a prosperous and well-organised spiritual empire collapse? The explanation is twofold: first, the leaders of the Church had become ambitious, arrogant, and contentious, and they soon set up rival establishments which not only split the West from the East, but fragmented the two resulting churches into a score of quarrelling sects. The classic schism was between the Catholics of the West and the Monophysites of the East. The ensuing wrangling was to make the realisation of the Christian World for ever afterwards unattainable. There was now very little brotherly love between Christians, but rather hostility and even hatred. Sectarianism, in turn, bred nationalism and, as we shall see, it was the nationalism of the Egyptian Christians, engendered by the enmity towards them of the Orthodox Catholics, that was largely responsible for the quick victory of the Arabs over the Byzantines, and the eventual defeat of Christianity throughout the Middle East and Africa.

The second destructive force was the loss of the primeval 'innocence' of the Early Christians and the growth of worldliness among their successors. 'Innocence' was manifested by these monks who possessed nothing but their cloak and sleeping mat; worldliness by the popes and bishops who now consorted with and lived like kings. The Desert Fathers believed implicitly in Christ's doctrine of love even to the extent of turning the other cheek. 'O athletes,' said the abbot Paul to his brothers when the Saracens were breaking down the door of the monastery tower, 'let not your souls be faint and do nothing unworthy of your cowl, but he clothed with strength and joy and manliness that you may endure with a pure heart and that God may receive you into his kingdom.' The priestly councillors of the emperors approved of and blessed the wars of conquest, apparently indifferent to the fact that the Christian armies were killing not merely pagans and infidels but Christians as well. So it was that Persia and Arabia, which by the sixth century were on the verge of becoming Christianised, were lost to the new gospel of love by the constant invasions and counter-invasions of those times, until it became impossible for non-Romans to equate Christianity with universal brotherhood. One assumes that the Buddhists and Shintoists of Japan must have reached the same conclusion when the Christians dropped their atom bombs on Hiroshima and Nagasaki. Doctrine and deeds seem irreconcilable.

And so the unusual and most interesting experiment in Christian fellowship ended in defeat, so total, it would seem, that few students even of Christianity are aware that there was once a thriving spiritual commonwealth in a region now regarded as empty desert. The physical remains are not impressive—certainly nothing to compare with the monuments of the Egyptians and of the Romans. Yet the commercial enterprises of both these peoples are of scant importance compared with the achievements of the Desert Fathers and of their disciples—the unknown hermits, ascetics, and monks whom the eighteenth- and nineteenth-century rationalists made it fashionable to deride. The truth of the matter is the Egyptian and Roman exploitation of the desert has had no effect whatsoever on the course of history; the occupation of the same wasteland by the early Christians has helped to determine the shape of Western civilisation.

It may be argued, of course, that these ideals and methods of primitive Christianity can no longer influence our world, since our culture is essentially secular and our economy essentially capitalist. In other words, it is no use extolling mysticism in a society where collective thinking frowns upon nonconformism; or, for that matter, to talk in terms of religious communities since the monastic system only survives, certainly in Protestant countries, as an appendage of medieval theocracy. In any case, Edward Gibbon seems to have had the last word on the subject in his famous description of the ascetics and mystics of the desert as:

> hideous, distorted, and emaciated maniacs, without knowledge, without patriotism, without affection, spending their lives in a long routine of useless and atrocious tortures and quailing before the ghastly phantoms of their delirious brains.

Gibbon's tremendous attack on the mystics and ascetics has dominated modern thinking to such an extent that the visionary, who was the most treasured member of religious and artistic society in the Middle Ages, is now the most despised. England, for instance, for a time the fountainhead of mysticism, has not produced a genuine mystic since William Blake, who seems to have been put away in the Bedlam madhouse for a period. We still equate the mystic with the lunatic; but it is only fair to give the view of a man who had seen these 'maniacs' at first hand and had, indeed, lived with them. Rufinus of Aquileia, traveller and translator, friend of St. Jerome, prefaces his *Historia Monachorum* with this account of his visit to the Egyptian deserts in A.D. 374:

> I have seen among them many Fathers that lived the life of heaven in the world . . . I have seen some of them so purged of all thought of suspicion of malice that they no more remembered that evil was still wrought upon the earth. They dwell dispersed throughout the desert and separate in their cells, but bound together by love. Quiet are they and gentle. They have indeed a great rivalry among them: it is who shall be more merciful than his brother, kinder, humbler, more patient . . .

REFERENCES

1 W. M. Flinders Petrie, *Researches in Sinai* (1906), pp. 46–7.
2 See *The Historical Library of Diodorus the Sicilian*, translated by G. Booth (1814), Book III, Chapter 1.
3 See Chapter 11.

2 To the Libyan Desert

The first journey I was about to take led to the borders of the Libyan Desert, to a valley called the Wadi Natrun, though with the usual confusion in the transcription of Arabic names into English, the place appears on maps and in books with a bewildering variety of spellings: e.g. Wadi Natroun, Wadi 'n Natrun, Wadi el Natrun, Wadi a'n Natrun, Wadi Natroon, and so on. The same valley was also formerly referred to as the Wadi el-Habin or 'Valley of Love'; and, if we want to go back as far as the Roman period, as Cellia (or Cellae) from the number of hermits' cells that studded it; or again, as Scete, the region of 'utter solitude'.

This Wadi Natrun is a dry river bed, possibly a western branch of the ancient Nile which today flows some forty miles to the east. For a long time there was a legend that the hulls of pharaonic ships lay buried in the sands of this valley, and Napoleon's scientists who were sent to survey the region looked, though in vain, for such interesting relics. But though there are no vestiges of ships and none of the life-giving waters of the Nile, there are six shallow lakes strung out along the valley—the famous natron lakes which formerly yielded 60,000 tons of salt and soda a year, requiring a bi-weekly caravan of 150 camels and 600 donkeys to transport the loads from the lakes to Cairo. But the natron industry is now abandoned, the camels and donkeys are gone; so is the light railway which replaced them; and so is the railway carriage used by the Empress Eugénie at the opening of the Suez Canal and bought by Mr. Hooker, British manager of the Wadi Natrun Salt and Soda Company. One wonders what happened to the railway carriage as well as to Mr. Hooker. Did he keep a diary during his sojourn in the Wadi Natrun? And if so, is it, like so many other historically valuable records, lying in some attic under the pile of souvenirs the manager of the Salt and Soda Company sent back from Egypt? But four of the Christian monasteries remain and there are still hermits living in their caves, so what one finds in the Wadi Natrun is not only a remnant of the world of the fourth century but four of the oldest and holiest shrines of Christendom—a region, in fact, which may have affected the course of Western history and the lives of men more than any other place outside Bethlehem.

The most extraordinary aspect of this valley is that the earliest description of it, that of St. Jerome writing as an eyewitness in A.D. 385, is still basically true today. St. Jerome says:

> The place is reached by no path, nor is the track shown by any landmarks on earth, but one journeys by the signs and courses of the stars. Water is hard to find. Here abide men perfect in holiness (for so terrible a place can be endured by none save those of absolute resolve and supreme constancy) . . . To this spot they withdraw themselves: for the desert is vast, and the cells are sundered from one another by so wide a space that none is in sight of his neighbour, nor can any voice be heard. One by one they abide in their cells, a mighty silence and a great quiet among them.[1]

The wadi itself, then, has not changed greatly since St. Jerome (accompanied by his disciple, the rich and pious widow Paula) visited it some sixteen centuries ago. But the desert is no longer so terrible a place, nor is the way thither particularly difficult. Indeed, the modern traveller can disregard the old guide-books which specified six days for the excursion, three for the outward and three for the homeward journey. Victorian and Edwardian 'Handbooks for Travellers' seem to have exaggerated the hazards and hardships of the trip, which was consequently not recommended except to those who were interested in primitive Christian monuments. The hazards consisted chiefly of the difficulties of obtaining reliable camels, donkeys and guides, with the possibility of harassment from the Bedouin tribes who controlled the desert which had to be crossed. The principal hardship was the lack of accommodation; and while it was conceded that tents were not absolutely necessary, these were advised, especially if ladies were included in the excursion. Women, one notes, were an additional complication to nineteenth-century travel in Egypt, whence the recommendation that 'where ladies are of the party, particularly on the Nile, the servants should be supplied with drawers, and an order given that the boatmen never go into the water without them'.[2]

However, the guides and camel-drivers who led the party to the Wadi Natrun were enveloped in their hooded cloaks and hence were unlikely to offend modesty. Tents, on the other hand, gave privacy. Otherwise travellers had to sleep in the waiting rooms of railway stations, or in the huts of the Egyptian Salt and Soda Company, which was a British enterprise that worked the salt lakes of the wadi for the natron once extensively used in industry.

The 1929 edition of Baedeker's *Egypt* was still recommending visitors to the monasteries 'to obtain board and lodging in the house of the manager of the Salt and Soda Company at Bir Hooker'. This advice is meaningless today, since neither the Salt and Soda Company nor the company railway which ran from the Nile to the Wadi Natrun nor the station called Bir Hooker exist. Factory, sheds, and workmen's huts have disappeared along with the rails, rolling stock, and the little station where a few tourists used to arrive aboard an open railway wagon.

Today the journey to this outpost of Christianity is neither as exciting, expensive, nor romantic as it was even thirty years ago, for the traveller can now reach the Wadi Natrun by the Desert Road which links Cairo with Alexandria. This road was begun in 1917 when the Egyptian Government provided the British engineer responsible for constructing it with five baskets, ten shovels, and a free hand in conscripting labour. The road took a long time to build, naturally, but it is today a good macadamised highway.

The traveller boards the north-bound bus outside the Nile Hilton Hotel in Cairo and crosses the desert at 60 m.p.h., stopping halfway between the two cities at a rest-house, whence he must find his own conveyance for the remainder of the journey across the open desert to the monasteries.

I had been told that there was a World War II jeep which ferried the occasional visitor to the convents, and while waiting for this vehicle to materialise I took coffee with Madame Katy, the widow of the erstwhile manager of the rest-house and now the manageress. Like most Greeks in Egypt, her second language was French. She spoke it fluently, at what sounded to me to be a thousand words a minute. It was soon apparent that she needed to talk fast to unburden herself of her *accidie*, which (as we shall see) is the special desolation of those who live in the desert cut off from sympathetic companionship. So the hour or more in which I drank coffee with Madame Katy was not long enough for her to tell me of her sadness, but also, at the same time, to show me all her souvenirs—the guest-book with its greetings and attempts at witty remarks—the inconsequential chatter of tourists passing swiftly through with just time to down a cup of coffee before going on to Alexandria, leaving Madame Katy looking down the road awaiting the next car or busload of Europeans. She is still waiting and looking, but I had been the only non-Egyptian passer-by for a long time, so I was shown the photos of her family—especially of her two grandchildren born in Montreal, far from Egypt and the beloved Hellenic homeland.

But the jeep had arrived. Madame Katy was still telling me about her grandchildren as I went out to the courtyard where the vehicle stood with its lid up as the driver tinkered with the veteran engine. Her son wanted her to join him in Montreal, but how could a Greek live in such a cold inhuman city? There was nowhere in the world for a Greek to live but in Greece. Ah, Greece! And the old Greek life! And the Greek artists and philosophers. And did I know the story of the philosopher Diogenes and the beautiful woman? . . . The driver had started his engine, and it was time to say goodbye to Madame Katy.

I left her standing in the courtyard outside the rest-house, a dumpy, grey-haired, black-bespectacled exile, a victim of that anguish which the fourth-century French monk Cassian has described from his own experience in the Wadi Natrun.

> When *accidie* besieges the unhappy mind, it begets aversion from the place, boredom, and scorn and contempt for one's brethren (Cassian writes). Also, towards any work that may be done within the enclosure of one's lair, we became listless and inert. We lament that in all this while, living in the same spot, we have made no progress, we sigh and complain that bereft of sympathetic fellowship we have no spiritual fruit . . . Finally we conclude that there is no health for us so long as we stay in this place short of betaking ourselves elsewhere as quickly as possible . . . One gazes anxiously here and there and sighs that no brother of any description is to be seen approaching: one is for ever in and out of one's cell, gazing at the sun as though it were tarrying to its setting: one's mind is in an irrational confusion, and no remedy, it seems, can be found. . . .[3]

Off we went in the dilapidated vehicle to the monastery called Macarius, the oldest of the four surviving convents and the farthest away. From the distance it appears across the rock-strewn sand as a small brown fortress, completely isolated in the wilderness of sand and rock. It has always been like this, the most remote of the great monkish colony of the Wadi Natrun—the most pillaged, and devastated and, as a result, the poorest of the remaining four convents.

The monastery of Macarius commemorates one of the first and greatest of the Desert Fathers who came to this valley in the second half of the fourth century. Macarius personifies in his life and philosophy the ideal of the early Christian ascetics who believed that the road to heaven was by way of total self-abnegation, the philosophical basis, of course, of all mysticism and mystical experience. Thus, during his sixty years' residence in the wasteland, Macarius excelled all the other hermits in the austerities he inflicted upon himself, for we are told that he lived only on raw vegetables and beans for seven years together; and for the following three years subsisted on an additional ration of five ounces of bread a day. I have often been asked when I reported cases of modern hermits I have seen who have survived for decades on a similar diet how this is possible. The answer is not as difficult or complicated as it seems.

First, the European diet, with its enormous quantities of meat, vegetables, fruit, bread, cakes, chocolates, et cetera, is as alien to desert-dwellers as the diet of, say, sheep or horses is to us. Millions of people can and do survive on 'a handful of rice' in many parts of the world; and, what is more, they live as long as the European on his enormous and varied quantities of food. Secondly, the climate in Lower Egypt makes far less claim on the constitution than it does in northern Europe. Nobody feels the need for a huge plate of roast beef, two veg, and a suet pudding either at midday or even in the cool of the evening. And thirdly, whether one approves of self-denial or not, it is certain that the mind can control the appetites of the body, especially in poor countries where scarcity is, in any case, a fact of life.

So the privations of Macarius in the matter of food are not all that exceptional, and we can well believe the story of Palladius, a disciple of the hermit, of how a present of a bunch of grapes was offered to the saint who personally carried it to the cell of a brother who was ill; and how this monk thanked the father and then sent the grapes to another whom he thought had greater need of a little treat; and so from cell to cell until the grapes came back to Macarius.

It is clear from this story that the Wadi Natrun was inhabited by colonies of monks and hermits by the second half of the fourth century, and there must have been enough of them and sufficient visitors for a hostel to be built, with a chapel for the weekly mass and the accommodation of travellers. The fame of the valley had, indeed, spread all over the Roman world, and hundreds of the curious as well as of the devout made their way across the desert to the cells and caves of the hermits. In fact, we hear on many occasions of princes, princesses, nobles, and high officials visiting the valley to ask advice of the holy men—on temporal as well as spiritual matters. As early as the time of Macarius, Apollinaria, a daughter of some legendary Roman emperor, lived for many years among the hermits disguised as a monk. She was only the first of many such noble ladies who earnestly desired the ascetic life. Apollinaria refused marriage, visited the holy places of Jerusalem, made a pilgrimage to the shrine of St. Menas,[4] and then declared her intention of setting out for Scete, the 'region of utter solitude'. She left the city of St. Menas in a litter, travelling by the once much-used road between that shrine and the Wadi Natrun, the same pilgrims' road later used by the Moslems on their *haj* to Mecca. Somewhere along the road she changed her dress for a monk's habit, and when a halt was made at midnight beside one of the natron lakes in the wadi, Apollinaria disappeared into the darkness. She is said to have remained around the marshy borders of the lake until she became unrecognisable as a woman and at this point presented herself to the hermits as a man called Dorotheus, a recruit to their community. Hospitality and kindness were always characteristic of the Desert Fathers, and no doubt some solitary was glad to move out of his cell to make room for the new 'brother', since neither he nor anybody else, including Macarius himself, knew that the new brother was really a 'sister'.

At all events Dorotheus soon gained such high repute for holiness and austerity that she was chosen to be the cell-mate and guardian of another visitor—no less than her very own sister. This unhappy girl was said to be 'possessed', and had, therefore, been sent to the desert for treatment by the saintly men who inhabited it. Indeed, a cure was soon effected and the princess was returned to her joyful parents in Constantinople. But alas! their joy was short-lived, for the devil caused her to be pregnant, to the great indignation of the emperor, who demanded the head of the monk to whom she had been entrusted. At this point Dorotheus-Apollinaria was able to step forward and thus save the reputation of the several hundred holy men, one or some of whom might otherwise have been suspected of unchastity.

No more heinous charge could have been brought against the ascetics of Scete for whom sexual purity was the greatest of virtues. In fact it was during Apollinaria's sojourn in the valley that a monk called Hierax epitomised the views of many solitaries in a doctrine that was later pronounced heretical: namely, that marriage and sexual intercourse were positively sinful and that only the perfectly continent (such as monks and nuns) were worthy of salvation.

It was, then, with great interest that I drove across the country once trodden by the feet of such saints and martyrs—yes, and fanatics—and so arrived at the monastery of Macarius or the Dayr Abu Makar, once the premier monastery of Egypt from which the pope of the Egyptian Church and principal prelates were often chosen. The monastery also housed in its great days the national library of the Copts, serving as a research centre for visiting scholars and so becoming famous throughout the Christian Orient.

One stops today, as the traveller has always done, outside the little postern-gate let into the high wall that surrounds the fortress, rings the iron bell, and awaits the slight opening of the door, with the hand that reaches out for the letter of introduction without which no visitor is allowed to enter. In due course the door was opened and I went inside the little fortified city to be welcomed by the abbot, an elderly monk in a faded blue gown and white knitted cap. Father Rofail conducted me to a reception room and called for coffee while we exchanged courtesies and I brought some news of the outside world. Then we began our tour, first stopping to pluck ripe oranges from the trees in the central courtyard, the sweetest and most perfumed fruit I have ever eaten. My Bedouin jeep-driver filled a small sack with these delicious oranges. There was no charge, and he was told to take all he wanted.

The church of St. Macarius goes back to the fourth century, though little remains of the original building except the traditional architecture of the early Coptic church. The ancient murals have long since disappeared and are replaced by brightly coloured modern tapestries reminiscent of the factory-made picture-cloths sold in the Cairo bazaars as tourist souvenirs. The monks, however, are delighted with these ikons and obviously indifferent to the genuine article, one of which, a triptych on wood, I found thrust into a dark corner. When I asked if I could see this ancient picture a brother dragged it from the wall, beat it vigorously with a duster so that flakes of paint fell off, and carried it outside for photographing in the sunlight. It was a very early ikon of great value in the history of primitive Christian art, and one could only imagine the sort of figure it would bring in the London auction rooms. It was sad to see it thrust back into its dark corner.

But the monks are not interested in the history of art, of course, and prefer those holy relics which constantly remind them of their predecessors, so near to them in spirit though separated by 1,500 years in time. In the main church, interred under the floor of one of the chapels, lie the Forty-Nine Martyrs who were slain by the barbarians in an attack on the monastery in A.D. 444. This atrocity is as of yesterday to the inmates of Macarius, for it typifies the glory as well as the terror of being 'an athlete of God'. Adjacent to these is the tomb of the patriarchs or popes, ten of whom came from the monastery of Macarius. They lie side by side, rather like logs, reverently covered by a pink counterpane. Above them, and elsewhere in the church, the ostrich eggs hang from the ceiling, symbols of spiritual dedication, for the monks told me that the female ostrich spends fourteen days not moving but staring at her eggs during the hatching period. The ostrich eggs are about all that is left of the hanging ornaments which once included great lamps of brass and glass chandeliers.

About these ostrich eggs. The first European traveller to visit the Coptic churches and monasteries after the closure of Egypt to Christians for almost a thousand years also notes the curious custom of hanging these shells in the churches and also received the same explanation from the priests as I did. Father Vansleb, writing in 1672, has this to say:

> I have read in an Arabian manuscript, a remarkable thing concerning the Austrich, which I cannot pass over without publishing.
>
> When it intends to hatch its Egs, it sits not upon them, as other birds, but the male and the female hatches them with their Eye only; and when either of them hath need to seek for food, he gives notice to the other by crying; and the other continues to look upon the Egs, till it be returned . . . for if they did but look off for a moment, the Egs would spoil and rot.

> The Church of the Copties hath learn'd an excellent custome from the practice of this bird. They hang up a lighted light between two Egs of an Austrich, over against the priests that officiate, to advise them to be attentive about their devotions. . . .[5]

Whether the Egyptian monks have learnt in the intervening 300 years since Father Vansleb visited them that the fable of the ostrich hatching her eggs in this manner is 'unscientific', I did not discover, for it was not my business to question their beliefs. But the tenacity with which the Copts, and particularly the priests, cling to their legends is understandable, for they have had good reason to shut themselves off from an always inimical outside world—the world of Islam on the one hand and that of Western Christianity on the other. In short, their superstitions, like their ancient ritual, have enabled them to survive.

After saying goodbye to the monks of Macarius (who obligingly came out of the monastery to push the jeep, which refused to start, but who objected to having their photographs taken while pushing, as this was undignified) we crossed the desert to the monastery of Suriani, or The Syrians, perhaps the most famous of the desert shrines. It was the great library of Suriani, with its 8,000 manuscript volumes, that the nineteenth-century bibliophiles ransacked to such good advantage for themselves and the national libraries of Europe.

When I arrived at Suriani, however, and handed in my letter of introduction, the doorkeeper informed me that the monks were undergoing a special lenten fast and no one was admitted. This was a considerable disappointment, as all travellers concur that the Syrian monastery is the richest and most interesting of the four. It would have been interesting, for instance, to have seen the staples to which its founder, St. Bischoi, used to fasten his hair in order that he could remain standing throughout the night in the *orante* attitude. This hermit and saint was one of the most redoubtable of all the ascetics and was, in consequence, richly rewarded for his self-denial. On one occasion the Saviour himself appeared to Bischoi who had the honour of washing our Lord's feet and of drinking the water afterwards. Understandably, Bischoi's fame and disciples increased rapidly. So great, indeed, was his reputation that he was visited by the renowned Syrian hermit Ephraem, who travelled many hundreds of miles from his native land to the Wadi Natrun expressly to converse with his holy colleague. Unfortunately Ephraem did not speak Coptic and Bischoi did not speak Syrian, but after the latter had said a short prayer, each was granted complete mastery of the other's language, and the two men spent several hours in reverent talk. Moreover, when Ephraem left his staff outside Bischoi's cell, it took root and immediately put forth leaves. Delighted with this succession of miracles, the two solitaries bade each other farewell, and Ephraem was carried homeward on a cloud specially provided for the occasion. The flowering staff grew into a great tamarind tree which I had looked forward to seeing in the courtyard of Suriani (for it is still growing there).

While outside Suriani, I watched the two camels which knelt outside the gate enjoying a meal of bread which is baked in the monasteries and then left to grow hard. This bread is given to all who ask for it, but after several weeks it is not in great demand and hence was being fed to the camels. The noise as these beasts crunched down on the rocklike substance was considerable, and I found myself wondering whether they found this bread harder to chew and digest than the date stones which they are usually fed. One never grows tired of watching camels.

I next made the short trip from Suriani to Bischoi, another monastery founded in the fourth century by the celebrated hermit Anba Bischoi—he who washed the Saviour's feet. The 'householder' here, as the Copts call their abbot, was a retired teacher of English, Abuna Mikail, who was glad to have a chance to use a language that, he said, was 'going rusty', though he refreshed his memory by reading the King James Bible. He was one of some twenty-five brothers, all of whom, I gathered, were meditating in their cells. Father Mikail, however, was happy to take me on a tour of his convent. He took me first, of course, to the shrine of the founder of the monastery. The saint lies side by side with his inseparable companion Paul under a very dusty red cloth. Father Mikail did not make the same claim for the dead Bischoi that was made to a Frenchman in 1778: that 'the body of the saint was as fresh and rosy as if alive'. But it used to be taken for granted that the bodies of holy men were incorruptible, and it was not considered exceptional for a saint courteously to reach out an arm from his coffin to shake hands with visitors—provided such visitors were true believers.

St. Bischoi's companion, Paul of Tamweh as he is called, achieved his great reputation for sanctity by having committed suicide seven times. As a result his relics have miraculous powers and, like the relics in the Coptic churches of Cairo, are kept in a sack which the sick can hold in the expectation of a cure. Thus, in the convent of St. George in Cairo, the abbess kindly let me hold the arm of St. George himself, neatly sewn inside a red sausage-shaped bag. From the feel and weight of this bolster-like object, I would say that the limb had become petrified in the course of centuries, unlike the body of St. Bischoi, reputed to be not only incorruptible but unwithered.

From Bischoi I went next to the last of the monasteries, the Dayr el Baramus, or Baramous, the northernmost convent of the four. Here I was to spend the next forty-eight hours, to attend pre-dawn mass, and to sleep inside the high walls of the convent. It is natural that Baramous should be my favourite monastery and Father David my favourite monk. I disagreed very strongly with my eighteenth-century predecessor Charles Sonnini, who wrote of Baramous: 'I do not believe there is upon earth a situation so horrible or forbidding', and then complained that the monks demanded visual proof that he was circumcised before they would let him in.

Father David, an elderly man with a splendid beard, informed me upon entering Baramous that this was the oldest of the four monasteries in the Wadi Natrun, dating back to A.D. 260. The date is highly unlikely, as all four monasteries are thought to have been founded during or towards the end of the life of Macarius, i.e. about A.D. 390. But 100 years more or less was of no importance. As for the name, Baramous is simply a transliteration of the Coptic *Pa-Romeos*, or '(Monastery) of the Romans', the Romans in question being two brothers Maximus and Domitius, sons of the emperor Valentinian, who were said to have made a pilgrimage to the desert of Scete about A.D. 381 where they occupied their cell along with other hermits, died in the odour of sanctity, and were commemorated in the Monastery of the Romans. Unfortunately for this legend, the emperor Valentinian had no such sons as Maximus and Domitius. In fact, he had no legitimate sons at all.

Father David, for his part, ignored the legend of the Roman brothers, for he had more interesting things to tell and show me. So we went first to the guest-house where I was to sleep that night in a vast canopied four-poster and afterwards to Father David's cell for a chat.

REFERENCES

1 *Historia Monachorum*, *Vitae Patrum* II, xxix. Translated by Helen Waddell in *The Desert Fathers* (1936).

2 Sir John Gardner Wilkinson, *Modern Egypt and Thebes* (1843), p. 37.

3 *The Institutes of John Cassian*, Book X, 'Of the Spirit of Accidie'.

4 See Chapter 11.

5 Johann Michael Wansleben, *The Present State of Egypt*, 1678, p. 64. See also Chapter 10, pp. 149 ff.

3 A desert monastery

Father David's quarters consisted of two snug rooms leading out on to a balcony which overlooked the monastery garden. They did not constitute a cell in the old sense. I had, in fact, seen some of these old monastic cells on the ground floor—mere holes in the wall not high enough for a man to stand up in. The brothers are not expected to live in these cells nowadays, for there is no compulsion to mortify oneself in the Coptic church. Self-denial and all forms of asceticism are a matter of personal choice.

Father David, who is now seventy years old, and most of the other twenty-four monks of Baramous, have comfortable quarters in which they live a somewhat austere bachelor's life, but not austere to the point of discomfort. Father David, for instance, has divided his room into a bedroom behind the curtain and a little kitchen-living room in front. Here he cooks his own food when and how he wishes. His front room contains all his personal treasures and a large work table on which he pursues his hobby of watch-making.

While he made tea for me, he told me about some of the distinguished visitors to Baramous—King Victor Emmanuel and his wife and family, King Farouk (always looking for loot), the American who rode away with the Bedouins, the tourist who borrowed the Father's £250 camera and forgot to return it. He told me about his recent operation for hernia and how before he went under the anaesthetic he could hear St. George galloping around the operating theatre—an experience which might have alarmed most men but cheered Father David up immensely.

Other priests dropped in while we were having tea until it was time to take a last turn round the ramparts and to view the desert in the moonlight, which was Father David's regular 'treat' before he retired for the night. As we leaned over the wall, looking out towards the west, I learnt that several of the monks were, even now, out there in the cliffs, pursuing their private orisons. One of these hermits, a former monk of Baramous, was of special interest, for he seemed to me to be a direct descendant of the original desert ascetics. His name was Abuna Abd el-Masih, and this is what I learnt about him as I stood on the monastery ramparts.

Around midnight, Abuna Abd el-Masih comes out of his cave in the Libyan Desert and stands with his hands held palm upwards in the same posture that the first Christians used when praying. His lips move as he looks up into the sky. Sometimes he kneels and touches the ground with his forehead. For the rest of the night he still continues his prayers and genuflections as he had been doing for the last thirty-two years.

Abuna Abd el-Masih is a Coptic monk and he is seventy-two years old. Forty years ago he walked the 1,500 miles from his village in Ethiopia to the monastery of Baramous on the edge of the Western Desert, some seventy miles north-west of Cairo. He spent five years behind the high walls of this Egyptian monastery, distinguishing himself by the severity of his penances, until he found the company of the dozen other monks distracted him from his aim of total mortification. He decided, therefore, to go out into the desert which surrounds Baramous, to dig his own cave, and to spend the rest of his life in complete solitude communing with his Maker.

In those early days when he was younger the Ethiopian hermit used to walk once a week three miles back to the monastery to get bread, beans, dates, and a jerry-can of water. Now that he is an old man, the monks of Baramous take his meagre rations out to him. He exchanges ritual greetings with his brothers, but that is all. He wants to know nothing about what is going on in the outside world and has no interest in that world any more. He refuses to see visitors, and the monks of the nearby monastery where I spent two days and a night were gently but firmly opposed to my approaching his cave.

I was told that the last person to try to visit him, a German, was dismissed with these words:

'If you are a German you are not a Christian, for Germans don't believe in God.'

He even scolds the monks themselves, saying to them:

'You monks should know that when you eat oil and fish [he is referring to sardines], the devil will visit you at night.'

I would very much have liked to visit Abuna Abd el-Masih, since he and several other hermits also living in caves in the region are the direct descendants of the famous anchorites of the Thebaid—of Paul, Antony, Macarius, and thousands of other solitaries who peopled the Egyptian deserts in the third and fourth centuries of our era. To us in the Western world, so totally oriented to a machine civilisation, the very idea of a man living and thinking exactly as the Desert Fathers did 1,600 years ago is almost incomprehensible.

But standing that night on the ramparts of the monastery at Baramous, and looking out across the silent wastelands, I did not find it so hard to understand. In fact, the monks were not in the least amazed by the spiritual feats of Abuna Abd el-Masih and the other 'athletes of God', as the hermits used to be called. We must remember that the Egyptian monks do not question the histories and biographies of the original Desert Fathers, neither the privations they suffered nor the miracles they were involved in. Athanasius tells us that one of the founding Fathers, Amoun, being too modest to strip off his clothes in Aden to cross the river Lycus, was wafted across to the other side on a gentle breeze. The monks of the Wadi Natrun monasteries see no reason to disbelieve this wingless flight, no more astonishing to them than the manifestation of the modesty of monk Pambo who burst into tears on seeing an actress pass by. The religious of the desert have always lived close to the supernatural, the aspect of their lives which we who eat three square meals a day find most hard to understand. The monk Pior, for instance, lived for thirty years on a morsel of bread and five olives a day. He would have seen nothing unusual in the ordeal of Macarius who spent six months naked in the swamps of the Wadi Natrun salt lakes where

Above The desert monastery of Baramous. The few monks in residence now live in rooms instead of cells
Below Coptic monks of the el Moharreq monastery

A monk of St. Macarius, oldest of the desert monasteries, with an ikon found lying against the wall of an abandoned cell

the mosquitoes (even today) 'pierce the hide even of wild pigs'.

Thus Macarius and many others entered into the company of the saints both by reason of their denial of the flesh and by the supernatural feats they were able to perform in consequence. Macarius gained great glory by curing the blind cub of a hyena who had beaten against the door of his cell with her head, seeking help: a delightful story, with a happy ending, too; for the next day the grateful mother, her cub having been cured by the saint, brought him a large sheepskin as a present. The hyena had no doubt enjoyed the sheep and hoped that the saint would enjoy a wool blanket.

Another holy man, Evagrius, abstained from all meat, vegetables, and fruit, interdicted himself from bathing, offered up 100 prayers a day, with genuflections, and overcame temptation by standing all night in a cistern of cold water. Moses the Robber (reformed and eventually one of the most revered of the early Fathers) when assailed by grievous temptations (he was a huge and virile Negro) used to spend all night carrying water to his fellow-hermits, many of whom lived five miles from the nearest well. Moses was often found lying as if dead somewhere in the desert; and the general opinion in such cases was that a demon had knocked him down with a club.

The extraordinary thing about nearly all these hermits, whether of the fourth or the twentieth century, is that they lived to a great age, despite their superhuman privations. One of the very first, and the greatest, St. Antony, lived to be over 100; Amoun to 97; Pembo, 70; Pior, 90; Macarius, about 100; Evagrius (always in bad health), 54; Moses the Robber, 75; and Abuna Abd el-Masih still strong and healthy at 72. We should not, then, think of the hermits as deliberately trying to commit suicide either by starving themselves or inflicting on themselves severe physical ordeals. In fact, in contrast to Abuna Abd el-Masih and his cave, the domestic conditions of the first hermits were considerably snugger, for we can piece together a picture of what the hermitages were like from the contemporary authors: a hut built of loose stones and covered with a roof of interlacing reeds from the salt lakes (no problem of rain, as it seldom if ever rains in the Wadi Natrun); a door on which visitors and pilgrims continually knocked for interviews; a reed mat on the floor and sometimes, as in the case of Macarius (thinks to his friend the hyena), a sheepskin for cover; a reed bolster used as a seat during the day and a pillow at night. These were the hermits' possessions, and if they moved house they took only their sheepskins, leaving the other items for the next occupant. In winter the hermit would light a fire of thorns, and these spots of light burning in the immense solitude must have been a comforting sight to those brothers who were new to the desert life. And while those ascetics who were farthest advanced along the road to complete self-abnegation existed on just a few mouthfuls of food, they none the less had in these huts jars of honey and wine and other pleasant foods, vegetables and fruits, which had been left by the pilgrims and which the Fathers pressed upon visitors as they will do to this day. There certainly must have been something of value in the monks' huts, because Macarius returned one night to find a thief ransacking his home. The saint saluted this rogue cheerfully, helped him load his donkey with the loot, and sent him away with his blessing. One can see why he was made a saint.

His Holiness Kyrillos VI, 116th pope of the Egyptian Church, and 'spiritual head of the town of Alexandria, all the countries of Egypt, of Jerusalem, Nubia, Abyssinia, Pentapolis, and all the lands in which St. Mark preached', was himself a hermit for ten years while a monk at the Baramous monastery. Yet when one meets the patriarch, sitting, as I found him, in his armchair beside his bed with a row of medicine bottles on the table nearby, one sees no marks of the extraordinary experience that he has undergone—an experience few other living men would care even to contemplate.

The example of Kyrillos VI is, of course, an inspiration to other monks, for they believe that the way to high office—to being elected pope or abbot of a great monastery—is by the hard road of complete spiritual dedication: in other words, by going to the limit of self-abnegation. It is not, then, surprising that his brother monks request Abuna Abd el-Masih to grant them the privilege of sharing his solitude, though the Ethiopian has now made it clear that he wants to spend the remaining years of his life alone in his desert retreat. But there are plenty of other caves in the cliffs of the Wadi Natrun; and according to the early historians thousands of hermits occupied them in the fourth century A.D. And even today no Copt, whether monk or layman, would find it unusual if a monk should walk out of his convent to live alone in the desert for months, or even years.

Alternatively, the brothers can mortify themselves within the confines of their own monastic cell, and Father David, my guide at Baramous, told me that the Ethiopians were renowned for the severity of their self-inflicted ordeals. One Abyssinian spent every night of his life, for twenty-five years, standing outside his cell, facing east, hands upraised, praying until the first rays of the sun came over the fortress wall. Others subject themselves to long fasts, though this is not in the least unusual, since all must fast most of the time, particularly during the Coptic Lent lasting fifty-six days. While I was visiting the Wadi Natrun monasteries, the rule prescribed only one meal of bread and bean soup a day.

In some monasteries, masses are continuous throughout the twenty-four hours, the one I attended beginning at four o'clock in the morning and continuing to six. I envied those old monks who had a tau-stick, or crook, to lean on, as we stood most of the time. On the other hand, the service and ritual in these Coptic churches, several of which claim to be built on the site where the Holy Family rested on their flight into Egypt, are so fascinating that I did not mind standing. The prayers and lessons are recited in Coptic, the direct descendant of the ancient Egyptian tongue, so that what one is hearing is a faint echo of the speech of the Pharaohs. I doubt, however, whether even a first-class scholar of Coptic would understand what was being said any more than the lay congregation, for I never heard words issue from the mouth of men faster than the liturgy did from the lips of the officiating priests. Prayers and liturgies are accompanied by the clash of a cymbal and the tinkle of a triangle and shouts of 'Kyrie eleison' repeated rapidly many times over.

Life in the desert monasteries is not, however, all austerity, and it is certainly not as severe as it used to be when these remote citadels of Christianity were completely cut off from Western Christendom. In fact, the convents are linked with the outside world by telephones, transistor radios, and above all, tourists, who have introduced a new note into monastic life. Concessions have been made to modern attitudes as well as to modern machines. Even ladies are welcome inside these ancient strongholds of misogynists.

As Father David and I walked on the ramparts to see the desert under the full moon, we were joined by a Father Ibrahim who brought along a dish of dates culled from the monastery palms, the trees whose dark green plumes are the first signs of life one sees on approaching Baramous across the desert. Father Ibrahim offered me both dates and cigarettes, for smoking is not prohibited. Alcohol, however, is forbidden, except for a glass of wine on feast days.

Listening to the murmur of prayers coming from some of the cells and looking out across the sand to the cliffs where Abuna Abd el-Masih was now standing with hands upraised praying outside his cave, I was struck by the curious disparity between what seemed like laxity on the one hand and extreme asceticism on the other. Inside the forty-foot-high walls, my two monkish companions appeared to be enjoying a pleasant and serene sort of life, while outside another monk was undergoing the severest conceivable penance. Both modes of spiritual service, however, are alike acceptable under the rules of Coptic monasticism, which has always left it to the wisdom of each man to work out his own salvation. Father David happened to prefer the security of the monastery, with his snug suite of rooms and a big table on which to set out the parts of the watches he was repairing and the tools he repaired them with. Father Ibrahim liked a gossip and a smoke before retiring. Both liked to play with the monastery cat—a queen with two kittens now gambolling about in the garden. The fondness of the two Fathers for their pet reminded me of the stories of how the first hermits shared their frugal rations with any animal that happened to drop in from the surrounding desert. In fact,

Macarius, the founder of the monastery of Baramous, once looked after a litter of orphaned kittens in a cave not far from here; and the great St. Antony himself, we are told, was always extremely courteous to wild animals. Thus, when he caught a gazelle eating the bean plants he had planted outside his cave, 'he took hold of it gently and said to it, "Why do you do harm to me when I do no harm to you? Go away, and in the Lord's name, do not come into my garden again." And ever afterwards', says Athanasius in the *Life*, 'the wild animals left his garden alone.'

Affection for an animal, a stroll along the ramparts in the moonlight, a cigarette, an evening repairing a watch, a simple meal, an hour with a book—such are the activities of these 'quiet men' of the desert, as characteristic of the tradition as the austere life of their brothers outside the precincts of the monastery in their caves. Their rule of life has not really changed in fifteen centuries; and what the visitor to the desert monasteries is seeing today is still the birthplace of the most significant movement in Christian history, as well as some of the oldest shrines of our religion. True, there is not much left to see in the case of most of them. The huge fortress-monastery of St. Simeon at Aswan is abandoned; the Red and White monasteries near Luxor are in a state of disrepair; and forty-six out of an original fifty convents in the Wadi Natrun have disappeared under the sands. Yet, cenobitic life in Egypt has continued almost uninterrupted for 1,600 years, sometimes under the most appalling difficulties and during periods when the monasteries were sacked or burnt and their inmates massacred. The evidence of these calamities is still seen in the high walls and blocked gates of these remote citadels of Christianity, and especially in the massive keeps within the walls, the last refuge of the besieged brothers to which they could retire over a drawbridge when attacked by Arab armies or Bedouin bandits.

And all through these centuries of persecution and outright destruction, the monks continued to feed any passer-by who asked for food. Their one concession to the hostility of the outside world was to lower food from the walls in baskets and to raise visitors in a net. Many a nineteenth-century traveller was hauled up over the ramparts in this manner. and even today one enters the desert monasteries through a small postern-gate which is unlocked by a massive key; and after sundown no one gets admittance at all.

So the Coptic monasteries of Egypt stand as the first models of Christian monasteries all over the world; and hermits like Abuna Abd el-Masih as the last descendants of the primitive saints from an age when saintliness was equated with the annihilation of all earthly vanities.

I was told that the Ethiopian was in his cave during the campaigns in the Western Desert and that he was under fire during Rommel's advance on the Nile. We have no way of knowing what he thought about the experience. Judging by his contempt of the outside world and all its works, the probability is that he dismissed the bursting shells and the showers of shrapnel as another trick by the devil to interrupt his prayers and meditations.

It is also reported that British G.H.Q. in Cairo apologised to the hermit for any inconvenience caused him—an ironic homage of the twentieth to the third century.

4 The beginnings of the Egyptian Church

I travelled north-east from the Wadi Natrun to Alexandria. It was to Alexandria that the apostle Mark came as the evangelist of the new religion. It was here that he preached and made his first converts; here that he became the first bishop of the Egyptian Church; was martyred (the legend is vague at this point as Mark, in any case, is one of the more obscure evangelists); and was commemorated in a cathedral bearing his name. Alexandria, therefore, is the Rome of the Copts.

I arrived in the centre of the city by the desert bus, avoided the horde of porters who were pouncing on the bags and parcels of the passengers, and strolled along looking for the Rue de l'Église Copte, not finding it until I fell in with a Greek gentleman out for his morning stroll who offered to conduct me personally to the Patriarchate, or headquarters, of the Coptic Church. Mr. Zaracoudi, my guide, was eighty-five years old, so at his request our progress through the busy streets of Alexandria was unhurried. Moreover, he had many things to tell and show me as we ambled along arm in arm. Here, for instance, a Greek barber, a passionate if unschooled student of archaeology, spent several years digging up the main road in his search for the tomb and sarcophagus of Alexander the Great. As the emperor's coffin was of gold, the dig would certainly have repaid the barber if his calculations had been correct. But the large hole yielded nothing. The barber had sunk his small fortune in that hole and the Alexandrians laughed at his foolishness; but my guide thought otherwise. The bold venture, he said, was characteristic of a true Greek.

Chatting pleasantly, we made our way to the Patriarchate, with my new friend stopping to rest at various corners while he talked of the old Alexandria, the pre-war city of the Greek poets, painters, and cotton merchants, of whom he had been one.[1] At eighty, he told me as we reached a quiet spot where he could rest and make himself heard, his wife died and he decided to take a second spouse, this one a Greek orphan forty years his junior. A *mariage de convenance*, of course; but like most such unions, a very happy and successful one, as he did not wish to live alone and his new wife had not wished to remain an orphan.

We had now arrived by slow stages and with numerous halts at the Coptic Patriarchate, an old building near the St. Mark's Cathedral, the parent church of the Egyptian Christians. The Archpriest Timothy received us enthroned on a wing-backed chair set on a dais; Mr. Zaracoudi and I sat on smaller chairs placed at right angles to his throne. A servant brought in small cups of Turkish coffee, a package of biscuits, and a packet of cigarettes, both of which our host opened himself.

After a few preliminary courtesies, the Archpriest launched into the history of the Copts from the time of Noah, pointing out that the Egyptians were direct descendants of Noah's youngest son Ham by way of the Mesram tribe. It was the sons of Ham, we learnt, who founded the greatest empires of antiquity, Assyria, Babylonia, Egypt, and Phoenicia until they were overcome in course of time by the races of Sem and Japhet. The Archpriest next rapidly enumerated the names of the biblical tribes, from which dissertation I gathered that he was explaining for us the origin of the various races of man.

Mr. Zaracoudi occasionally turned to me with some comment like 'Anthropology!' or 'Ethnology!', accompanied by a slight lifting of an eyebrow. Indeed, the 'science' of the Archpriest Timothy reminded me irresistibly of his distinguished predecessor, Cosmas Indicopleustes, also an Alexandrian theologian, who set out to prove fourteen centuries previously that the earth was a flat surface, its length twice its breadth, its elevation two stories high, the upper storey, or heaven, being supported by walls at the ends of the earth. Over this flat world moved the sun which disappeared nightly behind a mountain which stood somewhere 'in the north', though Cosmas does not specify where. He does however explain why God took six days to create the world: the deity could easily have done it in one, he says, but took longer for the sake of the angels whose weak intelligence would not otherwise have grasped the mechanism of the thing. These same angels, according to the old monk, are for ever running up and down a Jacob's ladder with a trap-door at the top which they cannot pass until mankind has paid for the sin of Mother Eve and so produced the key with which they get into the heavenly storey. I do not know whether the Archpriest Timothy had read Cosmas's *Christian Topography*, but much of what he was now telling Mr. Zaracoudi and me about the universe sounded as if he had not only read it but believed in it.

When his dissertation was over, he invited us to see the cathedral, dedicated to St. Mark, whose body, according to our guide, had been stolen from the original church in A.D. 790, but whose head refused to accompany the Venetians when they returned for this relic in A.D. 829: their ships had been unable to leave the harbour due to divine intercession, so that the saint's cranium remained in his own church. 'It's no use asking to see it,' Mr. Zaracoudi remarked. Mr. Zaracoudi, in fact, was giving a running commentary during our tour, and one detected a certain pagan irony in his attitude towards his co-religionists. Thus, remarking on the fact that in the Coptic churches the men sit in front, the women behind, so that the former should not be distracted from their spiritual reflections by the latter, Mr. Zaracoudi wanted to know whether the women were ever distracted by seeing the men.

But irrespective of whether the trunk of St. Mark is now in Venice and his head in Alexandria, the Coptic Church claims the apostle as their original evangelist and their first pope, a claim which like so many other legends, is hard to refute. According to the Copts, he came to Alexandria about A.D. 40 to begin his mission which immediately prospered judging by the number of churches, monasteries, convents, and hermitages which sprang up within the next three centuries, from the delta of the Nile as far up the river as Nubia and so, perhaps, into Ethiopia. Moreover, the success of St. Mark's mission can be assessed not only in terms of numbers but also in terms of faith, as witness the thousands of Christians martyred during the great persecutions of the pagan emperors of Rome. Even more significant was the survival of the Christian Church in Egypt after the Arab conquest of North Africa—the only Church to hold out against the appeal, let alone the menace, of Islam. As late as 1200, when Christianity had to all intents and purposes completely disappeared from the rest of Africa, an historian of the Arab world records 707 churches and 181 monasteries still existing in Egypt[2] In fact, through all its vicissitudes the Coptic Church has clung to its ancient faith, having never unconditionally surrendered to the tyrants who tried many times to wipe out both the faith and the faithful; and, for that matter, having never compromised with the Western Church on fundamental questions of creed and ritual. It still continues to style itself (an indirect challenge to the Catholic Church) 'spiritual head of the town of Alexandria and all the countries of Egypt, of Jerusalem, Nubia, Abyssinia, Pentapolis, and all the lands in which St. Mark preached'.

The Coptic Church, then, for the first four centuries a member of the Universal Church became separate from the fifth century onwards when the Egyptians rejected the findings of the Council of Chalcedon held in A.D. 451. The Copts held tenaciously to the principle that Christ was a single personality with a single nature, whence no distinction could be made between his divinity and his humanity. It is not a dogma about which modern theologians, much less laymen, are greatly concerned; but it is one that led to both controversies and crimes within the primitive Church. For men asked such alarming questions, as, if Christ was all-God, what then was his Mother? And did the Son exist at all before he was born of woman? And if he was all-God, how could he have suffered human pain on the cross? And so on—issues over which the early Churchmen not only argued but fought. At the so-called 'Robber Council' of Ephesus, soldiers attacked monks, bishops pummelled bishops, the pope of Alexandria kicked and trampled his fellow-priest Bishop Eusebius, and massacres resulted over a theory which the Eastern Church accepted as orthodoxy and the Western Church rejected as heresy.

In this long struggle for power and leadership, the Egyptian Christians gradually lost ground, until the Church of Rome became a greater enemy than the heathen hordes who were pressing on their frontiers as the old empire disintegrated. The pope of Rome was not only a spiritual enemy; he was a mortal foe as well, since it was through his hostility that the emperor Justinian is alleged to have caused 200,000 Copts to be massacred at Alexandria as heretics. The causes, like the numbers involved, are obviously obscure; but the result was that the Coptic Church broke away from both the Roman Catholic and Greek Orthodox communities whom it has never rejoined. In fact, the Egyptian Church is as separate and independent an organisation as the Protestant Church and still resists the appeals of both the Catholics and the Protestants for any form of union. Further, the Copts are definitely lukewarm towards the 'modernisation' of doctrine and ritual so characteristic of the Western Church. The idea of jollying up their services by introducing popular entertainers would be anathema to an Egyptian Christian. He prefers the ancient rites which sustained his forefathers in the darkest days of their persecution.

And what is noticeably absent from divine worship in Western churches, physical participation, is an integral part of the Coptic service. The people crowd up to the carved wood and ivory screen behind which stands the simple table the Copts use as their high altar, and they mingle with the priests who dash around the church shaking hands with their fellow-priests. Prostrations, too, strike one as elemental: no polite declination of the head or cushion-kneeling for the Copts, but down they go on all fours to the stone floor, touching the ground with their foreheads in their bendings. In one church where I attended a service, a large and corpulent young man joined in these prostrations evidently having come straight from his bed, because he was still wearing striped pyjamas which I had plenty of opportunity to examine as he knelt and genuflected directly in front of me. Neither the priests nor the congregation were struck, as I was, by the young man's informal attire. Their attitude towards religion is both simple and fervent, and reminds one of what a Christian meeting must have been like before there were any churches at all.

It has been this adherence to primitive ritual, like the unwillingness to compromise with original doctrine, that has distinguished and still distinguishes the Copts from their fellow-Christians outside of Egypt. As we have seen, the Egyptians refused to yield on the question of Christ's substance, though how much their stand was due to religious conviction and how much to political motives is arguable. For already, 200 years after the Founder's death, Christianity had become a political issue throughout the Roman empire, all the more so since the new cult had very early in its history become suspect to the authorities as a subversive movement. To the pagan Romans, the Christians, or Nazarenes as they were called, were merely another sect of the Jews, as their religion was merely a modernised version of Judaism. And this new cult, strongly nationalistic as well as messianic in content, was carried all over the Mediterranean world by merchant-travellers from Palestine to the Jewish communities in Alexandria, Athens, Carthage, Rome, and elsewhere. Moreover, the attraction of the story of the persecuted rabbi called Jesus was undoubtedly political as well as spiritual, particularly after the massacre and enslavement of the Jews following the capture of Jerusalem in A.D. 70. By A.D. 70, in fact, the persecutions of Rome and the ultimate defeat of the Jews in their long war for independence must have driven many of them into the camp of their Christianised co-nationals who appeared to be the only hope of a successful policy of civil disobedience by passive resistance.

At first, all this talk of a son of God born to a virgin and crucified as a criminal was a matter of considerable bewilderment to educated pagans like Gaius Plinius Secundus who, as Governor of Bithynia at the beginning of the second century A.D., had plenty of opportunity of studying the Nazarenes at close quarters. His bewilderment is apparent in a communication he wrote to the Emperor Trajan in A.D. 112:

> The Christians affirm that their only crime was that they were in the habit of meeting on a certain fixed day before it was light, when they sang in alternate verses a hymn to Christ, as to a God, and bound themselves by a solemn oath, not to do any wicked deeds, but never to commit any fraud, theft, or adultery, never to falsify their word, nor deny a trust when they should be called upon to deliver it up; after which it was their custom to separate, and then re-assemble to partake of food—but food of an ordinary and innocent kind . . . I judged it necessary to extract the real truth, with the assistance of torture, from two female slaves who were styled *deaconesses*; but I could discover nothing more than depraved and excessive superstition.[3]

Some twenty years later the emperor Hadrian had this to say of the Egyptian Christians in a letter to the consul Servianus:

> As for Egypt, which you were praising to me, my dear Servianus, I have found its people a mob of lightweight gossipers. The Christians appear to worship the Egyptian God Serapis whom the Greeks call Pluto; and there is not one of their priests who does not claim to be either a magician or a soothsayer. The very Patriarch himself is said by some to worship Serapis, by some to worship Christ. Their claim to worship the one and only true God is meaningless, since this God is common to Christians, Jews, and men of every race and religion.[4]

Hadrian's confusion as to which god the Christians were worshipping, whether Serapis or Christ, is understandable, since the former deity, a Hellenised version of the old god Osiris, was a sort of god of life-in-death, a concept which has obvious affinity with the doctrine of the Resurrection. Moreover, the Greek or Alexandrian version of Serapis as a mystic figure, crowned and bearded and regally enthroned, was so like the representations of the Greek Zeus or the Roman Jupiter or the Hebrew Jehovah or the new god, Jesus Christ, that it was difficult for a sophisticated pagan to differentiate between them.

Hadrian was not the only one to be confused. For that sect of the Christians called Gnostics did accept Serapis as symbolic of the universal godhead. More than that, the Gnostics dabbled in secret cults, obscure mysteries and magical practices involving seals, gems, and spells. Their version of Christianity, in fact, appears to have been largely a form of witchcraft based, as most witchcraft is, on incantations. Here is an example:

> Then Jesus stood with his disciples by the water of the ocean and pronounced this prayer, saying: aeaious iao, ora, psinother, thernops, nopsither, zagoure, pagoure, nethmomaoth, nepsiomaoth, marachachtha, thobarrabau, tharnachachan, zorokothora, ieou Sabaoth.[5]

This would make no more sense to a well-educated and travelled man like Hadrian than the howls of voodoo priests do to us, whence he dismissed the Christians, whether Gnostics or not, as typical of the Egyptians—a people who could worship a crocodile, a cow, a cat, and even a frog as gods.

But whereas Hadrian concluded that the new religion smacked of typical oriental chicanery and was no more of a threat to authority than the popularity of a dozen other Eastern cults, later emperors had reason to change their tune as they began to realise that the Christians were not a harmless sect consisting of superstitious old women, but a state within the Roman dominion, ruled by its own leaders and laws—a powerful opposition force, even if a passive one. At this point the authorities defined the Christian movement as disloyal and subversive, and threw in the description immoral to complete their anathema. The Establishment's distrust of the new movement was epitomised in the Edict of the emperor Decius in A.D. 249, an edict designed to liquidate Christianity by legal means.

The policy and the edict of the emperor Decius, who regarded himself as a Roman of the old school, were based on the belief that the Christians were using their religious freedom to organise an underground movement designed to overthrow the existing system. The pagans, both magistrates and philosophers, came to this conclusion largely on the grounds that the Christian gods were the same as the gods of all other peoples, though with different names. Why, then, were the devotees of this new creed unwilling to recognise, if not to pay homage, to the divinities of other nations? There was only one answer. The Christians were revolutionary totalitarians.

As a politician of the old school, Decius assumed that an ideology could be destroyed by the enactment of oppressive laws. These laws, promulgated in the Edict of 249, were given an appearance of justice. They simply required *all* citizens, irrespective of their race or religion (colour was not an issue among the Romans), to go in solemn processions to the temples and there to sacrifice to the official gods. Those who refused to do so—obviously, as Decius had calculated, only Christians could *reasonably* refuse—were to be punished by imprisonment, exile, and, in extreme cases, death.

By A.D. 249, the Christian population in Egypt was undoubtedly numerous, for the new creed must have had an enormous appeal both to the Jews and to the native peasants, for it was a gospel of revolution even if only in the form of passive resistance to the hated overlords. Certainly Christian Egypt was hard hit by the Edict, judging by the thousands of certificates of loyalty issued to Egyptian Christians who had apostasised. Some of these certificates, written out by official scribes with blanks left for names and called *libelli*, come from obscure villages in Upper Egypt, whence it follows that Christianity, by the year 250, had been carried to the remotest hamlets of the Roman Empire. The *libelli* also tell us something about the converts to the new religion, if only by implication. Here is the literal translation of one found in the Fayyum:

> To the Superintendent of the sacrifices of the village of Philadelphia:
>
> From Aurelius Syrus, Pasbes his brother, and Demetria and Serapias our wives.
>
> We have always been accustomed to sacrifice to the gods and we have poured libations and tasted the offerings in your presence and according to the edicts.
>
> We accordingly pray that you certify us as loyal.
>
> Fare you well.
>
> We Aurelius Syrus and Pasbes make this application for

clearance, which has been written for us by Isidore, as we are illiterate.

[Year of the Emperor Caesar Gaius Messius Quintus Trajanus Decius Pius Felix Augustus]

We can assume in the case of this certificate that the two men and their wives were simple people, uneducated and probably of the peasant class, too intimidated to refuse to make the sacrifice and too poor to bribe the officials to overlook them. In short, the alternatives for Christians in A.D. 250 were as follows:

(1) to refuse to sacrifice and to take the consequences—imprisonment, enslavement, exile, or death;
(2) to make the sacrifice and so publicly to renounce their faith;
(3) to bribe the officials to issue them a certificate of loyalty without their actually apostasising;
(4) to flee into the desert out of reach of the authorities.

It is with the last group that we are primarily concerned, since these were the Christians who shaped the future of Christianity.

REFERENCES

1 For a study of this now vanished Alexandria, see E. M. Forster's *Pharos and Pharillon.*

2 Abu Salik, *The Churches and Monasteries of Egypt* (1893), Appendix, pp. 347–52.

3 Pliny, *Letters* (No. 96). Translated by William Malmoth (1746), Book X, XCVI. The description 'food of an ordinary or innocent kind' is a reference to the rumours that the Christians sacrificed and then ate new-born infants at their secret rites. The pagans were obviously puzzled by what they thought of as ritualistic cannibalism, even though the eating of the Man-God's flesh and the drinking of his blood was only symbolic.

4 See A. F. Rudorff (editor) *De Juris Dictione Edictum* (1869) and J. Doublet, *Notes sur les oeuvres littéraires de L'empereur Hadrien* (1893).

5 For a discussion of Gnosticism see P. D. Scott-Moncrieff, *Paganism and Christianity in Egypt* (1913), Chapters VII and VIII.

Ruins of the 'lost' City of St. Menas in the Libyan Desert
Above The fourth-century Basilica of Arcadius
Below A Roman well

The eighth-century church of Abu Sarga in Cairo. Legend reports that the Holy Family rested here on their Flight into Egypt

5 The Desert Fathers

A little old man in a soiled white gown and skull-cap led me through the alleys of Old Cairo, a community of 29 mosques, 20 churches, one synagogue, 133,000 Mohammedans, 30,000 Copts, and 42 Jewish families. Old Cairo is some two miles up the Nile from the modern city with its complex of hotels, offices, and government buildings, and the two districts symbolise in their appearance and very atmosphere the difference between the past and present. The visitor will realise this the moment he enters through a gate pierced in the twenty-foot walls of the original settlement and descends a flight of steps to the level of the Roman citadel called Babylon.

The impression of a bygone age is strongest in the quarter of Old Cairo reserved for the Jews, a miniature ghetto of forty-two families housed in barrack huts on either side of a tree-lined avenue beside the synagogue of Ben Ezra. Placing me on a bench, my old man disappeared into one of the huts to look for the guardian of the Jewish temple. It was a good place to wait, watching the winter sunlight filtering through the trees in which the doves were murmuring, making of this courtyard a strangely peaceful and melancholy corner. However, my guide and the guardian who came to unlock the synagogue wore cheerful aspects, in keeping, I presumed, with the pamphlet which introduces the English-speaking visitor to the Israelite community of Cairo with these words, given here in their original form. (Why, one wonders, do the writers of these little guide-books not ask some English friend to make their translation for them?)

> The author of this modest work who has the privilege of exercing his mission in this beautiful Nile Valley, so well

known for its liberalism and spirit of relijious tolerance is happy to present to the Leaders of the Revolution, with this book, his respectful homage of loyalty. Patriotism and profound gratitude.

Although this population of different religious yet they are united and love each other as one family.

The history, like the appearance, of the Ben Ezra synagogue is confusing. The temple, both within and without, resembles an early Christian church, which is what it was from the fourth to the ninth century. Apparently the Copts were obliged to sell the church to the Jews in A.D. 868 when the Christians were unable to pay the tax of 20,000 gold dinars demanded by Ibn Tulun in order to build his mosque. A characteristic religious controversy ensued. The Jews claimed the site as the place where the synagogue of the prophet Jeremiah had been located and where Joseph and Mary worshipped during their exile to Egypt. The proof that this place was the original synagogue of Jeremiah destroyed by the Romans in 30 B.C. and wrongly taken from them by the Christians in the fourth century, they said, was the existence of an ancient Torah written on deer skin and hidden in its original *guenizeh*, or vault, within the walls of the building. The visitor is shown a roll of this *Torah*. The rest, says the little guide-book, 'is now spread over the Western world part in the Columbia University, part in the cemenery of New York part of the British Museum and the Bodleian University College and further part in Austria and Torino'.

A sad place, this empty synagogue with its few relics dutifully pointed out to the tourist by the guide—the 'Miracle Rock' under which the prophet Jeremiah is supposed to be buried; the arabesque ceiling dating from A.D. 1115; the old wooden clock; and the spring, or *mikva*, where we are told that Joseph and Mary drew water to wash the baby Jesus. Missing are the 100,000 books which once formed the library of the synagogue. But it suddenly becomes clear how Jewish and Christian history are intermingled in Moslem Egypt and how both groups need to shelter under 'the spirit of religious tolerance' referred to in the Foreword of the Ben Ezra Synagogue pamphlet—Moslem, Christian, and Jew 'united and loving each other as one family'.

Both ancient and modern history, of course, tells us otherwise. Certainly neither the Pharaohs, nor the Romans, nor the Christians, nor the Arabs, nor the Turks, nor the Egyptians today have felt loving towards the Jews who have wandered in and out of Egypt since the time of Moses. Perhaps the only period of respite these persecuted exiles enjoyed was during the first century A.D. when they settled in the cities and settlements of the Nile Delta. The evidence of this is seen in the flight of the Holy Family into Egypt, which must have been the safest refuge available. As the Ben Ezra pamphlet puts it: 'It is positively known that Joseph was Jew and that the logical thing for him to do was to go to his own people for a refuge for his family and himself.' Fifty years later, the apostles Peter and Mark, probably fleeing from the political and religious disturbances in Jerusalem, took the same road and arrived in Babylon, or Old Cairo, whence Peter sent his First Epistle General to Christian communities scattered throughout Pontus, Galatia, Cappadocia, Asia, and Bithynia. Peter ends his letter with the words 'the church that is at Babylon, elected together with you, saluteth you'.

Ecclesiastical historians have long disputed the whereabouts of this 'Babylon', the majority of them maintaining that the name is a metaphor for Rome. Rome is also preferred as lending credence to the legend that St. Peter was martyred in the Italian metropolis and, as that city's first pope, elevated that city into the capital of the Christian world. The opposing argument points out that Babylon was the Roman fortress and settlement on the Nile—the same refuge to which Joseph and Mary fled.

But whatever the arguments for or against St. Peter's visit to Babylon in Egypt, the evidence for several flourishing Jewish colonies in Lower Egypt during the first century A.D. is undeniable, whereas the Jewish population of Rome was, in comparison, small and unimportant. There were, for instance, several hundred thousand Jews living in Alexandria, or two-fifths of the citizenry. Moreover, this polyglot city in A.D. 50

was the philosophical centre of the Roman world, famous for its teachers, schools, academies, and libraries. And the leading scholar and metaphysician was Philo Judaeus, a Jewish philosopher steeped in both the Mosaic law and Platonic idealism and a disciple of the sect called the Therapeutae whose theory and practice of religion were so close to Christian doctrine that it was once thought that the Therapeutae were converts to the new faith. Could Peter have visited Philo Judaeus and told him of the new cult?

What, one wonders, would have been the future of Christianity if he had, and if a philosopher of the stature of Philo had helped to formulate the Christian ethic, synthesising the gospel of Christ with the speculations of the Greek philosophers? A profitless question, perhaps, since the Christians of the first and second centuries were suited neither by class nor education to regard religion as an exercise in metaphysics. The first Egyptian convert (according to the legend) was one Annianus, a shoemaker by trade. Such an artisan who lived and worked in an alley of the Alexandrian bazaars could have had little in common with an aristocrat like Philo, two of whose nephews were married to the daughters of King Agrippa, while his brother was the steward for Antonia, sister-in-law of Tiberius. Similarly, the hordes of exiles who fled to Egypt from Jerusalem after the sack of that holy city by Titus in A.D. 70 were not disposed to talk philosophy but demanded action to the extent that religion, whether Judaic or Christian, because another militant expression of their hatred of Rome. In fact, the Jerusalem exiles attempted to foment a Holy War on their arrival in Egypt, with the consequence that the rich, Hellenised Jews of Alexandria denounced the ringleaders to the authorities. Six hundred of their compatriots at least were put to death. This bitter internecine war must have spelt the end of any alliance between the followers of Philo, the orthodox Jews, and the Jewish converts to Christianity.

One result of this bitterness was a shift in Christian thinking from an emphasis on the doctrine of universal love to an obsessive hatred of the pagan world, which led observers like Tacitus to describe the new sect's hostility to other men as 'a detestation of the human race' and the emperor Hadrian to speak of Christians as 'seditious, vain, and spiteful'. The suspicion, hostility, or outright hatred of the converts towards the pagans soon led to a reciprocal loathing and so to the first religious persecutions of the ancient world, which had hitherto been remarkably free from this kind of bigotry. By the four edicts of Diocletian, for instance, all churches were to be demolished; all sacred books were to be burnt; all Christians who held any official position were to be stripped of their dignities and deprived of their civil rights (that they might thereby be legally tortured); and all Christians who were not officials were to be reduced to slavery. Such were the edicts; and one can imagine the state of mind of the Christians who read them in the market places of every town and village throughout the empire.

In Egypt, which had every reason to fear Diocletian and his legions (they had destroyed Alexandria in A.D. 292), the edicts were tantamount to death for the principal Christians and to slavery for the rank and file. Men had a choice, therefore, between martyrdom and flight. There must have been thousands of these self-exiles during the reign of Diocletian, as there appear to have been hundreds who preferred death. Eusebius speaks of scores of men with their wives and children being slain every day for several years. 'It would exceed all power of detail to give an idea of the sufferings and tortures which the martyrs of the Thebaid endured', he writes in his *Ecclesiastical History*, and then goes on to list some of the tortures, including scraping the bodies with shells, hanging up naked women by one foot, and lashing men's arms and legs to the branches of separate trees in such a way that when the branches were released they sprang back into their natural positions and tore the victims limb from limb.

Eusebius gives an average of about sixty martyrs a day for five years during the Diocletian persecution, which suggests a total of over 100,000 Christian deaths in Egypt alone. The number seems high until we compare it with the periodic slaughters characteristic of the ancient and, for that matter, of the modern world. There is no reason to doubt the figure, since by the end of the third century it is probable that a great number of Egyptians had accepted some form or the other of Christianity which made the persecutions all the more terrible. According to Coptic sources, 140,000 Christians were killed under Diocletian and 70,000 banished; and whether the figures are exaggerated or not (one learns not to pay too much attention to Oriental statistics), the Diocletian persecution made such an impression on the Egyptian Church that their calendar dates from the Era of the Martyrs, namely from A.D. 284, the year of the accession of the emperor Diocletian. From this time, the war between the pagans and the Christians was a war of unconditional surrender; and as in all wars of this kind, hatred and fanaticism, with their attendant forces of lies and distortions, replaced the original Christian concept of brotherhood and brotherly love.

There was only one way of escape for those Christians who still believed in that gospel to avoid the loss of their lives and their faith. That was to flee to the desert; and we may be sure that men did flee by the thousands, to begin a new life as far as possible from the cruelties and temptations of the old world. Their vision is summed up in the panegyric of St. Jerome, who spoke as a member of this new society:

> O Desert, bright with the flowers of Christ! O Solitude, whence come the stones of which the Apocalypse, the city of the Great King, is built! O Wilderness, gladdened with God's especial presence! What keeps you in the world, my brother, you who are above the world? How long shall gloomy roofs oppress you? Oh, that I could behold the desert, lovelier to me than any city.

But long before recognisable communities were established, individual ascetics had begun their journeys into the desert with the intention of fleeing from the world, choosing the most unattractive surroundings they could for the purpose. In the course of time disciples were attracted to their habitations, so that a collection of dwellings well scattered about the area grew up. These dwellings were, for the most part, caves, or holes hewn in the rock, or cabins built of stones and roofed with reeds. Two necessities of even the ascetic life eventually brought these solitaries together, at least on Sundays: one was the well of fresh water which even the most self-denying hermit had to visit and where, in consequence, he met his fellow-hermits; the other a communal place of worship where the *agape*, or love-feast of the early Christians, could also be held. The well, the little church, the kitchen, and perhaps some sort of shelter for pilgrims constituted the nucleus of what, by the fourth century A.D., had grown into a convent.

But even admitting the purely physical causes of this exodus to the desert, the phenomenon of men renouncing the world in the extreme manner of the first Christian hermits is not easily accounted for. Obviously, the occasional withdrawal of individuals from society is not in question here: such behaviour is usually explained as personal eccentricity. But the hermits of the Thebaid, as of other deserts in the Levant, were numbered in their thousands and constituted a people in themselves, almost a state, with their own government, laws, and sometimes armies. They even had a corporate name: they called themselves the 'Perfect'; or, alternatively, the 'Athletes of Christ'. It is clear, then, that we are not dealing with isolated social deviants; we are forced, rather, to recognise that the hermit communities consisted of men, and later of women, who were motivated by aims which the rationalist can scarcely comprehend and the materialist cannot understand at all. The issue is whether self-denial in its extreme form promotes a mystical union with God or the converse that self-indulgence separates man from God. The stubborn conviction that the former concept was the road to perfection is the key to the lives of the Desert Fathers, of whom St. Antony was the ideal.

6 The lost gospels of the Desert Christians

But even while admitting their profound influence on the faith we still nominally profess today, we must recognise that these primitive desert Christians are immeasurably remote from us not only in space and time, but in their basic beliefs. There are two significant reasons for this. First, they took Christ's doctrine and precepts literally and deliberately set out to practise what he preached; and secondly, the sources of their knowledge—their scriptures—were often different from ours, since they learnt about Jesus not only from the canonical gospels, but from gospels which are now lost altogether, or, if they survive in fragmentary form, are considered of no value from the orthodox point of view. On the other hand, it was these gospels, later suppressed by the Western Church, which were (a) responsible for some of the strange beliefs of the Desert Fathers and the early Church; and (b) a contributing factor to the great schism which split the universal Church first into two and then into a formidable number of rival sects.

There were at least a dozen of these forbidden gospels which were once freely read by Christians in the deserts of Egypt as well as the churches of Rome and which were gradually discredited by the more authoritative of the Catholic Fathers. In addition there were a great many other scriptures called Acts, Epistles, Teachings, Travels, Histories, Apocalypses, and Books which were damned *in aeternum* in a sixth-century decree emanating from the Vatican; but it so happened that many of these writings were the favourite story books of the Eastern Christians, while a number of them were greatly revered by devout and quite orthodox ecclesiasts. The publication of the so-called Gelasian Decree listing the 'heretical' gospels and scriptures led first to some very acrimonious arguments; then to charges of heresy; next to anathemas against a score of Eastern patriarchs and their flock; next to outright censorship; and finally to forbidden books.

All these happenings profoundly affected the Egyptian Christians since they found themselves being increasingly pushed outside the pale of the 'True Church', their beliefs denounced as heresies, and their scriptures condemned as spurious. Here we discover one more reason why the Copts withdrew into themselves, as it were, establishing their own Church which eventually broke all ties with other Churches and continues to do so today. We also understand why so many of the suppressed gospels have turned up in Egypt—on the shelves of the monastery libraries and in the graves of monks. Incidental to this strange and fascinating 'battle of the books' is the larger effect the controversy had upon social and political, as well as religious, practices. For we now arrive at the period of heresy and censorship, both of which have profoundly affected human destiny. When and how did these institutions originate?

We have a clue in the proceedings of the First Council of Nicaea in A.D. 325 at which the Fathers decided what books were 'acceptable' and what were not. The resultant brawling which went on in the Bithynian town was actually a battle of the books, a battle which would not have been won without divine intervention. For the bishops,

> having put all the books that were referred to the Council for deliberation under the communion table in a church, besought the Lord that the inspired writings might get onto the table, while the spurious ones remained underneath. And it happened accordingly.

This was certainly a novel way of censoring books, and it is not surprising that the supporters of those tomes which stayed under the table objected. They argued that many of the non-levitated texts were as authentic as those works which had defied the laws of gravity: in other words, they were as authentic in respect of their authorship, venerability, and acceptance by the primitive Christians. Some modern historians tend to agree with this reasoning, if only by implication. Dr. Montague Rhodes James puts the issue like this in his Introduction to *The Apocryphal New Testament*:

> It will very quickly have been seen that there is no question of any one's having excluded them from the New Testament: they have done that for themselves . . . (for) they do not achieve either of the two purposes for which they were written, the instilling of the true religion and the conveyance of true history.

Who decided what was true religion and true history in the fourth century? And on what grounds were the decisions made? Dr. James hints at the answer:

> The scholars of Alexandria, Antioch, and Rome, being 'tried money-changers', proved all things and held fast that which was good. Many a book, like the venerable *Gospel According to the Hebrews* which we should dearly have liked to possess for the light they would throw on primitive Christian history, has perished in consequence of their unfavourable verdict, and we regret the loss—no one more keenly than myself: but the verdict that consigned them first to obscurity and then to destruction I cannot quarrel with.

Without quarrelling we can still question the right of the scholars of Alexandria, Antioch, and Rome to *destroy* any of the evidence, since their action was the first step towards destroying the authors as well as their books. Thus the pious and learned Arius had all his works burnt under pain of death and was, perhaps, lucky not to be burnt with them, but only to be banished to the inhospitable mountains of Albania. And once the principle of suppressing unorthodox ideas had been established, it was not long before total censorship was in force. In A.D. 494, Pope Gelasius I finalised the work of the censors during the preceding two centuries in his decree *de libris recipiendis et non recipiendis*, a catalogue of prohibited books which proscribed at least sixty-one volumes and thirty-six authors together with their supporters, 'to be damned in the inextricable shackles of anathema for ever'.

Among these heretics and schismatics was Gelasius's rival Acacius, Patriarch of Constantinople, with whom the Western pope was engaged in an all-out struggle for the leadership of the Christian world. However, some of these books actually survived the anathema—the works of Tertullian and Lactantius, for instance. Some survived in papyrus fragments recently found in the sands of Egypt. Some have disappeared altogether. Probably there has been no great loss in either philosophical or literary content, judging from the titles of some of these forbidden books; but it would be interesting to have them all the same. What was the 'Book which is called The Home-going of the Holy Mary'? Or, the 'Book about the giant Ogias, of whom the heretics assert that after the flood he fought with the dragon'? Why did those early prelates not want us to read these fairy tales?

From the Decree of Gelasius onwards, the full weight of the Church's authority was behind the censorship not only of what men could read, but what they could think and say; and to ensure that its rulings were enforced, the penalties for disobedience became progressively more severe. By 1215, Pope Innocent III was calling for the 'extermination' of heretics; by 1252, Innocent IV was able to sanction the use of torture in heresy trials; and by 1563, the Council of Trent had declared that the Church was the sole arbiter of spiritual revelation; the Bible should be interpreted only according to the testimony of the orthodox Fathers; heretics should be anathemised; and books not approved by the Holy Office prohibited. In brief, censorship was now exercised in all departments of life, moral as well as religious, social as well as intellectual.

But long before the Council of Trent, the Egyptian Church had lost almost all ties with Western Christendom, so that all the anathemas, damnations, excommunications, and inquisitions passed the beleaguered Christians by. The monks in the remote convents of the Libyan and Arabian Deserts went on reading the banned books and believing what was in them. They were no doubt culpable of the most awful heresies, as some of the suppressed gospels clearly supported the Arian heresy, some that of the Gnostics, and some that of the Manichaeans.

But the cardinal inquisitors in Rome could certainly not reach the monasteries of the Wadi Natrun, for instance; and they were, in any case, too busy rooting and burning out heretics in their own domains to be bothered with what a few wretched monophysites were reading in their desert cells. As a result, a number of the 'lost' books have reappeared within the last fifty years or so—usually discovered in Egypt, occasionally in Ethiopia. The latest of them, *The Sayings of Jesus*, or the *Gospel According to Thomas,* was unearthed from the sands of Upper Egypt only twenty years or so ago.

Christians will ask today why so many of these ancient scriptures were anathematised and suppressed. First—and obviously enough—they were suppressed by the Roman Catholic Church because they contained the seeds of doctrines which had been pronounced heretical; and secondly—not so obviously since the books themselves are either lost or not easily available—they raise troublesome questions as to the facts and the interpretation of Christ's life and ministry. Indeed, the very foundations of traditional doctrine could be shaken by their treatment of such articles of faith as the Nativity, the Holy Family, the nature of Christ's teaching, the attitude of his disciples, the trial and crucifixion, the culpability of Pontius Pilate, the Resurrection, and even the divinity of Christ himself. (This last point, incidentally, throws light on the heresy of Arius who may have based his theory that Jesus was human on apostolic records that are no longer extant.)

The natural fears of the Church as regards scriptures which might undermine official dogma were summed up early in the fourth century by Eusebius of Caesarea (himself not immune from the charge of heresy):

> The thought and purpose of what is expressed in them [i.e. the disputed writings], being in the highest degree contrary to true orthodoxy, show clearly that in them we handle the concoction of heretics. Wherefore they ought never to be classed with the writings that are spurious, but ought to be rejected as wholly absurd and impious.

The operative words in Bishop Eusebius's condemnation of

the disputed, or 'non-acceptable' books are 'orthodoxy' and 'the concoction of heretics'. What the bishop meant, of course, was that the condemned scriptures contained a variant account of Christ's nature and ministry to that which the Catholic Church had decided was the most conducive to the firm establishment of a hierarchy. We can compare their concern with the present and future of their spiritual 'empire' to that of mundane imperialists who, through the medium of orthodox history, promulgate the myths surrounding national heroes. Thus we learn to think of mass-murderers like Alexander, Cromwell, Napoleon, and a hundred other successful war-makers as, in some way, benefactors of the human race; and as time goes on, the prime sources which describe their deeds (as, for instance, an account by a citizen of Tyre of how Alexander put to death 8,000 citizens in cold blood, crucified 2,000, and sold 30,000 into slavery) tend to be lost altogether, largely because the contemporary authorities suppressed them as 'subversive'.

However, as we have seen, many of the condemned scriptures have survived, mostly by accident, and it is only fitting that we should examine their claim to be genuine. Here one has to remember the manner in which all the gospels came down to us. The most reasonable supposition is that each of the apostles related his own account of the life and ministry of Jesus to sympathetic Jewish communities who regarded the crucified Nazarene as a victim of Roman oppression and a leader of a nationalistic movement. Some of the apostles seem to have travelled widely—in their hagiographies, at any rate; St. Peter as far as Rome, St. Matthew to Persia, St. Luke to Gaul, St. James to Spain, St. Thomas to India, St. Philip to Morocco, et cetera. Pious legend has the evangelists carrying the good tidings to the four corners of the known world.

What is certain is that the disciples told their story to many a sympathetic audience and that those who were converted (in the beginning Jews who travelled on business) carried the news of the new cult and its leader to Jewish colonies in distant lands. Biographies of the crucified Jesus were then written down and ascribed to various disciples, to Matthew, Mark, Luke, and John (the writers of the canonical gospels) and also to others of the Twelve. Hence, the congregations of the first and second-century churches had gospels according to Peter, Thomas, James the Less, Philip, Bartholomew, and even Judas Iscariot. These last six gospels, and a number of other so-called apostolic writings, began to be censored during the third and fourth centuries and were probably destroyed altogether in the fifth and sixth centuries. However, fragments of them have now accidentally come to light, and it is with them that we are concerned, for they help us to understand better the lives and beliefs of the Desert Christians.

Admittedly, the arguments for and against the genuineness of these rejected books belong in the realm of historical speculation. But the same arguments apply to all the early scriptures, since all our manuscripts of the New Testament, even the earliest, like the fourth-century *Codex Vaticanus*, are only copies and possibly translations of still older versions which eventually go back to oral tradition. All that we can say of these gospels, whether they are canonical or apocryphal, is that they were once read in Christian churches. The *Gospel According to Peter*, for instance, which survives only in a fragment discovered by the French Archaeological Mission in 1892, was undoubtedly in general use during the second century and is, therefore, as venerable as the canonical gospels. In fact, we first hear of it from Serapion, Bishop of Antioch, who, writing in A.D. 190 to the church at Rhossus, states: 'We find most of it of the right teaching, but some details are adventitious', by which he meant that the details in question did not agree with his interpretation of the events. But this did not cause him to condemn the gospel outright. To the contrary, he writes: 'If this is all that creates ill-feeling, why then let it be read.'

From the fragments of this Petrine gospel that have survived, we can glimpse the workings of the censors' minds. The text did not substantiate the version of events which the Church, still locked in a total war with the pagan world of old Rome, wished to perpetuate. Thus, the Gospel of Peter did not put the blame for the condemnation of Jesus and his mistreatment on the way to the cross squarely where the Western Fathers insisted it belonged. There is no mention of Pilate washing his hands, or of his delivering Jesus to be scourged. And it was not the Roman soldiers who stripped Jesus of his clothes, put him in a scarlet robe, and plaited a crown of thorns (as in Matthew, Mark, and John, but not Luke), but the 'people'. One suspects that this account of the trial was something of an embarrassment to those non-Roman Christians who had such good cause to hate their old masters as tyrants, to discredit them as pagans, and to exonerate the Jews as the authors of the Bible. As a result, the bishops smelled out the 'adventitious details', which were soon to be categorised as heresy, and the *Gospel According to Peter* was 'damned in the inextricable shackles of anathema'.

The same doubts as to the motives of the early editors are entertained as regards their suppression of another once-venerated gospel—that of the *Gospel According to the Hebrews*. St. Jerome himself states that he translated this book into Greek and Latin and adds that Origen often used it as one of his sources. There is even the suggestion in ancient commentaries that this scripture was the original of the *Gospel According to Matthew*. Why, then, was it suppressed? Catholic authority[1] replies, 'We are warranted in saying that while this extra-canonical material probably has as its starting-point primitive tradition, it has been disfigured in the interests of a Judaising Church.' 'Judaising Church' is a reference to the Palestine Christians known as the Nazarenes (the earliest sect that we have a record of), who used the *Gospel According to the Hebrews* as their main source for the life and teachings of Christ. But this hardly seems sufficient grounds for burning the book, as we are told Cyril of Jerusalem ordered one of his monks to do. More feasibly, the claim in this gospel that the Holy Ghost was a 'female force' called Mary who became the mother of Jesus Christ by God the Father, was not unnaturally rejected by the later ecclesiasts as smacking of paganism; for here we have a parallel with Greek mythology in the family relationship between Zeus, the chief god, his wife Hera, and their son Apollo.

Still another gospel which was to be anathematised was the one ascribed to James the Less, who styles himself 'the brother of the Lord Jesus, chief apostle, and first bishop of the Christians in Jerusalem' and who concludes his account with this interesting postscript:

> I James wrote this History in Jerusalem. And when the disturbances took place, I retired into a desert place until the death of Herod. After the disturbances had ceased at Jerusalem, I was able to write this gospel and send it to you who love God, to whom glory and power for ever and ever, Amen.

James's work, also known as the *Protevangelion*, was certainly accepted as scripture by some Christian communities in the first and second centuries, but, like the gospels *According to Peter* and that *According to the Hebrews*, was rejected by the Western Church as being tainted with Gnosticism. The objection to this gospel is that it purports to relate the events preceding the nativity; and, for obvious reasons, the account it gives was obnoxious to the early Fathers. For these learned men were undoubtedly harassed by the arguments concerning the Virgin birth, upon the acceptance of which depended the entire credibility of the new faith. Parthenogenesis in such manifestations as the offspring of gods and mortals was common enough in the pagan world, of course, though no intelligent person gave these legends the slightest credence. But the Christians abhorred everything to do with paganism, particularly the lascivious gods. But eventually those responsible for formulating official doctrine had to face the fact that their religion originated with an act of parthenogenesis, and it did not help them at all that the *Gospel According to James the Less* cast certain doubts upon that phenomenon. For this scripture discusses Joseph's relationship with Mary in much too frank a manner to substantiate the idyll of the compliant patriarch, the innocent maiden, and the mysterious Holy Ghost. It is no wonder the censors firmly suppressed it, outraged by the description of Joseph as an elderly widower obliged by the high priests to take a twelve-year-old girl into his household against his will.

> I am an old man and have children; but she is young and I fear lest I should appear ridiculous in Israel.

Obviously this kind of talk from a man who was to be canonised could not be permitted, nor could his displeasure when he returned from 'building houses abroad' to find his protegée pregnant. 'Smiting his face', he asks, 'Who has committed this evil in my house?' To which Mary replies, with a flood of tears, 'As the Lord liveth, I know not by what means.' She might well have made such a remark, since the canonical gospels themselves do not make the matter at all clear. Thus, the *Gospel According to Matthew* has an 'angel of the Lord' announcing the coming of the Messiah to Joseph; the *Gospel According to Luke* has 'the angel Gabriel' making the same announcement to Mary. In *Matthew*, Joseph sees the unnamed angel in a dream; in *Luke*, Mary sees Gabriel while she is awake. In *Matthew* the angel appears after Mary is pregnant; in *Luke* he appears to Mary before her pregnancy.

In contrast to all these contradictions, the *Gospel According to James the Less* gives a quite simple version of the events, portraying the widower Joseph as a confused and bewildered old man who, far from being the benign patriarch of orthodox scripture, behaves and speaks in a very human manner. For when he hears about the imperial decree ordering the poll-tax, he bursts out:

> I will take care that my children be taxed. But what shall I do with this young woman? To have her taxed as my wife I am ashamed; and if I tax her as my daughter, all Israel knows she is not my daughter.

The *Protevangelion* goes farther than this, giving the censors even more cogent reasons for suppressing it: it states that Jesus had half-brothers by Joseph's previous wife (or wives), an assertion which was more than enough to have the book banned, since by the time of Jerome (A.D. 340–420), the Church had decreed that there could be no offspring of either Joseph or Mary, since the former was supposed to be a lifelong celibate and the latter a perpetual virgin. The references to Christ's brethren in the canonical gospels, the fact that Mary designates

Joseph as Jesus's father, and Jesus himself refers to his parents were glossed over in order that the theologians could establish the doctrine that he was the literal son of God, sinless because untainted by original sin. Those 'apocryphal' gospels which threw doubts on this dogma were denounced as heretical, though many an early exegist had fallen into grievous error by attempting to solve the problem of the Virgin Birth. Thus Origen, the greatest of ecclesiastical scholars, made the mistake of comparing Christ's birth with the theory that Plato was the offspring of Apollo and a mortal woman; and then declaring that the Greek account of the philosopher's birth was, of course, ridiculous. Others like Tertullian also fell into doctrinal error by asserting that Mary, after she had given birth to Jesus, married Joseph, and had children by him. The heresy? A reflection on the purity of the mother of God. Hence even Tertullian is on the list of anathematised books in the so-called Gelasian Decree of the late fifth century.

And so we begin to see why so many ancient manuscripts that differed from the approved canon were, as Dr. James tells us, 'consigned first to obscurity and then to destruction'. Among them must have been all those accounts of the trial and crucifixion which tended to exonerate the Roman pagans. Condemned, too, were those which threw doubts, even if only by implication, on the supernatural character of the nativity. Others again, by reporting Christ's frankly political sayings, detracted from the portrait of a spiritual leader whose kingdom was not of this earth. Such, for instance, is the *Gospel According to Thomas*, also known as the *Sayings of Jesus*, unearthed in 1945 at Chenoboskion (Naga Hammadi) in Upper Egypt: a highly controversial book, for the portrait it gives, far from being that of 'gentle Jesus meek and mild', is of a philosopher-teacher whose opinions and precepts, like those of Socrates, were extremely repugnant to the conservative community in any society. Some of these *Sayings* are speculative, some humanitarian, and some definitely inflammatory. They are, in short, the reflections not so much of a divine personage above the petty problems and wranglings of mortal men, but the observations of a positive thinker deeply concerned with the human condition.

Let us examine some of these Sayings which are not found in the canonical gospels or which have significant differences in wording and import.

> Then saith he unto them, Render therefore unto Caesar the things that are Caesar's; and unto God the things that are God's. (*Matthew*, Ch. 22, v. 21.)

> They showed Jesus a gold coin and said to him, Caesar's men ask taxes from us. He said, Give the things of Caesar to Caesar, give the things of God to God, and give me what is mine. (*Thomas*, Logion 100.)

Is this what Christ actually said? Or is the third imperative an addition of some later commentator? It is impossible now to say, and it could be argued that the last clause doesn't make much difference to the general tenor of the reply, which was a shrewd retort to an obviously provocative question. On the other hand, if Christ actually did differentiate between God, Caesar, and himself, was he not disclaiming a divine status?

Whatever he said and whatever he meant, the bishops were not permitting the sceptical to quote evidence to support their argument that Christ was not the literal son of God; and the *Sayings* incurred their anathema. Understandably so, since this particular gospel (or *pseudo-Thomas*, as it is called) raised far too many controversial issues to be allowed to circulate freely, or even to circulate at all. It suggests, for instance, that Christ had moments of very human self-doubt, whence his concern with (in modern jargon) his 'image'.

> Jesus said, Make a comparison of me and tell me whom I am like.
>
> Simon Peter said to him, Thou art like a righteous man who brings good tidings.
>
> Matthew said to him, Thou art like a wise man.
>
> Thomas said, I am wholly incapable of saying whom thou art like.
>
> Jesus said, Then I am not the master.

From these replies, the heretics could argue that his disciples did not regard him as the literal son of God, but as an evangelist and a philosopher. Yes, and as a visionary, of course:

> His disciples said to him, Twenty-four prophets spoke in Israel and you speak with the voice of them all.

Jesus accepted these various titles, though he seems to have preferred the general description of himself as 'the son of man', an Aramaic expression which means neither more nor less than a 'man'; or, as our idiom has it, a 'human being'. However, the rumour that he was divine and not human had begun to circulate among the more superstitious or hysterical of his followers, which may explain Saying 15,

> When you see one who was not born of woman, prostrate yourselves upon your face and adore him. He is your Father.

Since none of his contemporaries could possibly have believed that he, Jesus, was not born of woman, his injunction must have been intended to scotch the talk that he was a god. Indeed, according to the *Gospel of Thomas*, he was only too aware of the irregularity of his birth, for it is difficult to explain otherwise the virulence of his attacks on the institution of the family. True, the censors allow us to catch glimpses of his resentment in the canonical gospels, though the quotations have been edited so as not to offend deep-seated traditions. Thus, according to *Matthew*:

> He that loveth father or mother more than me is not worthy of me; and he that loveth son or daughter more than me is not worthy of me.

The *Gospel According to Thomas* records the same pronouncement in a much harsher (and possibly the original) form:

> Jesus said, Whoever does not hate his father and his mother in my way cannot be a disciple to me.

Even allowing for the contemptuous attitude of philosophers towards women and the family in the first century A.D., the New Testament editors could hardly allow this and similar humiliating statements to go uncensored, any more than they could ignore the attacks on Judaic-Christian dogma as recorded in the Fourteenth Saying of the *Gospel According to Thomas*:

> If you fast, you will beget sins for yourself; and if you pray, you will be condemned; and if you give alms, you will do evil to your spirits.

In fact, a Jew could hardly have said anything more inflammatory, unless it was a condemnation of the sacrosanct rite of circumcision by which his people proclaimed their orthodoxy and asserted their superiority to the Gentiles. Indeed, the more the foreign tyrants had tried to suppress this ancient rite, the more the Jews clung to it as a test of faith. It is extraordinary, therefore, to find Jesus reported as stating, 'If circumcision were right and proper, men would be born circumcised.' On the other hand, St. Paul, who seems to have been conversant with this particular Saying (though it is nowhere reported in the canonical gospels) also promulgated the doctrine that the removal of the foreskin did not automatically bestow superior spiritual status, so the censors might have let this go, but decided that the safest course was to suppress the gospel of Thomas altogether and done with it. One can sympathise with their predicament. On the one hand, they had a vague spiritual comment about wealth—'It is easier for a camel to go through a needle's eye than for a rich man to enter the kingdom of God'; and on the other, a specific and, indeed, offensive attack on a large group of respectable citizens—'Tradesmen and merchants shall not enter the places of my Father' (Logion 64). Naturally, they chose the former.

But one can only guess at the reasons why such and such a book was 'not to be accepted'. In some cases, one may be sure that the editors felt justified in throwing out what they considered to be unmitigated rubbish. Such, no doubt, was their decision regarding the so-called *Gospel of the Infancy of Jesus Christ* which spins a series of yarns more suitable to an oriental bazaar than to a church congregation. It is obvious, moreover, that the writer of this hodge-podge had ransacked pagan literature for his 'gospel', even stealing Lucian's story of the ass to extol Christ's supernatural powers; for he tells how

Joseph and Mary, while staying at an inn, were surprised to find one of the rooms occupied by some young women and a mule. The latter was 'covered over with silk and wore an ebony collar hanging down from his neck'; while the former were kissing and feeding this animal who, they explained, was their beloved brother 'bewitched by a giddy and jealous woman'. Mary obligingly placed her son on the mule's back, whereupon a sort of palingenesis took place, and the young man was restored to his human shape. Not unreasonably, the Fathers, harassed in any case by scores of heresies, disapproved of this irreverent nonsense, though the later Church was quite tolerant of fables, as an examination of the hagiography of the Middle Ages will show.

It is important to recognise that many of these suppressed books continued to circulate and to be read by the early Egyptian Christians long after they had been totally forgotten in the West. Totally forgotten, on the other hand, is perhaps an exaggeration since those gospels which were obviously of the romantic or picaresque variety played a considerable role in medieval writing, both sacred and profane. In other words, the fairy stories involving dragons, young men turned into mules, palsied men waking dumb women in their beds, et cetera, passed into the stream of the folk tale and so into literature, to reappear in the new and more sophisticated versions of Boccaccio, Chaucer, and Dante.

But for the desert monks and hermits confined within their convents and cells the condemned books were not fairy tales but holy writ, as ancient and therefore as authentic as the canonical gospels. They constituted, moreover, the monks' only means of entertainment and relaxation, since they were read out at meal times and took a man's mind off his monotonous diet and continuous pangs of hunger. But most important of all, they gave a portrait of Jesus which appealed in particular to the simple Egyptian desert Christians. In brief, Jesus was presented to them as another St. Antony—that is, a man divinely inspired; godlike in all his thoughts, words, and deeds; an ascetic who rejected the world for the kingdom of heaven; a scorner of family ties, wealthy men, and politicians: in other words, a godly man in the desert tradition, of one character, one nature, and one will. Such was the simple, emotional appeal of Jesus to nearly all the ordinary Christians of the East, and it explains why these worshippers and their leaders were so passionately dedicated to Monophysite principles.

Not that the monks and hermits living in the Egyptian deserts were aware of the intellectual nuances of monophysitism, the controversy as to the single or dual nature of Christ. In any case, they did not know the Greek language in which the endless arguments about the *φύσις* and *ὑπόστασις* were conducted. All they knew was that their Lord and Master was of a piece in his life and his teaching, consistently denying himself and exhorting others to deny themselves not only the riches of this world, but even the simpler pleasures, like a home, wife, and family. Special emphasis was placed on those Sayings of Jesus which extolled chastity, continence, and celibacy—Sayings which we find quite frequently in the suppressed gospels, much less frequently (and in less offensive language) in the canonical gospels. The *Gospel According to the Egyptians*, for instance, has this curious condemnation of sex in an alleged statement of Jesus on the subject:

> For the Lord himself being asked by someone when his kingdom should come said, When the two shall be one, and the outside as the inside, and the male with the female neither male nor female.

And again:

> I came to destroy the works of the female.

It was undoubtedly *dicta* of this kind (who knows whether Christ ever spoke them or not?) that led to the emphasis upon sexual continence among the Egyptian monks, because 'female' symbolised in early Christian thought 'lust', an interpretation which seemed to be borne out by the story of Adam's fall due to the sinfulness of Eve. And as in confirmation of the uncompromising misogynist attitude, the gospels themselves, both the canonical books and those later suppressed, have many examples of Christ's disdain of, or diffidence towards, women, mothers, family, and so forth. In the suppressed *Gospel According to Thomas*, the gospel significantly found in a monk's grave in Upper Egypt and written in the Coptic language, we find this Saying of Jesus,

> Simon Peter said to them, Let Mary go out from among us, because women are not worthy of the Life. Jesus said, See, I shall lead her so that I will make her male that she, too, may become a living spirit, resembling you males. For every woman who makes herself male will enter the kingdom of heaven.

Continually subjected to such commands, the Egyptian monks could not fail to be obsessed by the innate wickedness of the contemporary Eves from whom they fled as far away as possible, refusing even to speak to their own mothers and sisters. And, as if in corroboration of the above Saying there were cases, as we have seen, where women did 'make themselves male' in order to join the company of the Elect in the desert.

It is certain that the Egyptians were not prepared to give up their books, even though they were pronounced spurious or heretical by the hated Western Church. They liked their gospels, Acts, Epistles, Apocalypses, and romances, especially as they had nothing else to read or to have read to them. Besides, these moral tales were exceedingly diverting while both inspiring and consoling to men who had given up the world for the sake of their master and his apostles. Some of the tales are quite beautiful in both content and style and were evidently written by novelists of genius, like the tale of St. Paul and the maiden Thecla in the so-called *Acts of Paul*. Here is the description of the apostle by a master-craftsman:

> A man little of stature, going bald, crooked in the legs, but powerfully built, with eyebrows joining, and nose somewhat hooked . . .

It was this dynamic little man who captivated with his oratory the young maiden Thecla, the betrothed of one Thamyris. Not surprisingly Thamyris and the girl's mother objected to Thecla's apparent infatuation with this little balding, bow-legged, and hook-nosed stranger; and the affair was eventually brought to the attention of the governor. The lover and the mother hoped to get rid of Paul by accusing him of being a Christian, that is, a subversive. Paul, however, escaped, leaving Thecla to be condemned to be burnt alive in the arena as a lesson to the other women who had, for the love of God, left their husbands or lovers. And as she went into the arena,

> Thecla, as the lamb in the wilderness looketh about for the shepherd, so sought she for Paul.

But she is saved by a miracle (a thunderstorm puts out the pyre) and follows Paul to the cave where he is hiding. So the story continues in a most romantic fashion—it reminds one vividly of Héloïse and Abélard—though Thecla and Paul has a happy ending, or what, perhaps, a devout Christian would call happy. But read between the lines . . .

> But Thecla yearned after Paul and sought him, sending about in all places; and it was told her that he was at Myra . . . And she departed into Myra and found Paul speaking the word of God . . . And Paul took her by the hand and brought her into the house of Hermias and heard all things from her. Then he said 'Go, and teach the word of God.'
>
> Now Thecla had much apparel and gold, and she left most of her possessions with Paul for the ministry of the poor.
>
> But she herself departed into Iconium. And she entered into the house of Onesiphorus and fell down upon the floor where Paul had sat and wept, saying, 'O God of this house where the light shone upon me. . . .'
>
> And she departed into Seleucia. And after she had enlightened many with the word of God, she slept a good sleep.

One asks oneself if such a subtle and sensitive study of a woman in love was not written by another woman, for the whole theme of the story is the passion and sufferings of Thecla, not the travels of Paul. We picture him, in fact, as a rather opportunistic itinerant preacher, obviously with tremendous sexual attraction despite his ugliness—a man who was to find the love and adoration of his young protégée becoming burdensome, as so many ambitious elderly men who have had an affair with a young girl have found before and since. 'Go, and teach the word of God,' he tells his pupil. She goes, falls down on the floor where her beloved had once sat, weeps, and realises that this is the end.

Legend reports that she lived to be ninety and was made sport of by young men who visited her cave expressly to torment her. The beautiful girl had turned, of course, into what they called a witch. . . .

The literature of the Desert Christians is full of similar stories of holy women whose passion for a father or monk was transmuted into what was supposed to have been a total surrender to Christ himself. We have arrived, at this point, at the phenomenon of Christian mysticism which reached its tremendous climax in the ecstasies of the women visionaries of the Middle Ages.[2] The fantastic experiences of St. Hildegarde of Bingen and Mechthild of Magdeburg are foreshadowed in the lives of women like Thecla, Hilaria, Melania, and Paula. Their stories are infinitely sad or infinitely joyful, according to the reader's own predilection. Let that of Hilaria as told in a Coptic manuscript sum up the life-story of them all.

> When she heard at the age of twelve of the desert and the monks living there, Hilaria left her father, King Zeno, and fled to the desert, disguised as a servant. The Father of the Desert [the reference is apparently to Macarius] received her; the Holy Ghost had revealed to him that she was a woman. But he concealed this fact and put her into a grotto where she remained thirteen years, praying with the monks till her skin grew black, her appearance became altered, and her bones grew thin. She reached a high degree of asceticism. At her death, her pure odour spread till the desert was filled with her perfume. And when they were stripping off her clothes, they found her breasts withered on her pure bosom like leaves wither beneath the trees.[3]

Why, we ask, did the primitive desert Christians enjoy such (to us) depressing stories? And what is the moral of such stories?

The answer is that men who were no longer tempted by women in the flesh were sorely tormented by those seen in the imagination and that they were consoled by the thought that even the youngest and most beautiful of women grew old and even the most desirable of their charms withered away. Adding to this physical fact the spiritual warnings against women ('I came to destroy the works of the female'), the ascetics were better able to deny themselves even thoughts of carnal bliss. For the moral of the tale of both Thecla and Hilaria was: banish women from your lives and thoughts and leave time to destroy them.

The most successful of all those ascetics to achieve complete release from the tyranny of lust was, of course, St. Antony of Egypt.

REFERENCES

1 *The Catholic Encyclopaedia* (1907). Article under 'Apocrypha', p. 608.
2 See Epilogue.
3 A. J. Wensinck, *Legends of the Eastern Saints*, Vol. II. Translated from the Coptic, Arabic, Aethiopic, Syriac, and Karshumi texts.

7 St. Antony of Egypt

The son of a village merchant, scarcely educated and even ignorant of Greek, the language of Egyptian scholars, officials, and gentlemen, Antony was the spiritual father of the greatest doctors of the early Church—of Athanasius, Jerome, Basil, Evagrius, Rufinus, and Augustine of Hippo. For more than a hundred years after his death, men and women inspired by his life and teachings were coming from the outposts of the Roman Empire to study religion in the desert as in our day they arrive from overseas to study history and economics in the universities. Some of these pilgrims stayed on in Egypt as hermits; some entered the monastic communities already forming in the wastelands beyond the Nile; and some returned to their own countries to establish convents which were to become the depositories of art and science throughout the Dark and Middle Ages. Fathers and doctors of the Church, founders of monasteries and religious orders, monks and nuns, pilgrims and Christians everywhere, all owed something to the Egyptian villager who went to find the kingdom of God by the mystical road of self-abnegation.

Antony was an orphan of twenty when he received the call to dedicate his life to God. The occasion was a text he heard in church: 'If thou wilt be perfect, go and sell all thou hast.' Antony obeyed this injunction literally, which necessitated his abandoning his home and family and living for the rest of his life on charity.

He began his life as a hermit by moving into an ancient Egyptian tomb near his village, and there it was that he underwent those strange conflicts with demons who attacked him so fiercely that he was sometimes left for dead. What the young hermit had to put up with during his vigils in his tomb is vividly described by Athanasius, his first biographer:[1]

> All at once the place was filled with the phantoms of lions, bears, leopards, bulls, serpents, asps, scorpions, and wolves. And each moved according to the shape it had assumed . . . And the noises emitted simultaneously by all the apparitions were frightful and the fury shown was fierce . . .
>
> Antony, pummelled and goaded by them, made bold to say, 'Do not delay! Up and at me! If you cannot attack, why excite yourself to no purpose. . . ?'
>
> So, after trying many ruses, they gnashed their teeth, because they were only fooling themselves and not him.

The modern psychologist will, of course, have a glib explanation of these incidents which Athanasius and his contemporaries saw more simply as a fight to the finish between good and evil, two terms which were not in disrepute in the fourth century. The psychologist would no doubt talk of hallucinations brought on by hunger, physical exhaustion, and an emotionally disturbed state of mind. The apologist for the mystics might reply that such a 'scientific' analysis of asceticism may apply to those who regard their physical wellbeing as the principal end of existence, but it does not apply to those who elevate the mind and spirit above the body. The controversy between the two opposing views of man and his fate is as old as human history and tends to become profitless with time. Today, for instance, the discussion is almost academic, since those of us who have been conditioned by a view of life that is almost wholly pragmatic cannot really comprehend the basic premises of asceticism much less the extraordinary claims of mysticism. One has only to read the revelations and visions of the medieval anchorites to see that this is so. But it was not always so. To the contrary, for about the first 1,500 years of Christianity even practical men who had not the least intention of giving up the world and its prizes still revered the mystics and still admired their teachings.

Thus Antony was revered and admired; and his fame quickly spread beyond the confines of his village throughout the whole of Egypt. Other would-be hermits and ascetics gravitated towards his tomb; and before long a colony of disciples had sprang up beside the Nile. Antony now had a choice between worldly and heavenly glory: he could have become, one supposes, a bishop and perhaps the patriarch of Alexandria; or he could continue his life as a solitary.

He chose the latter course, though before he betook himself into exile in the Arabian Desert, he seems to have done his duty by his disciples, for he organised and administered the colony, which became the prototype of the Christian monastery, the first in Egypt. The remains of this convent are somewhere in the mountains on the east side of the Nile, probably among the ruins of the old city called Aphroditopolis, a name with associations of cow-worship and sexual indulgence which Antony would have strongly disapproved of.

So about A.D. 294, Antony bade his fellow-monks farewell and set off with a caravan bound for the Red Sea, travelling east into the Arabian Desert. The courage and dedication of the saint are incredible, for the site he chose for his new hermitage was one of the most desolate in Egypt: specifically, the north face of a mountain called Colzoum, some twenty miles from the Red Sea. There was nothing here but a spring of sweet water. Not even the Egyptian ascetics could live on water alone, of course, so we wonder what he expected to do for food. The answer is simple. Holy men are always fed by primitive people; and since there was a spring on Antony's mountain, it follows that the Bedouin tribe who had squatters' rights to the pasturage and wells of the district supplied their visitor with the necessities of life. The same hospitality would be provided by the nomads today.

Secluded in his cave on the threshold of which the passing tribesmen left their gifts of bread, dates, and a handful of onions, Antony continued his private dialogue with God; and what is so extraordinary about the story is that the fame of this simple, uneducated hermit spread throughout the civilised world, reaching the court of the emperor Constantine the Great, who wrote Antony a letter asking for his prayers. Soon after his arrival at his cave on Mount Colzoum, in fact, he was visited by some of his old disciples, by various dignitaries of one sort and another, by pilgrims, and, of course, curious sightseers. The third century saw the beginning of the age of pilgrimages, which resembled our 'conducted tours', for we read in one of the early Lives of the Fathers that 'the deacon Baisan, who lived at Aphroditopolis, rented camels for those who wished to visit St. Antony's hermitage'. The system has not changed in 1,600 years, and even the dragomen who do most of the organisation of local tours are still Christians, even if not deacons.

High above the world in his lonely cave, with no companions but a few wild animals (in his day, and for that matter until fifty years ago, the ibex lived by the thousand in the Eastern Desert), Antony was still sought out by those who thought that he had discovered the secret of life itself. The coming and going of visitors and the presence of those who stayed to venerate the holy man soon led to the establishment of a caravanserai, which was the foundation of the later monastery—perhaps the most significant monastery of the Christian world.

Antony lived forty years in his cave, dying at the great age of 105. He died as he lived, with no earthly possessions beyond two sheepskins which he slept on, an old cloak, and his hair-shirt. His will, therefore, was very easy to make, and when the time came he named two of his disciples who were with him to execute his last testament:

> Shelter in the ground, hide in the earth the body of your father. And please do your old friend's bidding in this also: that none but you only shall know the place of his grave.

Having given these instructions for his burial (he obviously abhorred the idea of hagiolatry), he disposed of his goods and chattels:

> The sheepskin and old cloak I am lying on give to Athanasius the bishop; he brought it to me new. Let Serapion the bishop have the other sheepskin. Do you take my hairshirt . . . So farewell, ye that are my heartstrings, for Antony is going and will not be with you in this world any more.

These words, symbolic of his manner of dying as well as of living, help us to understand the profound influence of Antony the Egyptian in his own times and the troubled times to come. One must remember that the third and fourth centuries when he lived were dangerous and even chaotic, so that there was some justification for the Christians' fear that the actual physical end of the world was near. In A.D. 204 the African Septimus Severus had proclaimed an edict prohibiting Roman subjects from embracing Christianity. Less than fifty years later began the persecutions of Decius. In the meantime, a half a dozen upstarts had been proclaimed emperor by the Egyptians and had been killed. Each time the Roman oppression of Egypt became more severe. And for the next 300 years the country was raided by the Palmyrans, the Blemmyes, the Nubians, the Persians, and finally the Arabs.

In this kind of world, run by greedy politicians, ambitious generals, avaricious tax-gatherers, and brutal thugs, Antony stood out as a symbol of peace and stability, and even more, as the hope of virtue and sanity in an otherwise vicious and mad system. Where every other member of society, from the self-proclaimed emperors to the local administrators, was grabbing what he could at the expense of his fellow-men, Antony took nothing and gave everything he had away. While most men must have dreaded the distant if not the immediate future so that their lives became a series of compromises, Antony feared nobody and compromised not at all. In addition to these rugged virtues—virtues of courage, self-reliance, and godliness, he seems to have had a certain sweetness about him which was even more endearing than his absolutely blameless conduct. Indeed, this gentleness was characteristic of many of the Desert Fathers and is characteristic of them today. Antony's relationship with the wild beasts of the Arabian Desert is one aspect of this virtue: his love of God included a love for God's creatures; and love implied forgiveness. The ibex and gazelle which nibbled at his patch of corn were lectured and forbidden to do so again.

> He was happy that he should not have to trouble anyone for his bread and that in all things he kept himself from being a burden. But seeing that people were coming to him again [i.e. in his retreat near the Red Sea], he began to raise a few

vegetables too, that the visitor might have a little something to restore him after the weariness of that hard road.

At first wild animals in the desert coming for water often would damage the beds in his garden. But he caught one of the animals, held it gently, and said to them all: 'Why do you do harm to me when I harm none of you? Go away, and in the Lord's name do not come near these things again!' And ever afterwards, as though awed by his orders, they did not come near the place.

This particular anecdote tells us a great deal more about the actual life, character, and faith of the old hermit than the panegyrics about his conquest of demons. We see now that he was an independent, hard-working, generous, and merciful old man whose love for the world was of a positive kind, big enough, in fact, to embrace the wild animals who were, for the first time, regarded as God's creatures. When we remember how animals were treated in the Roman arenas, we realise what a new vision of nature Antony had acquired in his years of solitude and meditation. And so, despite the squalor of the hermit's life and the apparent irrationality of his asceticism, the virtues of love, mercy, and pity were plainly exemplified by Antony to a cruel and materialistic world despoiled by the last of the pagans. In the midst of wars and famines and terrible cruelties, we glimpse the figure of this gentle old man holding a gazelle as a punishment, then dismissing it with a short lecture. It was a tiny triumph of goodness, repeated by other Antonys, like the old monk who fed a starving lion with dates; the hermit who regularly shared his supper with a she-wolf; the solitary who accompanied a lioness to her den to examine her blind whelp; and a holy man who was taught by an ibex what plants to eat and what to avoid.

When, therefore, we come to examine the lives and beliefs of these 'athletes of Christ', we find, once we have overcome our repugnance at the squalor of their physical life, that these Egyptian hermits introduced a new concept of virtue into men's thinking, a concept based on loving-kindness. There certainly wasn't much of that in pagan society, and some observers might conclude that there isn't much in society today. But the hermits showed that extreme inhumanity to oneself can lead to the most perfect humanity towards others, selflessness being a sort of by-product of asceticism. But it is at this point that the modern Christian must part company with the mystics—he lives in an utterly different world from that of the Desert Fathers whose cells were visited by lionesses and whose followers came to number tens of thousands. A contemporary historian states that there were 10,000 monks in the region of Arsinoë alone; another 10,000 with 20,000 nuns at Oxyrynchus; while elsewhere 'the land so swarmed with monks that their chaunts and hymns by day and by night made the whole country one church of God'.

Egypt must have been a rather curious place in those days, admittedly a country with which modern industrial nations have little in common. In the first instance, the aims of these desert communities were different; in the second, they disregarded the economics of the market-place. All the same, they became in time well-regulated societies with their own laws and institutions; and a visitor to them in the fourth century did not look upon their citizens as a collection of freaks or eccentrics; to the contrary, he regarded them as a community of brothers who were trying to build a truly Christian civilisation, or, as he would have said, the kingdom of God on earth. For what alternative did practising Christians have but to seek the solitude of the desert since their choice was between a cruel and morally decadent society on the one hand and the kingdom of God on the other? The prospect of finding that kingdom seemed to be greater in the undefiled desert than in the corrupt cities.

It is only fair to remember this alternative in reviewing that period of our history which falls between the fifth and fifteenth centuries. For it is a curious fact of our historical consciousness that while we can extol the ancient Greeks and admire the ancient Romans, we seem ill at ease with the first millennium of our own era. The philosophical speculations of the Greeks and the technical achievements of the Romans are acceptable; the mystical viewpoint of the Middle Ages is not. The medieval belief that every tree and flower, every bird and fish, every star, in fact every object of nature, has an inner significance apart from its outer appearance belongs to a fairy-tale world as far as the modern scientist is concerned. This sort of view of the universe, which William Blake called a 'double vision', is 'unscientific' because it cannot be proven. And the mystic's ability to withdraw from the world, which *can* be demonstrated, is explained away as 'a subconscious wish to return to the security of the womb'.[2] With such pronouncements, suggestive of the hostility the materialist feels for all those who do not accept his standards, men of the stature of Gautama Buddha and St. Francis of Assisi are dismissed from the pages of history. It is obvious, therefore, that a world view based on a combination of rationalism, agnosticism, and materialism makes it almost impossible for us to understand the mentality of the visionary, though some lip-homage is paid in intellectual circles to those artists who have attempted to explore the invisible world beyond our sense perceptions. Some 'non-rational' cults have even gained a measure of acceptance. Schools of symbolism, imagism, vorticism, impressionism, surrealism, and so forth are now considered 'respectable'. The possibility of 'special truths beyond the rational world' is admitted. Even the mystic, if in fancy dress and eccentric in manner, is a feature of the contemporary artistic scene. It is only the actually genuine mystics of the Egyptian deserts and the medieval monasteries who remain almost totally outside our ability to understand or to sympathise with.

One reason is that the lives and legends of these extraordinary people have usually been presented in such a way as to excite either disgust or derision in the minds of Christians who place cleanliness next to godliness in the list of virtues. Certainly, as seen from a Victorian drawing-room or, for that matter, from a modern computerised office, the Desert Fathers were monsters rather than men of God. They did not eat five meals a day at set times, they did not wash, they were indifferent to comfort, and even their so-called miracles were ludicrous. It is easy to emphasise the absurdities, for their biographers, even brilliant men like St. Jerome, had this curious obsession with the bizarre which one might equate with the current obsession with violence. Consequently St. Jerome dwells much too long on the inhuman aspects of the ascetics' conduct—of St. Ammonius who burnt his penis with a red-hot iron when he was assailed by licentious thoughts; of others, like Origen, who went farther and castrated themselves altogether; of hermits who appeared to be suicidal, for we are told of Pachon deliberately inciting an asp to bite him, of Macarius who spent his nights in a swamp in order to be stung by hornets so that he was unrecognisable when he crawled back to his cell. We are told that some denied even the deepest convictions or instincts of men—Appollos by refusing to help his dying brother, Archelides by preferring death to looking upon the face of his mother.

> The desire and love of Thee hath conquered in me all other love and desire of parents and brothers and family. Now I beseech Thee, O Lord, to take my soul unto Thee that I may not be defeated by temptation.
>
> And when he had finished his prayer, he lay down on his mat and departed this life.

Moreover, many of the martyrs (according to their biographers, at least) enjoyed their sufferings to such an extent that the listing of tortures became the popular literature of the Middle Ages. The devout Christian of the fifteenth century evidently found the description of the sufferings of St. Clement first-class entertainment, for how else can this monstrous catalogue of cruelty be explained? St. Clement is reputed to have been hung up on a beam, his flesh torn with iron hooks, bound to a wheel, beaten with sticks, mutilated with knives, stabbed in the face with stilettos, his jaws broken, his teeth pulled out, his feet crushed with iron fetters, whipped with ox thongs, scorched with flaming torches, thrown to wild beasts, tortured by having red-hot needles thrust under his nails, burnt in quicklime, stretched on white-hot bedsteads, and then thrown into a furnace where he was left to burn all one day and one night, though still alive and, presumably, kicking. Brought out, he was beaten with iron hooks and flung against steel spikes, held while molten lead was poured over his head and his ears were pierced with needles, given fifty strokes with steel rods several days in succession, and finally—anticlimax! —beheaded. Only when his head was severed from his body was his biographer satisfied that he was dead and martyred.

One can only laugh at this gruesome tale; and if it is laughter one wants to clear the air, there is the account of St. Rumwold who repeated his profession of faith the day after he was born, preached a long sermon to his parents on the second day, and died on the third. Or there is the blessed Marianus who had no need of a candle to see by since the tips of his fingers gave out the necessary light. Or the two skeletons which lay side by side in the crypt of the monastery of St. Catherine's on the Sinai Peninsula and became involved in a fight as one skeleton, disliking the proximity of the other, continually threw it across the crypt until it was officially ordered not to do so. Commodianus, on the other hand, persuaded a lion to make a speech in support of the apostle Paul, while St. Menas simultaneously cured a paralytic man and a dumb woman by putting them both in the same bed for the night. The paralytic regained the use of his limbs, the dumb woman of her voice. It is a story worthy of Boccaccio!

One recognises that all of these ridiculous legends were nothing more than fairy tales, sometimes sick like the accounts of tortures, sometimes charming like those involving the talking animals. There is manifestly not a word of truth in most of them and those anti-clerical historians who have used them to scoff at the old monks and martyrs are wasting their breath. The childish fantasies which went under the name of miracles did no harm to anybody, despite the fact that they flouted the laws of nature. The mystic might argue that man interferes with the laws of nature every day of his life; so God, or his chosen servant, is entitled to do likewise. But it was not so much the account of fantastic miracles that damaged the reputation of the ascetics as certain dangerous doctrines which nearly wrecked all the good work of gentle spirits like Antony and Macarius. Men like the Armenian Eustathius of Sebaste, born about A.D. 300 and, like so many anchorites, dying a very old man, were regarded even in their own time as both absurd and potentially dangerous, for some of them went so far as to declare that no married person could be saved: in other words, that marriage was a sort of private hell on earth, a point of view that was neither flattering to those already married nor acceptable to the State inasmuch as it was liable to lead to the complete extermination of the human race if carried to its logical conclusion. But even though wiser doctors of the Church thought that men like Eustathius had gone too far and did, indeed, anathematise their doctrines, much damage was done to the cause by exacerbating the Christian sense of guilt in all matters pertaining to sex.

But the mystic is not concerned with this sort of logic, which, in any case, is the quintessence of man's egocentricism. For the same man who feels indignant about any threat to his survival has exterminated innumerable species of other animals and appears to spend a great deal of his time inventing weapons to exterminate himself. He is scarcely justified, therefore, in scorning those solitaries who never injured anybody but themselves, doing so in the belief that knowledge of ultimate reality comes only to those who have killed out the Old Adam and reconciled the personal will to the will of God. Obviously the primitive Egyptian hermits like Paul, Antony, and Macarius stumbled upon the technique of self-purification without which the final steps towards union cannot be taken. One says 'stumbles' advisedly, since some of the more simple-minded fugitives from the Roman persecutors had no specific vocation to the mystical life and in their case the natural conditions of the desert enforced the mortification of the flesh, whether they intended it or not. But the more spiritual of them discovered a basic truth of mysticism: that he who wishes to attain to a oneness with God must first rid himself of selfhood.

Christians in the fourth and fifth centuries believed this was true, and this explains why rich, influential, and scholarly men and women came from all over the Roman world to live for a time in the Egyptian deserts. They included some of the greatest names in the history of the Church, Basil, Chrysostom, Athanasius, Jerome, Cassian—the creators of Christian philosophy and institutions as we know them today. They included, too, those saintly women who aroused the indignation of Gibbon. On the one hand, the great historian did not readily approve of females taking part in public affairs, whether political, social, or religious; on the other, a man of his temperament was not capable of understanding the motives which led aristocratic Roman matrons like Paula, Melania, Blesilla, Eustochium, Laeta, Marcella, and Olympias to give up their homes, their husbands, their children, and all their possessions to live and die in eastern convents as nuns. They should have been doing their 'duty' as rich patrician ladies keeping an eye on their house-slaves.

Gibbon puts the blame for their rejection of the world on the Desert Fathers whom pious women from all over the empire visited in the course of pilgrimages. For in those days it was easier to travel in the desert than it is today, or was to be for the next thousand years. Indeed, it would be roughly true to say that a British subject in the fourth century of our era could travel from London to the monastery of St. Antony in the Arabian Desert with fewer hindrances and formalities than he could in this year of grace. And when he arrived, he did not find a population of bearded wild men living in caves like animals, but a well-organised community, a sort of straw-hutted village with a roughly built stone church for Sunday mass, hostels for pilgrims, a bakery, wine-shop, and even a lending library. This was the nucleus of the monastic settlement which left the more zealous hermits free to meditate and pray in their cells, some of which were individual caves, some huts shared by two or more like-minded religious. The point was that the ascetics could suit themselves as to the degree of their mortification. Their brothers who preferred the mundane tasks of drawing water from the wells or hewing wood or making baskets and curios to sell to the pilgrims so that they, the monks, need not ask for charity bore no grudge against those solitaries who did nothing at all yet had to be fed. This was what was meant by love and brotherhood. And those religious who were skilful at medicine, surgery, calligraphy, architecture, and so on gladly contributed their knowledge to improving the amenities of the colony, without expectation of reward. In such a community laws and penalties for breaking the law were scarcely necessary.

Pilgrims and visitors who came in their thousands during the fifth and sixth centuries were housed and fed to the best of the monks' ability. Those who stayed beyond a certain time were gently requested to help in the community tasks in some manner or the other, even if it was only watering the vegetable garden. But there was no objection to lazier people sitting in the shade reading a good book. And those who decided to remain and join the colony were at once given the hut or cell of a regular inhabitant who quietly rolled up his mat and his sheepskin rug, collected his few possessions, and walked off into the desert filled with happiness because he had been 'more merciful, kinder, humbler, and more patient' than his brother.

This was the concept of the fraternal life which led to the creation of what we have called a Christian commonwealth, a sort of spiritual empire which took as its earthly domain first, the deserts of Egypt, then the wastelands of the Near East. It was an empire without kings or armies which explains why it was finally overthrown and why its once flourishing monasteries, towns, estates, orchards, vineyards, and magnificent irrigation systems are now abandoned except for occasional outposts in the mountains or deserts.

REFERENCES

1 Vita S. Antoni, 9.

2 The theory of the German psychologist Walter de Gruyter as expounded in *Die Askese*.

8 St. Antony's desert

The old road to the Red Sea hermitages—the one that St. Antony and the pilgrims followed during the early Christian period—starts on the eastern bank of the Nile upriver a mile or two from the town called Beni Suef. This road is no longer used by tourists to the monasteries, and the authorities would laugh at a traveller who asked for camels and Bedouin guides to make what used to be a three-day trek across the desert from the Nile to Mount Colzoum where stand the twin monasteries of St. Antony and St. Paul. Tourists now reach the shrines along a concrete road which runs from Cairo to Suez and then down the Gulf for sixty miles, then westwards into the mountains. All the adventure and excitement which travellers enjoyed up to fifty years ago can only be experienced nowadays in the imagination.

A hundred years ago the guide-books gave several pages of advice to those willing to undertake this expedition, adding: 'This journey is not likely to be undertaken by the ordinary traveller.' However, for those who insisted, the list of requirements was long and detailed:

> A party of four should have two large tents, one for feeding and sitting in and one for sleeping in and one smaller one for the kitchen and servants. All water for drinking should be carried in barrels kept strictly locked, and the Arabs never allowed to draw from them. The taste of the water will be one of the traveller's greatest hardships. To be constantly imbibing a fairly powerful solution of Epsom salts is an amusement one soon grows tired of. All sorts of plans are used to disguise the flavour—lime-juice, brandy, strong tea, or Arab coffee as thick as cream. So what with the naturally

> villainous taste of the water, its strong purgative properties, the little extra goatish flavour imparted to it by the goat skin, the traveller must become pretty well hardened before he can be said to enjoy it.

In addition to a long lecture on how to disguise the taste of the water, advice was offered on the subject of provisions, travellers being warned that absolutely nothing could be bought in the desert except occasionally a sheep. They were therefore admonished to take a stock of live fowls, turkeys, and pigeons with a plentiful supply of brandy and wine, an extra camel being recommended to carry the crates. What with the frequent warnings about lacing the water, even when boiled, with brandy and the load of claret that was taken along, these old travellers must surely have wandered along in an alcoholic daze much of the time, whence the hints about camel-riding.

> Much of the comfort in a desert journey depends on having a good camel and a comfortable seat. The camel should be chosen and tried beforehand; and the quieter he is and the easier his paces, the better. You may then sit in any position you please, sideways, or astride, or lady-fashion, or even lying down . . . A great relief to the uncontrollable feeling of *ennui* and a sense of monotony which comes over most people during a long day's ride on a camel's back under a broiling sun is reading. A book is an agreeable companion, not a stiff book either, but a novel or some such light reading. Stanley, Warburton, Miss Martineau, Lord Lindsay, and as many others should be taken and read daily, and a stock of still lighter literature in the Tauchnitz edition which can be thrown away as read.

One envies these Victorian travellers wandering across the desert at two to three miles an hour, reclining on the top of their camels, replete with a turkey dinner, flushed with claret, and slightly befuddled with brandy. No doubt the words of the novel they were reading danced before their eyes which must soon have closed in slumber. At thirty shillings a day ('for everything except wine'), one could think of worse fates than wandering back and forth across the desert, even if one were not going anywhere in particular.

The Victorian travellers, however, while placing great store on their physical comfort, seldom journeyed without some stern moral objective, their sanctimonious descriptions of nature on the one hand and their contempt of foreigners on the other. On approaching the monastery of St. Antony along the wide desert plain, they automatically jotted down some purple passages about the grandeur of the scenery, whereas their references to the monks were invariably derogatory. The fact that these poor, rather dirty, and ill-educated men who appeared to know and to do nothing but pray and meditate, none the less represented the last of the Desert Fathers who had made the rich monasteries and splendid cathedrals of Europe possible does not seem to have occurred to them.

They were, of course, weak on the history of the Egyptian Church and, in keeping with contemporary taste, unimpressed by the Byzantine frescoes which covered the walls of the basilicas. The poverty, squalor, and, above all, the apparent uselessness of the monkish inmates of the convent offended them. The ladies were affronted at having to stay outside, while the men were not amused at having to be hauled up over the walls in a basket. Inside the visitors found a chaos of crumbling buildings and a large garden abounding in vegetables, date palms, and fruit trees, all watered by rills conducted from a spring that burst out of a cleft in a rock. According to the tradition, Miriam, the sister of Moses, bathed in this spring at the time of the Exodus. The more energetic of the tourists set off to see the Cave of St. Antony, high up in the precipice of Mount Colzoum. Standing on a ledge, overlooking the loneliest outpost in all Christendom, the tourists no doubt tried to find adjectives to describe the scene and the sentiments they felt obliged to include in the journal they hoped to publish. But once out again in the desert, swaying along on their camels, taking sips of their brandy and water, these travellers no doubt sank back into the pleasant state of ennui from which they had been temporarily awakened in order to see the sights.

But this halcyon method of travelling was strictly limited to the last fifty years of the nineteenth century and the first fifteen of the twentieth. Before the time—that is, before the British occupied Egypt—travel anywhere in the country, if not dangerous, was certainly complicated. In fact, there were few visitors other than those explorers who were interested in the Pharaonic monuments and the loot which came out of them. Travel was more or less restricted to the Nile Valley, and there are no records of explorers crossing the Egyptian deserts as British, German, and French pathfinders were crossing the Sahara to the west. The first recorded European of modern times to reach the Monastery of St. Antony, for instance, seems to have been a Sicilian friar called Brother Bernard who carved his name and date (1626) on the wooden altar screen in the church and then passes from history. His *graffito*, if genuine, implies that Western Christendom had not completely forgotten about this desert outpost, though there is no record of anyone having visited St. Antony's before Brother Bernard. St. Catherine's across the Red Sea on the Sinai Peninsula, in contrast, was never lost sight of and seems to have been on the itinerary of those medieval pilgrimages which combined danger, adventure, and piety in a manner which travellers will never know again. Sir John Mandeville, writing about 1350, has a reference to St. Catherine's in his *Voyages and Travels*:

> In that abbey no flies, toads, or lizards, or such foul venemous beasts, nor lice nor fleas ever enter, by the miracle of God and of our Lady.

If it was difficult to reach St. Catherine's, it was even more hazardous to cross the Eastern Desert to St. Antony's as long as Egypt was under the dominion of the Turkish pashas and the Mameluke beys: that is, while the cities and Nile villages were administered by these usurpers and the deserts beyond the green belt of the river were controlled by the Bedouin. The problem confronting the would-be visitor to the monastery of St. Antony, then, was first to get a *firman* from the Turkish authorities in order to be able to travel at all; and then to get permission from the sheiks to cross their particular territory. Since the Bedouin did not recognise the Turkish pashas as their rulers, neither a *firman* nor a guard of Turkish soldiers was of any use in the desert; so to mount an expedition to any of the

Coptic monasteries, whether in the Western or Eastern Desert, was a formidable enterprise and one that was only undertaken in the seventeenth and eighteenth centuries by those now-forgotten soldiers of fortune who first explored Africa, often at the cost of their lives.

To most such adventurers there were, in any case, more rewarding journeys than crossing the empty desert between the Nile and the Red Sea. In the first place, there seemed to be nothing worthwhile to explore.

The Eastern Desert is a roughly oblong stretch of country of which the top corners are Cairo to the west, the town of Suez to the east, while the bottom corners are demarcated by Aswan to the west and the ancient port of Berenice to the east. The country rises slowly from the Nile, towards a backbone or range of mountains, some of whose peaks rise to 6,000 feet. The western or Nilotic side of this central mountain range is a rainless, scorched plateau of sand and rock interspersed with dried-up wadis. The eastern or Red Sea side gets what rain there is when the clouds burst against the granite peaks and send torrents of water leaping down the mountainsides.

This region was formerly inhabited by two Bedouin tribes whose ancestors were certainly herding their flocks of sheep and goats in the time of the old Kingdom of Egypt, 3,000 and more years before Christ. The two tribes continue to lead almost exactly the same life as they did when St. Antony went into their country—a life based on courage, endurance, and strict compliance with tribal law. Like the Tuareg of the Sahara, they scorn to live in a house, or even a hut. The tent is their home.

The Eastern Desert today, however, is beginning to feel the effects of westernisation, though large areas of it, in particular the central range of mountains, are relatively unvisited and untouched, for it seems to the tourist crossing the desert 8,000 feet up in his aeroplane to be an empty wasteland, devoid of interest or profit. He could not be more mistaken. The Eastern Desert was once the most highly industrialised region of Egypt.

It was the Pharaohs who opened up this forbidding country, both as a vast mining enterprise and as a trade route from the

East to the Mediterranean. This trade route was one of the richest highways of the ancient world, for it joined India with Egypt by way of Persia and Arabia. Beyond India lay China; and above Egypt, the emergent Greece. The Eastern Desert, then, was the land bridge between the Far East and West, and it remained so until the Portuguese discovered the sea route to India via the Cape in 1487.

The existence of a well-organised system of forts, roads, and wells indirectly helps to explain how the original hermits managed to survive in the desert. Whatever their state of holiness and whatever their strength of will trained by years of self-abnegation, their contributions to religious life and thought would have been in vain if the system of communications left over from the Roman period had not kept them in contact with their fellow-Christians as far away as the capitals of Rome and Constantinople. But the road was still open for the coming and going of an increasing number of disciples and pilgrims whose requirements led to the establishment of settlements which eventually became the actual monasteries which have lasted to this day. Indeed, the extent to which the Egyptian deserts were frequented during the third to the seventh centuries is proven by the existence of other monasteries of which we have no precise record apart from a few stones and several vague place-names. Travelling in the Eastern Desert in 1823, Sir John Wilkinson mentions several of these *deirs*, or convents, now evidently completely lost and certainly unexplored, though they are marked on the Wilkinson map printed in the Royal Geographical Society's *Journal* of 1832. Wilkinson was unsympathetic towards the monks of the two still-surviving monasteries, St. Antony (Deir Antonios) and St. Paul (Deir Bolos), and terms them 'uncouth, inhospitable, ignorant, and consequently suspicious, scarcely condescending to answer the usual questions of the traveller'. It is unfortunate that this early traveller felt (and probably showed) contempt for the sixty-three monks who were then in residence at the convent, for he had an opportunity of seeing the community and of studying the buildings before the era of 'modern improvements'. The churches of St. Michael and of the founder were then still adorned with their thirteenth-century wall paintings, notably of Christ in glory, the Virgin, Moses, the saints, and a curious picture of Santa Sophia, though all these superb paintings were obscured by the smoke of the fires lit by the Bedouin who occupied the monastery after the murder of the monks in the fourteenth century. Some books of the priceless library also survived the sacking of the convent, for Wilkinson speaks of some 'worn-out bibles' which the brethren were unwilling to show him. Other travellers, whose manner was more sympathetic, had more luck, for a few years later the bibliophile Richard Tattam, Archdeacon of Bedford, was able to examine these books and bring some of them away with him.

However, Wilkinson, with his companion James Burton, whose manuscript account of their wanderings resides unpublished in the British Museum Library, did discover the ruins of other monasteries. The three most important are in the Wadi Gareya, about twenty-five miles north-east of the Nile at Keneh. Sixty years ago traces of the monks' cells and the arches of cloisters were visible, but nothing is now known of this convent except what the local Bedouin report, that it was destroyed during the Mohammedan invasion. A second monastery was located in the porphyry quarries of Djebel Dokhan. The church of this convent survived intact except for the roof at the time of Wilkinson's visit in 1823, when the explorer found an inscription in Greek which read:

> Flavius Julius, the renowned Governor of the Thebaid, built this Catholic Church in the time of——, Bishop of Maximianopolis.

One is at first disposed to wonder if this church was not built by the Christian slaves who worked in the quarries nearby, for evidence of shrines and the worship of Jesus has been found in other quarries in Africa, notably those at a place called in Roman times Simuttu (Chemtou) on the Algerian-Tunisian border. But it is unlikely that the overseers in charge of production would ever have allowed the Christians enough time or freedom to build a church of this size. It follows that the monument must date from the third or fourth centuries when the quarries seem to have been abandoned and the Christians flocked in large numbers into the desert. This was the period of the greatest disturbances in Egypt when the desert tribes were attacking the fortresses and stations on the highways across the Arabian Desert from the Red Sea ports to the Nile. The Romans could no longer afford the men to garrison the forts and look-out stations which controlled the thousands of slaves housed in camps all through the mountains. The legionnaires withdrew, the slaves escaped, and the persecuted or frightened Christians took advantage of the situation to set up a state of their own.

Today there are only some half a dozen active monasteries surviving out of the hundreds which once housed tens of thousands of monks in the Egyptian deserts. There is only one in the Eastern Desert—that of St. Antony. The neighbouring monastery of St. Paul has long since been abandoned. We have vague evidence of others—like the ruin located near the Mons Claudianus and called by the local Bedouin the Convent of the Deaf Men. It is doubtful whether the remainder will ever be located now.

A curious story illustrates the ephemeral nature of the archaeological conditions obtaining in this region. In 1823 Wilkinson reported the following:

> I ascended the rock and arrived at a stone building which, from its appearance, is not very ancient; it consists of three rooms and a kind of portico, or covering, supported on two pillars, nothing but the roof is wanting—the walls, windows, and doorways being all perfect. The Arab sheik, my guide, at length pointed out a 'written stone', which proved to be a Greek inscription, showing the building to have been a church. It lies on the ground, on the outside, and is broken, but few letters, I believe, are lost. The words are as follows:
>
> *φλαύιος Ιούλιος ὁ διασημότατος ἡγεμὼν, Θηβάιδος ὁ κατασκεύασας . . . καθολικὴν ἐκκλησίαν. 'Επι . . . ητος ἐπισκόπον Μαξιμιανπόλ [εως]*[1]

Seventy-nine years later J. T. Hardwick, making a geological survey for the Egyptian government, reported:

Above The Monastery of the Syrians, richest of the Wadi Natrun convents. *Right* A few Coptic monks still live in the ruins of the Red Monastery

The White Monastery in Middle Egypt was one of the oldest and most important centres of the early Christians. It has fallen into disrepair

On the right of the road, on a piece of raised ground, were some small granite pillars, and in the path itself a slab bearing an inscription which possibly at one time had been borne on the pillars. The presence of this record is of special interest, as the inscription is in Greek, opening with the words *ΚΑΘΟΛΗΚΗ ΕΚΚΛΗΣΙΑ*. If circumstances permitted, it would be well if this unique memento of Christian influence at Dokhan were obtained for the Cairo Museum, as it now runs imminent risk of being swept away in one of the rain storms.[2]

Are Wilkinson and Hardwick talking about the same monument? The location is the same and the Greek inscription must surely be from the same stone. Yet Hardwick's version *opens* with the words 'Catholic Church', while Wilkinson's places these words in the middle of the inscription. The whole thing is a puzzle which will probably never be solved now, as the inscribed stone must long since have disappeared.[3]

With the disappearance of the monasteries and the coenobitic communities which had sprung up throughout Egypt from the fourth to the seventh centuries, there ended one of the most remarkable periods in the religious history of mankind. For during those 300 years, the world saw a spiritual commonwealth established on a scale which had never been realised before and will never be realised again. This commonwealth grew and eventually extended beyond the borders of Egypt eastward across the Sinai Peninsula up through Palestine and Syria to the Black Sea. During the same period, the ideal of a theocratic society was carried back by European ascetics who had experienced the eremitic life in the Egyptian deserts to their native lands, until almost the whole of Europe was covered by monasteries which gave a characteristic flavour to life and learning during the Dark and Middle Ages.

This commonwealth and the ideals it was founded upon have, to all intents and purposes, disappeared, particularly in Moslem countries, but the vestiges of it can be traced in the ruins of hermitages all over the Middle East, while a few of its outposts actually still survive as operative centres of Christianity as far east as the borders of Kurdistan where stand the monasteries of Rabban Hormuzd and Mar Mattai. And this Christian commonwealth was not a union of isolated and ill-organised communities, but a state within the secular Roman Empire, recognised as such by the Christian emperors; for these rulers had no reason to fear a rival power or to be jealous of its dominion, since the capitals of the commonwealth were invariably in the most inhospitable regions, like the Libyan and Arabian Deserts, the Sinai wilderness, Cilicia, and Upper Mesopotamia. These spiritual kingdoms had neither armies nor dreams of territorial conquest. Yet all these communities, whether in the full desert or in the greener zones, were self-sufficient, even though they were dedicated to the religious life and remained indifferent to earthly things.

Perhaps this is why they aroused the scorn of the eighteenth-century rationalists and nineteenth-century economists on the grounds that they neither enriched themselves nor their nation. Their critics went farther and alleged that they contributed nothing to the welfare of their fellow-men by subjecting themselves to outrageous austerities and self-abasement. What, for instance, was to happen to the human race if so many thousands of men and women made celibacy a condition of godliness? What was to happen to society if the rich and influential abandoned their wealth and positions and buried themselves in convents, as the Roman ladies Paula and Melania did? What was to happen to industry and trade if honest working men left the workshops and markets to spend their lives prostrating themselves before altars?

But much, if not all, of this criticism is based on an assessment of the primitive Christian monasticism taken from the usually ridiculous accounts of the hagiographers, the biographers who concocted the lives of the early saints and martyrs to entertain what would be called today a 'mass audience', an audience which enjoyed sex, science fiction, and violence as much as a 'mass audience' does today. The facts as revealed by what is left of these coenobitic communities tell a different story. A traveller to any of the deserts once occupied by hermits, monks, and their lay disciples can see for himself what these colonies achieved, particularly in the Negev which escaped the continual wars of the Byzantine period, though it did not escape the sword of Islam. In other words, the evidence of these Christian communities, even in the region now known as the Wilderness of the Wanderers, remains to prove that the monastic ideal was not only practicable, but successful, for there in the wasteland are the vestiges of the terraced hillside, cultivated fields, orchards, and the ruins of towns. And these communities had nearly always grown up around the hermitage of some holy man whose disciples had lived beside him in their cells, built a small church for the communal worship, then rest-houses for pilgrims, until, in the course of time, a whole agricultural community was established.

In short, those sceptics or cynics who condemn the Desert Fathers and their successors for having wasted their lives in a sordid routine of self-abasement overlook the achievements as well as the teachings of these strange mystics. Most of them recommended their disciples to undertake some useful labour, even if it was only weaving mats and baskets to be sold in the local markets and the proceeds given to the poor. In fact, as the community grew, there was something for every able-bodied man to do—wells to be sunk, cisterns hewn out of the rock hillsides to be terraced, fields cultivated, and houses built. The organisation and economy of such settlements was based on a simple communist or perhaps vague anarchistic system, whereby each man did what he could according to his degree of good will or religious zeal. Human nature being what it is, and always was, there is no doubt that these desert communities were the retreat of both criminals and idlers; and there was also a sect of vagrant ascetics who ostensibly gave themselves to prayer, but actually refused to do any kind of work and lived by begging. They were later censured at the synod of Ephesus in A.D. 431. But judging from their physical achievements alone, the hermits and monks also included skilled engineers, masons, architects, farmers, scholars, and writers who created between them homes, schools, and libraries, once the pride of the great monasteries. The Egyptian libraries, in fact, became the literary centres of world Christianity, partly because of their calligraphers and partly because of their polyglot scholars. Three Fathers of St. Catherine's in Sinai, for instance, spoke Latin, Greek, Syrian, Coptic, and Persian.

An archaeologist who visited one of the most characteristic regions of this old Christian commonwealth sums up what he saw and felt like this:

> The chief impression that remains with me from the examination of several hundred hamlets, villages, and cities in the Negev is the passion for the worship of God which seems to have possessed their inhabitants. Wherever we turned in settlements large and small of this period [A.D. 400–600], we encountered the remains of Christian sanctuaries. Whether the Byzantine Christians of the Negev were immensely pious, or enormously rich, or both, the fact remains that they delighted in building numerous and elaborate churches and magnificent basilicas . . . No town, however small, however remote in the desert, seems to have been without one or more churches.[4]

REFERENCES

1 J. Wilkinson, 'Journey in the Eastern Desert', *Journal of the Royal Geographical Society*, 1832.

2 T. Barron and W. F. Hume, *Topography and Geology of the Eastern Desert of Egypt* (1902), pp. 27, 28.

3 I inquired about it in both the Cairo and the Coptic Museum, but nobody knew anything about it—or, for that matter, to what exactly I was referring. It is, of course, possible that the stone (either Wilkinson's or Hardwick's) is actually lying around in the cellars of one or the other of these two museums.

4 Nelson Glueck, *Rivers in the Desert: the Exploration of the Negev* (1959), pp. 278–9.

9 Sinai and St. Catherine's

A continuous pilgrimage from the monasteries of the Wadi Natrun across Egypt to those of Sinai is now impossible, since the Egyptians will not allow travellers to go east of the Nile to visit St. Antony's in the Arabian Desert and the Israelis cannot guarantee the safety of tourists going to St. Catherine's along the western side of the Sinai Peninsula.

However, in the spring of 1969 the shelling across the Suez Canal stopped long enough for a party of us to make the dash along the exposed part of the road to Suez and Port Tewfik to the safety of the coast road which runs south to El Tur and Sharm el Sheikh. On the first day of this trip, we passed through Gaza and El Arish whose ancient history is now overshadowed by the events of the Israeli–Egyptian wars. The ruins today of these two oases are Russian tanks and guns burnt out or toppled over beside the road and under the orange groves; the historical ruins of El Arish (ancient Egyptian, *Zaru*; Roman, *Rhinocolura*) seem to have disappeared altogether, though the nineteenth-century sailors, Irby and Mangles, who passed through the oases in 1817 speak of 'notable Roman remains'.

We had no time to stop and look for these remains, notable or otherwise, and had to be content with a glimpse of 'the palace of Jarvis, the last British governor of Sinai'. The announcement recalled an echo of a period as remote now as the Roman occupation of this same troubled area. However, one saluted the memory of that last British governor, Major Claud Scudamore Jarvis, who so efficiently yet good-humouredly administered his little empire with 145 police on camels and 104 on foot. His 'palace' is now a large, crumbling villa, missing its front wall, and it tells us little of El Arish once renowned as the seat of a bishop, with two large churches whose high walls remained standing in the eleventh century and whose marble columns were beautiful enough to have been looted by sultans and carried off to the mosques of Cairo.

The talk among the party with whom I was travelling, however, was not of the ancient history of this region, but of the recent destruction of the Egyptian Army whose equipment, bombed and burnt out, stretched along the roadside from El Arish to the canal. The Mitla Pass, in fact, looked like Armageddon, with hundreds of heavy vehicles knocked out by the Israeli Air Force. With such dramatic events so spectacularly presented, the traveller has difficulty in visualising the old wars and the old armies which marched back and forth across this wilderness in the continuous tradition of conquest—Israelites, Hyskos, Syrians, Assyrians, Hittites, Babylonians, Persians, Greeks, Romans, Arabs, Crusaders, French, British, and so on until today. Nobody seems to have the slightest idea of how long the pattern will be repeated, and perhaps all we can predict, on the basis of past experience, is that what one generation builds up the next will knock down.

What we see very clearly in the Sinai Peninsula, then, is the debris left by two currents of history: first, the castles, watch-towers, highways, and devastation of the wars; secondly, the abandoned cities, monasteries, churches, farms, and orchards of two centuries or so of the Christian commonwealth. Seeing these latter remains, one might surmise that if only the wars would cease in this part of the world, the wilderness of Sinai could become a fertile land as it had been twice before in its history. It had been prosperous during the period of the Nabataeans, a somewhat mysterious people who appear for a short time on the periphery of the classical world. It is not surprising that the Arab historian Makrizi confused them with the Magi, though western scholars had a better idea of who they were from the writings of the ancient historians. But the Nabataeans were never wholly 'real' until their capital city Petra was discovered by the Swiss explorer Johann Burckhardt in 1812. So, too, the Garamantes of Libya, first mentioned by Herodotus as the people of the Fezzan who chased the Negroes in four-horse chariots, were regarded as quasi-mythical until their capital Garama (modern Germa) was located by the Oudney-Denham-Clapperton expedition of 1822. Such were the breath-taking discoveries of the early-nineteenth-century explorers.

Once Petra was found, historians and archaeologists were able to piece together, albeit slowly, the story of the rise and fall of this Near-Eastern empire whose kings held their own against the rival monarchs of Judaea from 200 B.C. to their conquest by Trajan in A.D. 105. The Nabataeans were primarily caravaners and as such controlled both the east–west and north–south routes to and from China, India, Arabia, and Egypt. Their wealth was in tribute exacted from the gold and spice caravans which grew to enormous size as the demands of the Roman world increased from the Mediterranean to the Atlantic. In fact, the Nabataeans employed camels in such numbers that the Greek geographer Strabo describes the caravans as resembling great armies on the move. One is reminded of the German explorer Heinrich Barth's account of 10,000 camels mustered at Agadez to cross the Ténéré Desert to the salt-pans of Bilma.

The vast commerce thus organised by the Nabataeans did bring a certain prosperity to the whole of the Middle East, including the Sinai Peninsula which the caravaners used for pasture land, seeking out the long wadis where the camel-thorn grew after the winter rains. Here along the ravines, the herdsmen left a record of themselves which we can still see, many thousands of inscriptions, drawings, and vague graffiti known as the Sinaitic Inscriptions. These rock pictures are incised on boulders all along the valleys and consist of a great many crude depictions of camels, gazelles, and cattle. To anyone who has seen the great art galleries of the Acacus Mountains in Libya or the Tassili n'Ajjer in Algeria, these Sinaitic engravings are obviously fairly recent, if only because of their crudity, for it seems to be a first principle of rock art that the older the etching or drawing, the more skilful the execution. The first travellers to see them thought otherwise, however. The Spanish pilgrim, the lady Etheria, noted them first in A.D. 450 while on her way to visit the Christian monasteries; and a century later they attracted the attention of the sixth-century traveller Cosmas Indicopleustes, he who claimed that the sun retired behind a mountain to spend the night.

Cosmas writes:

> In that wilderness of Mount Sinai one can see at all the halting places all the stones that have been broken off from the mountains, inscribed with Hebrew letters, as I myself can testify, having travelled in these places.

The Egyptian monk's description of the Sinaitic Inscriptions is not altogether accurate. Most of the writings are actually in Aramaic or other Semitic scripts, including Nabataean. A few are in Greek or Latin. They do not tell us much more than the modern graffiti one finds on every monument all over the world, adding up to an announcement that 'Kilroy (or his equivalent) was here'. The character of the inscriptions is shown by such statements as 'Remember Zailu, son of Wailu, grandson of Bitasu' and 'Think of Sambu, son of Nasaigu'. But how does one think of Zailu and Sambu?

Major Jarvis, who browsed in his day among the graffiti of the Wadi Mukatteb, sums up the layman's view of these scrawls. One can imagine the difficulties and perplexities of historians 2,000 years hence, he says, when, after weeks of labour, they decipher a present-day English inscription such as 'Coronach, a snip for the Derby' or 'Put your shirt on Dark Warrior for the Lincoln'.

The historians, however, have learnt something about the early Christian period from these writings, which indicate that pilgrims were visiting the hermitages of the Sinai Fathers even before the lady Etheria travelled across the peninsula in A.D. 450. Egyptian monks, in other words, had settled around the holy mountains some time during the third century, one of the first being St. Onophrius who dwelt in a grotto south of the Djebel Musa, surviving to the good old age of ninety, as so many of his fellow-ascetics managed to do, despite the extreme rigour of their life. In fact, these same hermits were described by an early traveller as being 'naked and covered with bristles'. Being naked on Mount Sinai on a winter's night is an ordeal which few men could survive today. But that they did survive, in great numbers, is proven by the cells still to be seen in the cliff faces all over southern Sinai and particularly in the oasis of Pharan (Feiran) which was the first great hermitage and monastery of the peninsula.

The visitor to the oasis of Feiran can still see the last ruins of this once famous cathedral city built in a long valley whose mountains of granite are said to be the oldest in the world. Millennia ago, the oasis was a large lake which burst through its limestone dam and rushed down the wadi to the sea. The springs which fed this lake still rise to the surface of the valley floor, however, and create a little green spot known in the guide-books as 'the Pearl of Sinai'. Certainly the dates and vegetables grown here are delicious and must have made life a little more agreeable to the first hermits who arrived on the spot quite early in our era, attracted to Sinai as the country of Moses and the Ten Commandments. In fact, the earliest identification of the mountain on which the leader of the Israelites received the Tablets of the Law was Mount Serbal, which rises directly above the oasis of Feiran, and this huge granite mass is covered with the ruins of churches, hermitages, and the cells of solitaries. One can still enter these little caves, usually only big enough to enable a man to lie down. On the other side of the valley stands the ruin of the great cathedral-monastery, once the residence of an archbishop in the heyday of the Sinaitic Church.

What kind of life was it for the monks and hermits of Feiran during the three centuries that they occupied the monasteries and hermitages throughout Sinai? Quite simply a life based on the literal interpretation of Christ's teaching—even to the extent of turning the other cheek to their enemies, the barbarians of the surrounding countryside who periodically took advantage of the Christian's pacifism. We have an eyewitness account of one such attack on the monastery of Feiran from the pen of an Egyptian monk who was visiting 'the holy mountain called Sinai'. (He meant Mount Serbal, not the mountain later called by the Christians the Mount of Moses.) The monk, Ammon, made his visit to Feiran about A.D. 380. He wrote his report in Coptic, which was later translated into Greek, Syriac, and Latin.

He says that as he sat one day in his little cell at the place called Canopus near Alexandria, he decided to go on a journey to the holy mountain called Sinai. While he was there, the Saracens came through the country in raiding parties, killing or wounding all the hermits who were not able to take refuge inside the stone towers which the monks had built to serve them as both churches and fortresses. Thirty-eight hermits were slain in the region of the Mount of Moses.

> For who [writes Ammon], even if his heart were of stone, would not weep for the holy martyrs who had grown old in the garb of Christians, flung upon the ground in merciless suffering; each one of them struck down, one with his head cut off and another [cleft in twain and another] with his head split in two. What can I say about the number of merciless blows which struck the saints who were killed limb by limb and were flung upon the ground?[1]

In the meantime, other barbarian raiders had crossed the Gulf of Suez and attacked the settlement on the west coast of the peninsula in the neighbourhood of the oasis of Feiran. Those hermits who lived alone in the mountains were killed in their cells; the monks of Feiran were besieged in their church towers. The barbarians, encountering no resistance in the shape of missiles, scalding water, and hot lead poured from the embrasures of the fortress, heaped tree-trunks against the wall outside and so burnt down the great door through which they burst looking for loot. Inside the tower the abbot, Paul of Petra, comforted his companions with a speech typical of his time.

> Ye all know that we have dwelt in this place for the sake of our Lord and Master, Jesus the Christ, cut off, because of his love, from the habits of this vain world, in this rough and fearful desert, living in hunger, in thirst, in dire poverty and misery, despising certainly, if I may so, everything earthly and this vain world, that we may deserve to be his

worthy companions in the kingdom of heaven . . . O athletes of God, let not your souls be faint and do nothing unworthy of your cowl, but be clothed with strength and joy and manliness that you may endure with a pure heart, and may God receive you into his kingdom.[2]

Paul's words help us to understand a little better how the holy men died with such a minimum of fear and even rancour. The abbot addresses his appeal to their belief in God and his kingdom; the modern equivalent of this, one assumes, is the statesman's appeal to the people's belief in king and country. The monks of Pharan, at all events, died bravely, one of them, Jeremiah by name, refusing to identify abbot Paul and in consequence being stripped of his clothes and used as a human target for the bowmen. When they found abbot Paul, the old man said quietly, 'I assure you, my children, I own nothing but this old robe that I am wearing'; at which the barbarians knocked him about, but, learning nothing, split his head open with their swords. Several score of the brothers were butchered to death, only three hermits escaping; Andrew who was wounded but later recovered, Domnus who died of his wounds, and Psoes who hid under a wood pile in the tower and lived to tell the tale to Ammon, his fellow-Egyptian.

It is apparent from this and many similar accounts of the killing of monks that these holy men refused to use arms to defend themselves, for they took Christ's commands in this matter as literally as they did in others. In the case of Sinai, they were so harassed by the Saracens that eventually they had to ask Justinian for protection and the emperor's response was to build fortresses to which the hermits could retire in times of danger. Eventually, as the holy men came under constant attack, their monasteries became fortresses proper, and such is the origin of St. Catherine's.

There were other fortress-monasteries at Clysma (Suez) and Raithou (Tur), but no trace of these buildings survives.

The task of finding any traces of ancient Tur is not made any easier today by the fact that the modern town has been utterly abandoned by the Egyptian population who were ordered to evacuate this important port on the Sinai side of the Gulf of

Suez during the Six Day War with Israel. And so one finds oneself gazing at a modern city with the same melancholy thoughts that one looks at the ruins of ancient places like Leptis Magna and Timgad, stepping carefully into deserted houses and public places and wondering what the people were like who lived in them.

All this has happened to Tur within the last two years: before that, it was a great clearing centre for Mecca pilgrims coming from all over North Africa via Egypt. The beautiful old boats which brought these pilgrims—they were mostly the poor people who could not afford plane and train fares—lie all round the shore, quickly rotting in the manner of unused boats left out of the water. The caravanserai which housed the travellers are empty: their shutters bang back and forth in the wind. The shops, souks, and modern apartment buildings are all abandoned, lock, stock, and barrel. The Lazaretto, or quarantine station, which looks like an enormous cattle market, houses not a single pilgrim. One enters the police station. The records lie scattered about the floor, and one picks them up mindful of booby-traps. They say there is now only one resident left in Tur, the priest of the Greek Orthodox Church which is an outpost of St. Catherine's monastery. But a few Bedouin arrive with sea shells for which Tur was always noted, and these men sit on the pavements with their gee-gaws on display for the tourists who arrive by the weekly bus. Otherwise Tur, which has the best harbour along this important coast, is a dead city.

Evidently the same fate befell the port after the Arab occupation of the Sinai Peninsula, for the Christian population—mostly monks in the monastery and hermits in the nearby caves—were killed, fled into the mountains, or sought sanctuary in the fortress-convent of St. Catherine. Such castles, built by Byzantine architects, were to be the only centres of the Western faith to survive during the next thousand years of practically continuous religious wars between Christendom and Islam; and it was only due to the foresight of the emperor Justinian and his consort Theodora that we can visit an outpost of Christianity in Sinai today.

The actual building of St. Catherine's began in A.D. 535 and was ordered by Justinian probably at the instigation of his wife Theodora who was occupying herself with that fierce controversy over the one versus the two natures of Christ. It is strange to think of an actress-harlot who became an empress worrying her pretty head with doctrinal questions which are today almost incomprehensible even to the learned: the arguments concerning whether the nature of Christ was single or double, and if double then 'neither mixed, transmuted, divided, nor separated'. But obviously Theodora had made up her mind, or had it made up for her, and having opted for the 'single nature' of Christ, joined with her husband in strengthening the monophysite faction whose exponents dwelt in Sinai and were, at the time, being harassed by the Saracens, as the local Bedouin were then called.

By great good fortune, we have an account of the transactions between Justinian and the monks of Sinai written by the emperor's secretary, Procopius—he who kept two sets of books, one for public and one for private consumption. In his book *The Buildings of the Lord Justinian* this cynical and perhaps pagan writer describes the activities of Christian monks as 'a life devoted to a careful study of death'—an extraordinarily equivocal statement. 'They therefore sought the solitude that was dear to them', he continues, 'and persuaded the Emperor to send architects and stone-masons out to Sinai to build three fortified monasteries.'

The convent built at the foot of the Mountain of Moses up which the pilgrims have toiled their way since the sixth century is a magnificent example of Byzantine military architecture. The massive fortress, 280 by 250 feet, is constructed in its lower courses of blocks of granite five feet square, and neither sieges nor conflagrations have managed to overthrow this part of the original building.

In order to safeguard the splendid new castle, Justinian wisely despatched a detachment of 100 Bulgarian slaves, with their wives and children, to act as the defenders and servants of the monks and hermits in the local caves. The descendants of these Europeans are now a tribe called the Djebeliya, and it is indeed true that these people are different in appearance from the other Bedouin tribes who inhabit Sinai. Their features, apart from their dark skins, are more European than Arab, which is understandable since the amount of intermarrying between these Djebeliya and the other tribes is negligible: the former are still tarnished with the disgrace of being the 'slaves' of Christians. At the same time, even while one can, with the aid of the imagination perhaps, discern an Aryan look to the Djebeliya, the official guide's explanation that blood tests have shown them to be of Norwegian stock takes a bit of swallowing, though it will no doubt become part of the mythology which surrounds St. Catherine's, the Mount of Moses, the Burning Bush (called by the guide 'the bruning bush' and corrected by a visitor to 'the burning brush'), and the rock where one sees the footprint of Mohammed's camel. One's impression of all these fairy tales is that the Christians laugh at the Moslems' legends, the Moslems laugh at the Christians', and the Jews laugh at both.

Whereas all the monasteries in Egypt proper, even those of the Wadi Natrun, were attacked, looted, and burnt so often that little remains of the original buildings, St. Catherine's has been rather more fortunate, though there have been short periods in the 1,400 years of history when it has been abandoned. There were no monks inside the convent, for instance, when a party of German pilgrims arrived there in 1565, and parties arriving after 1570 found the gates walled up. From that time until the British occupation, entrance into the monastery was by a basket hauled up by sturdy monks working a pulley on the rampart above.

Still, St. Catherine's did manage not only to survive the rage and hatred of Islam for the Christians, but even to grow more prosperous. There were two main reasons for this: first, the Bedouin in whose country it stood themselves reverenced the whole region as the country of Moses, one of the principal prophets of the Moslem religion; and secondly, the monastery had close ties with European convents, particularly those in France. In addition, a cult of St. Catherine swept across Europe during the eleventh and twelfth centuries, and the oil which was supposed to exude from her bones became the most prized of all relics. To us today, and even to churchmen, the extraordinary fervour of this saint's cult is puzzling and the tendency of the Catholic authorities is to dismiss her legend as practically worthless.[3]

The legend claims that Catherine was of royal birth and one of the most learned women of her time. At the age of eighteen she presented herself to the emperor Maximianus, who in 306 was violently persecuting the Christians. Catherine upbraided him for his cruelty, and undertook to confute any pagan philosopher the emperor might like to pit against her. The result was that every one of her opponents was not only conquered by her eloquence, but converted to the true faith, for which they were at once put to death. Even the emperor's wife, yielding to Catherine's exhortations, was baptised, and she, too, 'immediately received the martyr's crown'. Thereupon Maximianus ordered Catherine to be broken on the wheel and beheaded. Her body was carried by angels to Mount Sinai where it was kept in a casket in the Church of the Virgin and exuded the holy oil, a small phial of which was given to visiting pilgrims, until the flow was reduced to three drops a week in 1489, after which date it ceased altogether.

For some reason or the other, the young saint was invested from the eleventh to the sixteenth centuries with a halo of profound veneration, miraculous power, and charming poetry. Not only was she the patroness of young maidens, female students, philosophers, preachers, apologists, wheelwrights, millers, and others, but she was regarded as one of the fourteen most helpful saints in heaven. Together with St. Margaret, she was Joan of Arc's close adviser; and many theologians, philosophers, and scholars, before beginning their work, implored St. Catherine to purify their thoughts. One asks, 'And why not?'

It is not surprising, therefore, that her cult brought thousands of pilgrims throughout the Middle Ages to Mount Sinai, so that the monastery grew rich from gifts and was able to feed hundreds of visitors as well as the local nomads every day of the year. Thus it escaped the fate of so many monasteries in Egypt proper and was never really lost to the Western world.

On the other hand, as relations between Europe and the Ottoman Empire deteriorated during the sixteenth century, the monks periodically abandoned the convent altogether, though where they went is not clear; apparently to the seaport, Tur. In fact, by 1600, the monastery had become a colony of quasi-exiles, their number dwindling to thirty where once there had been hundreds, not counting the hermits and brothers in outlying cells and settlements. The archbishops of the convent, once the resident stewards of the shrine, preferred to serve God in more civilised places, making only an occasional visit to Sinai. From 1782 to 1872, no archbishop visited the monastery at all; and the few monks who occupied the convent were either old men who had nowhere else to go, or young men who longed to escape. The golden era of the Christian desert commonwealth was ended; and the era itself, the religion it avowed, and the men who practised it are almost as remote and alien to modern Christians as the Homeric age itself.

Thus it is that a visit to the monastery of St. Catherine's today only emphasises the remoteness of that primitive Christian world which the priest Antoninus described in A.D. 570 as 'the abode of a multitude of monks and hermits who came to meet us bearing crosses and singing psalms and falling upon the ground to reverence us. And we did likewise, shedding tears.'[4] No such welcome can be expected from the seven overworked monks of St. Catherine's today, since four of the seven are old and ill and the other three must manage the multifarious affairs of the monastery, which include the daily tours for the tourists. It is not surprising that there are no longer, as in Antoninus's time, 'abbots learned in tongues—that is to say, Latin, Greek, Syriac, Egyptian, and Persian'.[5] The youngest of the seven, who acts as the guide, speaks only his native Greek and some Hebrew, the latter a useful accomplishment since the majority of the visitors today are Jews. But not all Jews speak Hebrew, and very few indeed, one imagines, understand modern Greek, so a great many of those going round the monastery to see its ancient relics and treasures receive very little information about what they are looking at.

Because of this, but much more because of the unmonastic

Above The Nile just below Aswan, as seen from the monastery of St. Simeon
Below The *reis*, or skipper, of a Nile felucca

Two views taken inside the eighth-century monastery of St. Simeon which once housed 300 monks and several hundred pilgrims. Now in ruins

atmosphere of St. Catherine's—the constant coming and going of tourists, the absence of monks, the disuse of the various churches, and the general air of neglect—one comes away from the great convent with the presentiment that its active spiritual life is over and that it will never be anything more than a tourist attraction. Tourism is no doubt commendable, even if it is reducing a once-variegated and amusing world into a dull, standardised replica of Main Street; but no one would presumably argue that tourists visit St. Catherine's in a spirit of reverence. The great shrine is only too obviously another 'sight', like the pyramids. But how different the spirit in which the early pilgrims visited the monastery, travelling overland from Spain like the nun Etheria in A.D. 460 or journeying by sea from Genoa or Venice in the manner of the medieval voyagers! In those days the visitors, innocent of cameras, knelt reverently before the shrine of St. Catherine whose head (writes Sir John Maundeville) 'was rolled in a blood-stained cloth which I looked at carefully and often with unworthy eyes'. Were our forefathers incredibly naïve? Or did they believe that miraculous events were simply a manifestation of holiness? In either case, they were delighted to receive the gift of a small phial of the oil which oozed from the ends of the saint's fingers, which, however, fell off some time in the eleventh century and were taken as holy relics to the abbey which was being built at Rouen. The holy oil was considered an adequate souvenir of the long, arduous, and expensive journey.

In those days, in 1384 for instance, when a party of Italian pilgrims arrived at the monastery, there were 200 monks in residence, of whom 150 served the convent chapels and fifty the outlying chapels on the Mount of the Law. Food was cooked in the convent kitchen every day for 400 persons in huge cauldrons. Bread and alms were distributed every day to a thousand Bedouin of the desert, and nobody who passed the convent ever went away unfed.

That was St. Catherine's in the fourteenth century. Today the seven monks in residence are not enough to serve either the convent chapels or the outlying churches; no food is cooked in the monastery kitchens; bread and alms are no longer distributed; and passers-by must bring their own food. One could say that St. Catherine's, one of the greatest shrines of Christendom, resembles today a rather ill-run motel to which few travellers come as pilgrims and devotees of the girl who defied an emperor. And as if ashamed of Catherine and of her relics, the young monk who acts as guide never refers to his patron saint at all and certainly not to her severed head 'rolled in a blood-stained cloth'. And during the visit to the charnel house, one sees from his irritable face that he is as sceptical about the piles of skulls and thigh bones which represent the mortal remains of his predecessors as the tourists who fiddle with their light-meters preparatory to getting a shot of this strange and gruesome necropolis.

REFERENCES

1 Ammon, *The Forty Martyrs of the Sinai Desert*. Translated by Agnes Smith Lewis. (Horae Semiticae, No. IX). p. 3.
2 op. cit., p. 8.
3 In May 1969 dismissed as *wholly* worthless and entirely legendary.
4 *Of the Holy Places Visited by Antoninus Martyr*, Palestine Pilgrims Text Society, Vol. ii, p. 29.
5 ibid.

10 The end in the desert

The old guide-books, give them their due, were full of curious titbits of history. Thus, Murray's *Handbook to Egypt* (1888) informs us that Eratosthenes in the third century B.C. discovered the rays of the sun during the summer solstice fell vertically to the bottom of a deep well at Aswan, while, at the same hour, a shadow was cast at Alexandria, enabling the astronomer to make his calculations for the measurement of the earth. It is the sort of snippet of information which enables some travellers —and I am one of them—to see local history in terms of people rather than monuments. And in a town like Aswan, distinguished today by hideous monolithic buildings, it is pleasantly nostalgic to remember Eratosthenes and his successor Juvenal, exiled here three centuries later. Their lives and activities seem somehow more interesting than those of the nameless Russian engineers quarantined in the modern hotels.

The traveller to Aswan today will find no trace of Eratosthenes's well, or of Juvenal's fifteenth satire; nor will he hear mention of Syene, the ancient name of the town. For that matter, all vestiges of the more recent British presence—fortresses and garrisons from which the British troops left on the Nile Expedition of 1884–5—have disappeared along with the majority of the Pharaonic and Roman monuments. The visitor is expected to reserve his enthusiasm for the High Dam.

However, once the visit to this stupendous engineering feat is over, he can wander down to the river below the first cataract. Here in a little rock-bound bay wait the feluccas which, in better days, took the tourists to see the local sights, notably the Island of Elephantine, the temple of Philae, and the Agha Khan mausoleum. My destination was a ruined monastery called St. Simeon on the west bank of the Nile, a place to which the *rais*, or skipper, of the felucca I hired seldom visited. But he said he knew how to get there. I hoped he did and on examining his face, decided he was an honest-looking fellow. The large carbuncle on the side of his nose gave one confidence, as physical defects or disabilities in another man often do.

The *rais* was quite content to let me sail his boat down the river. The feluccas are gaff-rigged, the gaff being used as an upward extension of the mast, giving great height and grace to the sail. Sailing on the Nile is, in general, a matter of tacking downstream with the current and running back against it, so that one can be sure of travelling in both directions in all seasons. Tacking downstream past the islands, we put into a sandy cove whence we climbed the cliffs to the Agha Khan mausoleum, which I had no interest in seeing. Here, however, the local guardian was supposed to hand over the key which admitted us to the monastery of St. Simeon. Having obtained the key, we marched upwards across the bare plateau until the tower and walls of the great eighth-century convent came into view. From afar, St. Simeon looks like a Byzantine fortress, and a fortress it had to be, exactly like the monasteries of the Wadi Natrun, those of St. Antony and St. Paul in the Eastern Desert, and Christian strongholds all over Egypt and the Near East.

Arriving at the portico, the *rais* produced a very large key, inserted it into the lock, and discovered that it would not fit. The guardian had given him the wrong key. This seemed to be standard practice, for my guide took me along to a place where we could scale the walls and enter in this manner. The *rais* climbed the rough walls barefooted, and urged me to do likewise.

Inside the monastery the visitor is confronted with a small city which has not evidently been systematically destroyed but has simply decayed through the centuries—the principal damage having been inflicted on the site by passing vandals who defaced or desecrated the murals in the main basilica. Of these murals I could only discover that of the Christ Triumphant painted on the central apse. The rest of the interior of the monastery was a confusion of vaults, cells, staircases, walls, workshops, and pilgrims' quarters, the whole dominated by an enormous keep three storeys high. The place has never been systematically excavated and its history remains obscure. Yet it is the finest example of an original Christian monastery in Egypt and to wander around in it alone is an evocative experience.

What do we know of St. Simeon? First, this name is of recent date and actually has nothing to do with the Simeon the Stylite, for instance. There were, in any case, two, if not three, pillar-sitters of this name: Simeon the elder, A.D. 388–459, who spent thirty-six years of his life on top of a fifty-foot column; Simeon the younger, born 521, died 597, sixty-eight years atop his shaft; and a more obscure Simeon reputed to have lived as a stylite near Hegca in Cilicia, to have been struck by lightning, and subsequently revered by the Greeks and Copts. However, the founder of the monastery appears to have been not Simeon but a Bishop Hadra of whom nothing is known except his name. Perhaps he was one of the fourth-century martyrs, from the year of whose death (A.D. 304) the Copts base their calendar; in that case his tomb in the mountain overlooking the Nile may have been a pilgrims' shrine which eventually led to the building of rest-houses for monks and visitors, as in the case of the city of St. Menas.[1] The structure dates from the eighth century and apparently survived, along with other monasteries in Upper Egypt and Nubia, into the Middle Ages, despite the persecution of the Christians and the wholesale destruction of their churches by the Arabs. Why St. Simeon was not destroyed in A.D. 1321 when eleven other Christian churches were knocked down in Aswan alone is not clear; but even so the monks were certainly killed or driven out and we can date the abandonment of the fortress-city from the fourteenth century.

In the great days of this convent, there must have been thousands of monks and hermits in the desert hereabouts, for everything about the monastery is on the grand scale: the ring-wall built of dressed stone was thirty feet high; the inner keep is three storeys high; there are cells for 300 resident monks and dormitories with three beds to a room for several hundred pilgrims; and outbuildings (mills, bakehouses, workshops, et cetera) for regular community life. Outside the monastery were the caves of the hermits, and all the way down to the Nile the fields and gardens which fed this large community. The explorer wandering about among the massive ruins of St. Simeon asks how it was possible for this little corner of Christendom to have reached this dismal end.

The answer is that primitive Christianity, which was the literal acceptance of Christ's teaching, largely destroyed itself, first by the *doctrinal* controversies of the fourth and fifth centuries; and secondly by outright *political* rivalries. Eventually, as doctrine became equated with politics, no one could any longer say with complete certainty what particular cause a spokesman was advocating, whether the cause of the kingdom of God, or that of an earthly faction. A classic example of this is the tremendous struggle for power between Gelasius, pope of Rome, and Acacius, patriarch of Constantinople, during the latter half of the fifth century. While this controversy had some vague doctrinal basis (the vexed and vexatious business of the 'two natures'), the real issue was the leadership of the Christian world—was it to be Roman or Byzantine? On behalf of the former claim, Pope Gelasius argued that his city had been given by God the rights and honour of the Chair of Peter. (That there was no proof whatsoever that Peter lived and died in Rome was irrelevant, since all Christians now accepted this legend as divine truth.) On behalf of the Byzantine faction, Patriarch Acacius contended that Constantinople was now the capital of the empire and the residence of the emperor, who was the *pontifex maximus*: therefore he, Acacius, was the proper spokesman for the Church. Pope Gelasius, in a rather weak position politically, replied by anathematising his rival in perpetuity. Patriarch Acacius countered this by removing the pope's name from the document and by even converting the pontiff's emissaries to the heretical monophysite doctrine. So the war between Western and Eastern Christianity dragged on until religion became more and more tainted with nationalism.

The political attitude of the Egyptian Church at this period (around A.D. 449, the year of the great heresy trials at the Council of Chalcedon) manifested itself in two forms: first, in outright nationalism based on a hatred of the Roman occupiers; and second, a struggle for leadership between the pope of Rome and the patriarch of Alexandria. The two are directly related, since the Egyptian patriarch came to personify more and more the ghostly leader of the hoped-for liberation, a liberation from both Rome and Constantinople, the 'new' Rome. The tragic and bitter finale to this politico-religious struggle between Egypt and the West, was the decision of the Egyptians, through their church and its leaders, to throw in their lot with the new invaders, namely the Arabs, against the old Roman occupiers. This, of course, is an episode in Egyptian history which is not recognised by the sympathisers and defenders of the Copts.[2] But whether collaboration is admitted or not, the seventeenth-century Egyptian historian, Abu Dakn, specifically states that 'the distressed Jacobites [i.e. Copts], who by their daily ill usage had been too much exasperated, had as much cause of fear of their fellow-Christians as of the blasphemous enemies of that sacred name and fled to Mahomet for succour . . . [And] the Ægyptian Copht, easily submitting themselves to the Mahomet yoke, being mildly used, found a much more gentle slavery than the other Christians.'[3] It was as though the Egyptians won the last battle by destroying both the foreign and their own church; and their reasons for doing so could hardly have been wholly spiritual ones. They were, rather, the culmination of many centuries of repressed nationalism and the emergence of a policy of Egypt for the Egyptians.

This curious and discreditable phase of Christian history, during which nearly everything that the Desert Fathers and their successors had built up was destroyed, can be studied in the ludicrous accounts of the heresies, great and small, of the fourth and fifth centuries. But it soon becomes obvious that men's passions were not aroused merely by arcane definitions as to the nature of Christ, but by the manifest ambitions of the various supporters of the definitions. The Council of Ephesus held in A.D. 431 led to the first of these outright battles between rival prelates. The expression 'battles' is not exaggerated, for these early councils were the scenes of actual physical violence as well as of religious controversy. The charges, counter-charges, arguments, and abuse hurled about at these Church conferences are so absurd that few historians trouble to examine them today, partly, no doubt, because Gibbon in the forty-seventh chapter of his *Decline and Fall of the Roman Empire* left them nothing more to say:

> The emperors enforced with arms and edicts the symbol of their faith; and it was declared by the conscience or honour of five hundred bishops that the decrees of the synod of Chalcedon might be lawfully supported, even with blood . . . Jerusalem was occupied by an army of monks; in the name of the one incarnate nature, they pillaged, they burnt, they murdered; the sepulchre of Christ was defiled with blood; and the gates of the city were guarded in tumultuous rebellion against the troops of the emperor . . . Superstitions were inflamed on either side by the principle and the practice of retaliation: in the pursuit of a metaphysical quarrel, many thousands were slain, and the Christians of every degree were deprived of the substantial enjoyments of social life . . . 'The people of Alexandria and all Egypt were seized with a strange and diabolical frenzy: great and small, slaves and freedmen, monks and clergy, the natives of the land, lost their speech and reason, barked like dogs, and tore with their own teeth the flesh from their hands and arms.'[4]

But the basic cause of the 'diabolical frenzy' of the Egyptians was not, of course, the argument concerning the single or dual nature of Christ; it was the hatred of the Roman oppressors—the magistrates, tax-collectors, army, and a host of public officials, including the Catholic priests. This hatred was political: it was the outcome of that nationalism which was replacing the old 'One World' concept of both the Roman Empire and the primitive Christian commonwealth. The same narrow regionalism was to lead to the fragmentation of the entire European world during the next thousand years and more, and was to determine the course of history far more than religion. In other words, by the end of the sixth century, genuine internationalism, the universal brotherhood of man, as firmly believed in, and advocated by, the Fathers of the Church, had ceased to be a driving force in human affairs; and though the Catholic Church of the Middle Ages tried once again to introduce the theory and practice of theocracy, the passions of nationalism proved far stronger than the fear of God and his priests. The division of the Church into innumerable schisms and sects which seem to have nothing in common other than a claim to the same divine sponsorship is the end result.

In Egypt the initial result was the undoubted collaboration between the Copts (particularly those in high places) and the Arab invaders; and it is reasonably certain that the armies of the new prophet would not have been able to conquer and occupy Egypt without the help of a Fifth Column. Even so, the number of actual collaborators was small, and the fate of Egypt was certainly not decided by the rank and file of Christians, who were unarmed, oppressed, and indifferent to who won the battles that were continually being fought on their soil. If anything, their sympathies probably lay with the Arabs, for these invaders from the East at least belonged to a circumcised nation and believed in one God, which could not be said of the Romans. In fact, to a seventh-century Copt, the Arabs must have seemed like semi-Christians, particularly as Jesus Christ was revered by them, along with the major prophets of the Old Testament. In addition, the new religion of Islam preached the gospel of 'the surrender of the individual will to the law of God'; and this surrender, or resignation, to God was precisely the faith of the Desert Fathers from whom the basic creed of the Coptic Church was derived. So it is little wonder that the apostles of Islam were not at first regarded as spiritual enemies; to the contrary, the Mohammedans, compared with the Catholics, were the better monotheists.

Whatever the pros and cons of the controversy as to who was responsible for the loss of Egypt to the Arabs, it is certain that the final surrender was negotiated by Egyptian churchmen who were understandably elated with the terms of a treaty which promised them freedom of worship, non-interference in their religious affairs, and protection for their places of worship, rights and concessions which the Byzantines had never granted them. Little they knew that they were only exchanging one set of tyrants for another, for within a hundred years they were no better than the serfs of the Arabs. Indeed, the Christian population of Egypt dropped from several millions in the seventh century to several thousands by the end of the fourteenth. The fact that the Egyptian Church survived at all under the circumstances was a triumph of faith and loyalty, particularly since the Copts were almost completely cut off from the rest of Christendom for well over a thousand years. During that period they received neither help nor comfort from their western co-religionists who, to the contrary, made life much more difficult and precarious for them by continual crusades against the Moslems. It is no wonder that the Arabs, though at first well disposed towards their subject Christians, began to accuse them of disloyalty, treachery, and hatred of Islam. In short, the Eastern Church paid for the zeal of the Crusaders with their lives, their property, and their peace of mind.

But in the beginning all was kindness and understanding between the invaders and the invaded. Amr, the Arab commander-in-chief, received with antique courtesy every kind of supplicant—philosophers, scholars, librarians, and an extraordinary embassy of 70,000 Nitrian monks, each with his staff, who had marched from their desert monasteries in the Wadi Natrun to request that their churches and cells be left unmolested. Amr received all these importunate Egyptians with patience and, indeed, generosity, for he promised the monks his protection, their freedom to worship the one God (he happened to worship the same deity), and the right to reinstate their patriarch Benjamin as their leader. And as long as Amr governed Egypt, Christians had their religious and civil liberty.

Moreover, the Arabs, though semi-barbarians in the eyes of the Romans, had the intelligence to recognise that the Egyptians, though no soldiers, were skilled doctors, artists, architects, engineers, craftsmen, and artisans and, as such, were to be treated with respect. This respect for learning, in fact, is the explanation of why and how the Arabs excelled in art, architecture, mathematics, astronomy, alchemy, and so forth from the seventh to the twelfth centuries: their reverence for art and science made them the patrons of Greek, Armenian, Egyptian, and Circassian craftsmen and scholars who contributed to the golden age of Islam.

As long as Egypt was governed by soldiers like Amr and the old-fashioned men of Mohammed's age and outlook, the people enjoyed peace and liberty. Indeed, their principal troubles were still caused by internecine struggles between the National Church (the Monophysites) and what remained of the Orthodox Byzantine Church (the Melkites), since the leaders of the two sects continually quarrelled to the extent of accusing each other of treachery, with the result that the Arab overlords began to suspect, then to fine them, and eventually to imprison their leaders. Otherwise, the Moslems still had no doctrinal quarrels with the Christians, the proof of this being the sponsorship by the Emir Abd el Aziz in A.D. 695 of a church council convened to consider the question of Christian divorce—already settled, of course, in Koranic law.

But once the old desert aristocrats had been replaced by petty tyrants and opportunists, the situation changed. The Arab politicians discovered that they could make the rich Christians pay for the religious liberty of the poor by fines and bribes; and then, with oriental cunning, they argued that if their victims could produce so much gold, they must have access to more. Rich men always did. And it was not long before fines and bribes were legitimised in the form of tribute. We now have the spectacle of the patriarch of the Copts spending his entire time travelling about collecting this tribute from his impoverished co-religionists in order to escape imprisonment.

Over a thousand years of this kind of harassment now lay ahead for the Copts. Indeed, the story of oppression now becomes so tragic that the historian is puzzled as to how any Christians survived at all in Egypt, Nubia, and the Sudan—as none survived in the western lands of North Africa—Libya, Tunisia, Algeria, and Morocco. At one point, Moslems were actually authorised to kill any Christian they met in the street, and Christians were compelled to wear blue turbans in order to proclaim their faith. In addition, they had to wear a bell round their necks to announce their entry into a public place. They were not permitted to ride horses or mules and were only allowed to mount on a donkey provided they rode facing the animal's rear. Thousands of Christians apostasised in those days, or never went out of their houses at all, or borrowed the Jews' yellow turbans if they had a Jewish friend. For a time, the desert monasteries were the only sanctuaries for Christians. The churches in cities all up and down the Nile were burnt down. The historian Makrize (1363–1442) lists eleven churches destroyed in Cairo, four in Alexandria, and thirty-five elsewhere, together with a great number of monasteries—all this in one year, 1328.

The remainder of the story of the Coptic Church is confused and obscure, for on the one hand the Christians were persecuted and taxed almost out of existence by tyrannical Moslem governors, both national and local; and on the other they survived in sufficient numbers to prove that the Saracen tyrants were not as ruthless as the tyrants of recent history. Probably the mass slaughter of Christians during this middle period in Egypt was limited by the lack of communications: in other words, Christians in the villages of Upper Egypt were out of the reach of the fanatical mobs in Cairo. Moreover, the old faith was kept alive by a few monks in the desert monasteries, though these shrines were now periodically looted and burnt by the Bedouin.

Yet it was the desert which saved Christianity from utter extinction in Africa. The monasteries of the Western Desert in the Wadi Natrun, those in the Eastern Desert on Mount Colzoum, and a few in the Sinai Peninsula managed to survive from century to century, though all of them were completely abandoned at one time or another. The monasteries and churches along the Nile, however, as far down as the Sudan were destroyed or totally abandoned by the end of the fourteenth century and have since disappeared into the desert sands. Typical of them, and significant as showing the former power and glory of the Egyptian Church is the basilica of Faras, excavated in 1962–3 by the Polish archaeological mission under the auspices of U.N.E.S.C.O.[5] Professor Michalowski, head of the mission, reported:

> We discovered a complete basilica at Faras. Engulfed by the sands, it had been abandoned in the 12th century when northern Nubia came completely under Moslem rule. It is built of stone and fired brick in contrast to most other buildings of the period, including the many churches scattered along the Nile. Its stones were taken from the ruins of Pharaonic temples. This basilica dates from the 7th century and is dedicated to the Virgin and Saint Michael.

As the archaeologists cleared the sand and rubble from the building, they uncovered artistic treasures which have never been surpassed in the history of excavations in Christian Egypt—169 paintings, most of them still in their pristine state, one of them a fresco of the Nativity measuring twenty-two by thirteen feet; twenty-seven of them portraits of the bishops of the diocese, all with their names and racial characteristics clearly depicted. Attached to the cathedral of Faras was a monastery, at least six other churches, a large citadel, and various administrative buildings, showing how rich and flourishing the Christian culture was in a region which is now an abandoned wasteland and is soon to disappear under the man-made lake required by modern progress.

Certainly by the modern period when the first European travellers penetrated into the closed Islamic world, Egyptian Christians had been reduced to the status of a cruelly oppressed minority, particularly in the villages. The first European to give a general account of the Copts was Johann Michael Wansleben who visited Egypt in 1670.[6] This is his description of the people he calls 'the Copties':

> The Copties at present in Egypt are not numerous in comparison of what they have been heretofore; for in the days

of Amru ibn Aff, who took this country from the Greeks there was of this nation 600,000 that paid him tribute: but now, according to the relation of their own Patriarch, there is scarce ten or fifteen thousand . . . After this, the Mahometan kings and princes that have governed Egypt since the Christian emperours, when they found them [i.e. the Copts] rebellious against their government, have not spared them. They have killed the chief (=the Patriarch), sold for slaves the wives and children of the others, so that the weaker sort have been forc'd to turn Mahometans. By this means, after so many evils, this nation is reduced to a very small number.[7]

After his tour of Egypt, Wansleben, or Vansleb as he is often called, went to say goodbye to the Coptic patriarch, 'one of my best friends':

I had often intreated him to come and dine with me, but he answered me he had not been out of his house a year for fear of the Turks. He complained that all the Patriarchs of the other sects had the liberty to go about the town, but he was so narrowly observed by the Turks that he could not so much as go out of his house. . . .

I must confess that there is no nation in Egypt so much afflicted as are the Copties, because they have nobody among them who deserves to be honoured for his knowledge, or feared for his power and authority; for all that were rich and wealthy are destroyed by the cruelty of the Mahometans: therefore the rest are now looked upon as the Scum of the World, and worse than the Jews. The Turks abuse them at their pleasure; they shut up their churches and the doors of their houses when they please, upon light occasions, altogether unjust, to draw from them some sums of money.[8]

Judging from the reports of later travellers, the condition of the Copts showed no improvement until the end of the nineteenth century, but, if anything, deteriorated with time. We repeat, that when one reads of the unbridled cruelty and corruption of the Turkish rulers—during the eighteenth century the Emirs murdered each other sometimes at the rate of one a month—it is phenomenal that this tiny religious minority was able, let alone had the will, to survive. They were saved by their genuine faith which had remained almost unchanged from the time of the Roman persecutions; by their intellectual superiority to the Mamelukes, making them almost essential to the running of the state; and by the continuous civil war between the rival political and military factions within Egypt itself. By cowering within their homes in Cairo and Alexandria, or lying low in their shacks in the villages on the banks of the Nile, the Egyptian Christians somehow managed not only to stay alive, but to retain their ancient faith.

Beyond the Nile, the last strongholds of Christianity, the great monasteries of the desert were also in mortal danger from the attacks of the barbarians who controlled the country once policed by the legions. St. Antony's and St. Paul's in the Eastern Desert were deserted from 1500 to 1580 after the massacre of the monks by the descendants of the slaves sent by the emperor Justinian in A.D. 536 to be the servants of the religious. The convent Arabs were said to object to the celibacy imposed on them by the priests, but it is more likely that they were resentful of the endless privation and ritual imposed on them by the strict discipline and were covetous of the sacred relics, vessels, ornaments, books, and ikons. These treasures were either looted or destroyed by the savages who murdered the monks, carried off the gold and silver ornaments, and burnt pictures and manuscripts in the monastery ovens. However, when Father Vansleb reached St. Antony's in 1672, he found the convent occupied by two priests and seventeen lay monks. He gives this description of the conditions under which they lived:

> Their cells are very little, and poor, of yellowish earth, without timber, plaster, order, or symmetry: they are so low that a man may easily reach up to the top with his hand: therefore the monks cannot very well stand upright: there is a little light that enters in through holes in the wall, about a foot long; the doors are so low that one must stoop to go in. . . .
>
> Their rule obliges them to renounce matrimony for ever, all carnal desires, their parents, to possess no estate, to dwell in the wilderness, to be cloathed with wool, to be girt with

a leathern girdle, to eat no flesh, nor drink wine all their lifetime, to shorten their dinner and to deny themselves all the nourishments without which the body is able to live. It commands them to imploy all their time in fasting, and prayer, and worship, to have always their mind running upon God, to apply themselves to the reading of the Holy Scriptures, and to understand the truths that are there contained.

It obliges them to sleep upon a mat, or the ground, their Superior excepted, and such as are sick; not to take off their Cloaths, and their girdle, never to sleep two upon the same pillow, nor near one another. In short their rules oblige them to repeat the Canonical Prayers, to prostrate themselves before they go to bed 150 times, with their faces and bellies to the ground, to spread out their arms in a cross, with the fist shut, and at every rising to make the sign of the cross . . . which renders them very lean, and cast down; so that they appear like so many skeletons, rather than men.[9]

Of the nineteen inmates of the monastery, says Father Vansleb, almost all were either blind, deaf, lame, halt, or worn out with old age. The very thought of this company of old and decrepit men spending their last days in the dreadful wilderness of Mount Colzoum in the Eastern Desert is appalling to those who have no concept of monastic life, and this is apparent enough in the comments of all the European visitors to the desert monasteries. Those travellers without exception report the monasteries occupied by a body of monks ranging in numbers from six to twenty, living in conditions of great hardship. In fact, by 1912 the Egyptian monasteries which numbered hundreds in the sixth and seventh centuries were reduced to eight; and the monks who were counted in hundreds of thousands before the Arab invasion totalled 400. Moreover, nobody, it seemed, was interested in either the ancient monuments themselves or their inmates. Once the libraries of the convents had by 1912 been ransacked, the buildings themselves were considered to be of no importance either historically or architecturally. A few archaeologists and scholars like Alfred Butler and Somers Clarke had done their best to draw the outside world's attention to these ancient relics of Christianity, but, in general, everything Coptic, including its art and architecture, tended to be despised by the Egyptologists. In consequence, some of the oldest shrines of the Christian religion were allowed to be used as tenements, or to crumble away altogether. The White Monastery, the mother church of Schenoudi, founded in the fourth century and still the noblest church in Egypt, was in 1907 when Somers Clarke visited it 'foul and disgusting beyond description. . . . The narthex was the common cesspit, and even inside the church, whilst holy offices went on at the altar, filth accumulated in the transept, and chickens marched about unmolested.'[10]

I was mindful of my predecessors of early days when I arrived at Soohag en route to the Red and White Monasteries. One feels that a small Nile town like Soohag has not greatly changed since Father Vansleb passed through 300 years ago. True, there is now a railway station whereas the old travellers came by boat; but they must have found the noise, dust, and confusion about the same as I did. And no doubt the same sort of urchins fought to carry their bags, and no doubt the fight was won by the more sturdy of these ragamuffins. The Palace Hotel was not there in Vansleb's day, of course; but it was probably in existence when Robert Curzon passed through in 1837. It certainly looked as if it might have been.

On the advice of a Copt who had come to meet me together with a priest who marched ahead with his ebony walking stick with which he parted the crowds, I sought out the Atlas Hotel, which the old guide-books would certainly have classified as modest. Here began the usual pantomime with my passport which the manager of the hotel handled as though it were a time-bomb set to go off in five minutes or thereabouts. This man proved to be an officious and unsmiling xenophobe, and my Copt guide, seeing that we had reached an impasse over the passport, suggested that we report to the police and so get this phase of my visit over with. At the police station there seemed to be at least a score of policemen and perhaps fifty spies and informers awaiting my arrival, already announced by the hotel telephone, unlocked with a key for this purpose.

At first my presence in the police station was studiously ignored, as several smartly dressed officers began feverishly writing in large ledgers. Protocol was being observed. Eventually my passport was inspected, and the more people who examined it, the more it seemed to become obvious that I was a dangerous spy, for why else should I come alone to a place like Soohag? But what can one do in these circumstances but play the part of an innocent old lady, while producing documents galore and answering questions about one's grandmother's maiden name? Finally, with a grand flourish, the headman stamped my smallpox vaccination certificate with the official seal of the city of Soohag, I signed a long screed in Arabic, and was allowed to go on my way.

My way led out of town along the dirt roads towards the desert where stood the Red and White monasteries. We proceeded across fields of sugar cane and over canals, where, according to my antique guide-book, 'very good duck hunting may be had, and the ornithologist above all should make the excursion if he is desirous of obtaining the Egyptian eagle-owl (*bubo ascalaphus*) or the brown-necked raven (*corvus umbrinus*)'. What killers these Victorians were to come to Egypt to shoot the last surviving owls and ravens—though who are we to criticise them, our record being the extermination of one species of animal per annum?

Naturally, we saw no birds of any sort, but dogs, donkeys, chickens, and children, all tumbling in the dust of the village squares.

At last we reached the Dayr el-Ahmar, or Red Monastery, though what one actually sees now is the church attached to the conventual complex of cells, guest houses, gardens, and community buildings all once contained within a high wall. Everything has gone but part of the great church said to have been founded by the empress Helena. The Coptic histories state, on the other hand, that the sanctuary was built in memory of a robber called Bischoi, who turned Christian and atoned for his wicked life by prayer and fasting. Until recently, Bischoi's club was one of the holy relics of this shrine, but who knows what became of that? The club has gone, and the impression is that it will not be long before the church itself goes too, for it is in the last stages of dilapidation. Its massive walls, of classical Roman brick, dark red in colour, still stand, surrounded by mud hovels.

Inside, vestiges of its ancient grandeur are still discernible in the fallen columns, the three apses, and a central and two side altars in the Byzantine style: that is, semi-circular chambers two storeys high and surmounted by half-domes. The domes are supported by six columns for each storey, twelve in all, with niches between each of the pillars, probably to house statues of the apostles. Columns and walls were once covered with frescoes, leading up the main picture on the half-dome of the central altar—a large portrait of Christ Pantocrator. But these murals were so blackened with the smoke of incense and candles that they are scarcely discernible. One assumes that they could be cleaned; and if they were, they would no doubt rank as unique treasures of Egyptian–Byzantine art of the tenth century.

My tour of the Red Monastery was enlivened by the company of two priests who lived in nearby hovels with their families. Every time I took a photograph, these good men posed with their little gold crosses held aloft in the right hand, while beside them, as conscious as film stars of their image, the several toddlers in their little flowered dresses from which projected their skinny legs and bare feet, posed with the solemnity of animals in front of a camera. Cups of sweet tea appeared frequently; the atmosphere was festive; and it was difficult to concentrate on either the architecture or the history of this venerable place. This was even more the case when I arrived at the nearby White Monastery, for by now all the inhabitants of the villages had joined us, and all climbed into the old Dodge car for the ride. The priests of the White Monastery were waiting for me, ready to pose for their picture, eager to run me round the church and to get the formalities over with. Priest, villagers, and infants hurried me from place to place, lighting wax matches to reveal the secrets of this fifth-century church, pointing out the stones taken from Egyptian temples and still covered with hieroglyphs. Again it was difficult to examine the frescoes on the walls and domes of the apses, though I was able to perceive a great picture of Christ with four evangelists in attendance— and noted in my hurriedly scrawled notes: 'Another masterpiece of sixth- or seventh-century art going to pot.'

Yet this was the monastery founded by Schnoudi (Schenute, Schenudi, Sinuthius, et cetera), Coptic saint and father of the Egyptian Church. When he was abbot in about A.D. 400, Schnoudi was head of a colony of some 20,000 monks, 2,000 of whom lived in or around the White Monastery. What, one wonders, was the attraction of the life, particularly as regulated by a bigot and tyrant like the head of the White Monastery? Perhaps the answer is that austerity and discipline comfort men in times of trouble. Or perhaps those old Christians really believed that a good life was rewarded in heaven. At all events, the monks of the White Monastery all took this vow at the altar of the ruined church where the archaeologist Somers Clarke saw chickens marching about unmolested and children relieving themselves in the transept:

> I vow before God in his holy place as the word of my tongue is my witness: I shall never sully my body in any way; I shall not steal; I shall not take false oaths; I shall not lie; I shall not do evil secretly. If I transgress what I have sworn, I shall not enter the kingdom of heaven, for I know that God before whom I pronounce this pledge will thrust me body and soul into hell-fire.

It is the first monastic vow of which we have any knowledge and it sounds typical of an abbot who personally flogged erring monks and even flogged one man to death. He would have flogged the nuns, too, if it had been seemly, because these sisters were often worse than the brothers. In fact, despite Schnoudi's whip and his ranting and raving, monks and nuns appear to have led a relatively pleasant life. They had ways and means of supplementing their meagre diet of beans, bread, and water with sweetmeats smuggled in from outside. Indeed, the White Monastery sounds more like a public school in Victorian times than a religious community: there seems to have been the same combination of ferocious discipline and laxity.

By 1670 when Father Vansleb reached the Red and White

Monasteries, he found them 'altogether ruinated' and occupied by a few monks who spent their time 'seeking for the philosopher's stone and in works of Chymistry—an excellent employment' (he adds in one of his rare moments of cynicism) 'for such as have left the world and forsaken their riches.'[11]

The tourist today will not find monks in any of the surviving convents seeking for the philosopher's stone. Both men and buildings have surrendered to progress. The traveller is no longer hoisted up over the walls in a basket. He will no longer have his feet washed by the abbot when he is inside; or be required to give proof that he is circumcised; or be asked, 'When will you European Christians kill all the Arabs?' He will be received by a monk who speaks his language fairly well, shown to the guest house, and fed corned beef or sardines from tins. If he stays the night, he will sleep in a clean bed covered with a mosquito net and will suffer none of the torments of the nineteenth-century travellers, one of whom reports that the bugs 'walked by day as by night', or, as Robert Curzon, afterwards Lord Zouche, wrote in 1836 that he could not sleep a wink, even though 'the poor monks, hearing my exclamations, crept out of their holes and recommended me to go into the church, which they said would be safe from the attacks of the enemy'.

Some things have not changed, however—notably the ritual. If the visitor attends mass, he will experience the same long vigil that the earliest travellers describe, three hours of chanting, beating of cymbals, bell-ringing, genuflecting, and continuous shouting of *kyrie eleison*. Constantine Tischendorff, the German scholar and bibliophile who made the greatest haul in book history by obtaining the Codex Sinaiticus from the Monastery of St. Catherine on the Sinai Peninsula, gives us the best description of the monasteries in the mid-nineteenth century. On his visit to the Wadi Natrun in 1844, he found some fifteen brethren living in the monastery of Macarius—'all sallow and several of them a sickly yellow; they almost all suffered in their eyes, and the superior was totally blind'. Like all travellers who stay overnight in one of the desert convents, he attended a night mass, which lasted—as it still does—three hours. He noted the little humorous incidents which make the Coptic service so human and so *sympathique* to the visitor from the far-away outside world: the argument between a reader of the liturgy and a brother who corrected him; the comedy of the Eucharist as the officiating priest took the grape juice out of a glass vessel with a spoon, popped the holy liquid into a deacon's mouth, then scraped out the dregs with his fingers, which he licked, and finally touched his fellow-worshippers on the forehead and cheek with his still-sticky fingers.

Tischendorff sums up the Victorian protestant's abhorrence of the monastic regime:

> They live on carelessly from day to day. To such an existence, what is the past and what the future? . . . In all these monasteries my advice and aid were in request by people with sore eyes, many of whom were hastening towards total blindness. If there be a mode of life which leads directly to blindness, it is certainly that of these monks . . .
>
> Thus the entire existence of these Coptic communities is an unnatural and unscriptural penitence. There the spirit of Christianity slinks stealthily about like a gloomy demon, infusing poison in life's joyless draught. The path it indicates as the road to heaven is a sunless shaft. . . .[12]

Tischendorff was expressing his honest opinion; and those of us who have stayed in one of the desert monasteries know whereof he speaks, even though the monks no longer 'creep out of their blackened holes' where they spent all their time praying and genuflecting when not praying and genuflecting in their incense-reeking churches. Yet one has an odd sensation that something has been overlooked in this condemnation of 'an unnatural penitence'. Tischendorff himself expresses it best in his description of the abbot of Amba Bischoi, a man said to be 120 years old, blind, confined to a bench in the monastery garden where he sat all day and most of the night 'singing aloud'.

> This evening of life has something pleasing in it. To this old man heaven hangs down its holy lamps so low that his

eye, already closed to the world, sees God only, and his lips do nothing but pray . . . Upon taking my departure from the monastery, he came forth, supported by his staff and appeared to speak to me with perfect intelligence. A benediction from these aged lips deeply affected me.[13]

One wonders why a rich, healthy, well-fed German traveller should be 'deeply affected' by an old blind Copt's blessing. Perhaps the answer is that the abbot of Amba Bischoi possessed a quality called holiness.

REFERENCES

1 See Chapter 11.
2 See, in particular, A. J. Butler, *The Arab Conquest of Egypt* (1902.)
3 Josephus Abudnacus, *The History of the Cophts*. First published in a Latin text in 1675; translated into English and published 1692. Abu Dakn was a Jesuit and consequently unsympathetic to the Copts.
4 Edward Gibbon, *The Decline and Fall of the Roman Empire*, ed. by J. B. Bury, Vol. V, pp. 127–8.
5 See *The Unesco Courier*, December 1964, pp. 72–76.
6 See Chapter 12, pp. 182 ff.
7 J. M. Wansleben, *The Present State of Egypt* (1678), pp. 10–11.
8 op. cit., p. 174.
9 op. cit., pp. 184–5.
10 *Christian Antiquities in the Nile Valley* (1912), p. 159.
11 Wansleben, op. cit., pp. 222 ff.
12 op. cit., pp. 53–4.
13 op. cit., pp. 52–3.

11 The lost city

The place we were going to see was one of the truly lost cities of the ancient world, lost for a thousand years and rediscovered only some fifty years ago. The place is called the City of St. Menas. It is, or was once, an oasis, though when one sees it today, it is almost impossible to believe the description of it given by El Bekri, an Arab geographer of the eleventh century. In fact, this panegyric about a city he calls 'Mina' was considered to be the rather typical fantasy of oriental geographers, always partial to mythical oases, a number of which explorers have looked for in vain over the years. 'Mina' seemed to be such a figment of the imagination, for this is how El Bekri describes it:

> Mina consists of three cities abandoned in the middle of the dunes but identifiable by the buildings which still remain standing. The Bedouin hide in these buildings in order to ambush the passing caravans. You can see there superb and beautifully constructed palaces surrounded by battlements. They are for the most part built in the form of roofed colonades and some of the buildings are occupied by monks. There remain a few wells, but water is now scarce. Further off, one sees the Cathedral of Saint Menas, an enormous building ornamented with statues and the most beautiful mosaics. Inside, the lamps burn day and night. At one end of the church, there is a huge marble tomb with two camels and, above it, the statue of a man with a foot on each of the camels: one of his hands is open, the other closed. This statue, they say, represents Saint Menas . . . The façade of the church is sculpted with all sorts of animals and men of every profession—among others, a slave trader who holds his purse turned upside down. Over the church is a dome

covered with paintings which, they say, represent the angels.

At the side of the church is a mosque with its mihrab turned towards the south. The Moslems come here to say their prayers.

The whole countryside round about is planted with fruit trees which produce excellent fruit and there are also many vines which are cultivated for wine.

Travellers in the Libyan Desert where this fabled city was situated somewhere south-west of Alexandria and north-west of the Wadi Natrun could find no evidence of either palaces, churches, orchards, or vineyards, and the very aridity of the Marea region militated against the possibility of a metropolis in the middle of the dunes.

On the other hand, there was not the shadow of a doubt that a saint called Menas existed, had his cult, and possessed a shrine somewhere in the Western Desert—a shrine which was one of the great centres of the pilgrimages of the fifth, sixth, and seventh centuries. The souvenirs of the pilgrims' visit to this shrine, brought back in their hundreds, have been found all over Europe and Africa. The 'Souvenir of St. Menas' was a little earthenware ampulla in the shape of a flat, two-handled jug which contained the holy water of the sacred well. Most of the national museums of Europe have an assortment of these Menas flasks, most of which have a crude portrait of the saint standing between two camels as El Bekri describes him in his account and bearing the standard inscription: 'Blessing of St. Menas'.

Nobody, however, was clear as to the original provenance of these jugs, for the cult of this saint had been wholly abandoned by the western church and the man himself began to take on a mythical character. It was the reverse process to what had happened in the legend of St. Peter for whose visit to, and martyrdom in, Rome there was no contemporary evidence whatsoever. Later hagiographers and historians produced the evidence themselves and then declared it 'historical fact'. The existence of St. Menas and of his city in the desert, though attested by contemporary records, began to be doubted, particularly as his hagiography was of the plainly ridiculous variety which tends to relegate such martyrs to the ecclesiastical limbo. For according to the legends Menas was an Egyptian soldier who suffered martyrdom in A.D. 296 by having the soles of his feet torn off, his eyes put out, his tongue dragged out by the roots, and his body cut up into little pieces. Despite these mutilations, he was still able to stand up in the arena and address the spectators for four consecutive hours. At the end of that period, the emperor Maximinus slew Menas with his own hand, placed the body in an iron coffin, and set it adrift on the sea. Two angels guided it to the North African shore west of Alexandria where some Bedouin loaded it on a camel and proceeded to march into the desert. At a certin place, which was afterwards to become the shrine, cathedral, and City of St. Menas, the camel carrying the coffin refused to get up from the ground: the animal was, in fact, glued, as it were, to the soil so that it was impossible for it to rise. So the coffin and body of the martyr were left in the place he himself desired for his sanctuary; and here at a spot on the caravan route between Cyrene and the Nile grew up one of the most frequented centres of the early Christian pilgrimages.

All this fantasy about the tortures Menas was supposed to have undergone, his four-hour speech in the arena before the emperor Maximinus, and the floating coffin crewed by a couple of angels was forgotten by the late Middle Ages and dismissed as pious fraud by modern exegetes. Yet neither the evidence of the Menas flasks nor the specific statements of contemporary historians could be dismissed. For instance, Sophronius, the patriarch of Jerusalem in A.D. 634 and before that a monk in one of the Nitrian monasteries, describes the City of St. Menas which he himself may have visited as 'the pride of all Libya'. Severus, a tenth-century Egyptian monk, reports in his *History of the Patriarchs* that the Coptic patriarch Benjamin, fleeing his enemy Cyrus, the Greek patriarch, in A.D. 630, journeyed to the monasteries of the Wadi Natrun, passing by way of the City of St. Menas where he prayed to the martyr in the cathedral. In fact, Severus gives us Benjamin's itinerary: the patriarch left Alexandria by the west gate, went on foot to

Marea and thence to Mina, and from there on the ancient caravan route to the Wadi Natrun. Explorers, therefore, had this fairly specific clue as to where the lost city was located: it had to be on the highway between Marea (once the chief city of north-west Egypt and still identifiable by the ruins of its three jetties and quays) and the Nitrian monasteries.

Despite all the clues and the specific references to the once-famous city's location, the site was not found until June 1905, when the German archaeologist, Monsignor Carl-Maria Kaufmann, more or less stumbled upon it during his wanderings in the Libyan Desert. It is interesting to note that even in this century travel in this region of Libya and Egypt was both difficult and dangerous. The Turks were still the masters of Cyrenaica in 1905, and they were still hostile and suspicious towards Christian travellers. The particular area which Monsignor Kaufmann wanted to search was especially hazardous, and there was talk of his expedition party (himself and his young cousin, J. C. Ewald Falls) travelling disguised as Arabs. In fact, the problem was how to get to the Mareotis at all, since none of the authorities, either Turkish or Libyan, would give the necessary permission, the famous *firman*, or passport, required for travel in the Turkish dominions.

Eventually the two men set out from Alexandria, and then, partly by judgment, partly by luck, came to a place in the Auladali desert called Karm Abum and sometimes Bumna. There were ruins scattered over the ground here and there, larger stones among the customary rubble of the stony desert. These ruins had been remarked by previous travellers, notably by the French explorer, M. J. R. Pacho, in 1824.[1] It is strange that nobody, including the amateur British archaeologists who were wandering about in the Mareotis region, recognised in the Arab name Karm Abum, or Bumna, the Coptic title of the old Egyptian saint, Abu Mina—Karm being the Arabic word for 'vineyard'. The geographer who had described the place in the eleventh century had, after all, specified that the oasis in his day was fruitful in vines. On the other hand, Bumna was absolutely waterless, and it needed a great deal of faith, or imagination, to see this dreary wasteland with its odds and ends

MAREOTIS

Site of the MONASTER
ENATON and the
CHURCH OF ST GEOR
TEMPLE OF OSIRIS; 4th century B.C., port at west end of Lake Mareotis; visited by ALEXANDER THE GREAT; JUSTINIAN built baths here; jetties; western wall against the barbarians; and ARABS' TOWER, a Roman watch, signal and light tower. Here was signed a treaty between KARAMANLI (Tripoli) and EATON (U.S.A.) 4th March, 1805
CHERSONESU
"Martello towers" (recent)
TAENIA
Ancient stone jetty, quarry, remains of NICIUM (?)
Gulf of Plinthine or Arabs' Gulf
PLINTHINE
MAR
Once the ch
of N.W. EG
with three
jetties, qua
Maryut
TAPOSIRIS MAGNA
Lighthouse erected by ISMAIL PASHA to placate some foreign power. Not in use. Formerly an Arab castle (13th century) here.
BAHIG A jetty i
Lake for old ferries.
Mallaheret
BORG EL ARAB
EL BORDAN
ST MENAS
Identified 1905 by RALPH CARVE
excavated KAUFMANN 1907
described by EL BEKIR 1086
BASILICA OF ARCADIUS (395-4
N
EL IMAYID
EL QASSABA EL SHARKIYA
Ruins of a fort
KHASHM EL EISH
Ancient fortress
W
E
QASR EL QATAGI
Christian chapel here, on the route St Menas to Wadi el Natrun?
S
0 5 10 15 20 miles 25

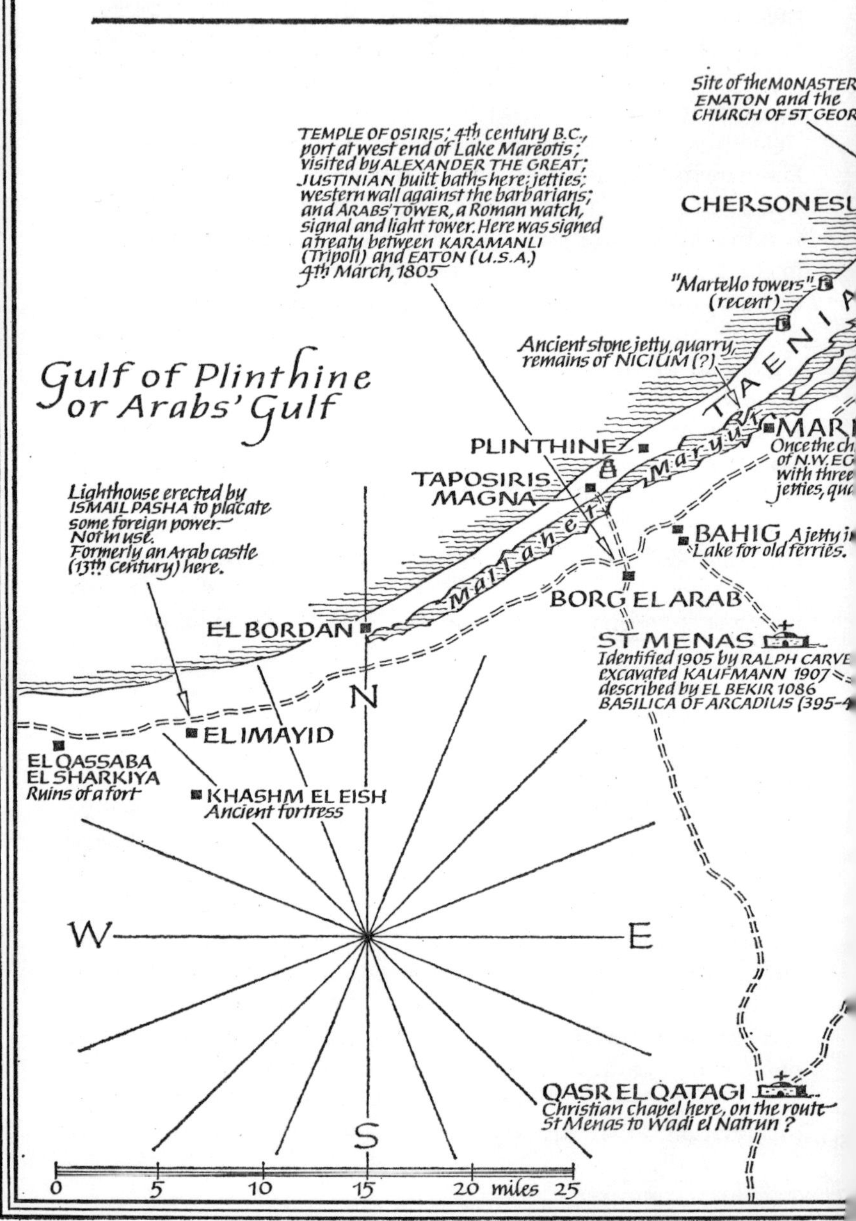

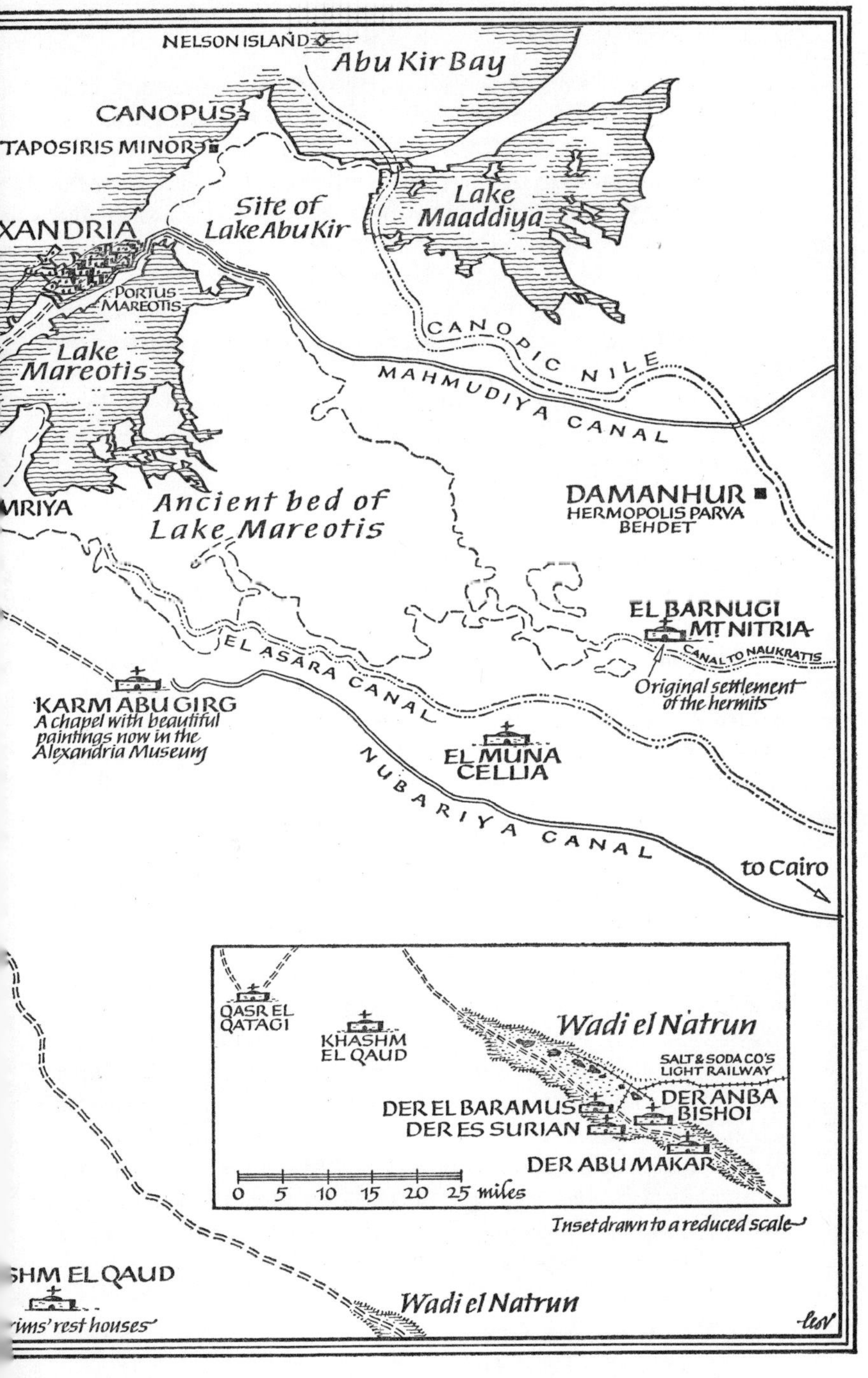
NELSON ISLAND
Abu Kir Bay
CANOPUS
TAPOSIRIS MINOR
Site of Lake Abu Kir
Lake Maaddiya
XANDRIA
PORTUS MAREOTIS
Lake Mareotis
CANOPIC NILE
MAHMUDIYA CANAL
Ancient bed of Lake Mareotis
MRIYA
DAMANHUR
HERMOPOLIS PARVA
BEHDET
EL BARNUGI
MT NITRIA
CANAL TO NAUKRATIS
Original settlement of the hermits
EL ASARA CANAL
KARM ABU GIRG
A chapel with beautiful paintings now in the Alexandria Museum
EL MUNA
CELLIA
NUBARIYA CANAL
to Cairo
QASR EL QATAGI
KHASHM EL QAUD
Wadi el Natrun
SALT & SODA CO'S LIGHT RAILWAY
DER EL BARAMUS
DER ANBA BISHOI
DER ES SURIAN
DER ABU MAKAR
0 5 10 15 20 25 miles
Inset drawn to a reduced scale
SHM EL QAUD
rims' rest houses
Wadi el Natrun

of masonry as a great pilgrim-city, with two cathedrals, churches, a monastery, hotels for travellers, public baths, orchards, and vineyards.

As for the honour of discovering the site, we find that the strong rivalry and, indeed, hostility between the English and Germans in the early years of the century make themselves felt in the claims of the two nationalities. Ewald Falls, companion of Monsignor Kaufmann, in his popular account of the Expedition, *Three Years in the Libyan Desert*, takes every occasion he can to discredit the English: his indignation at not being allowed into the dining-saloon of the P. and O. liner *Isis, en route* from Brindisi to Alexandria because he and his cousin, the Monsignor, were not 'properly dressed for dinner' (tails and white tie) is understandable. He describes this as 'a curiosity of civilisation that so many travellers in the English sphere of interest bitterly complain of and which almot spoiled our voyage—the stiff British etiquette that prevails on all their boats'. In return, a British critic of Herr Falls pours scorn on the Germans' claim to have found the city of St. Menas and maintains that the site had been identified early in 1905 (i.e. before Monsignor Kaufmann announced his discovery to the world) by a British resident of Alexandria, Mr. Ralph Carver; and adds,

> Monsignor Kaufmann reaped the benefit of this discovery, and it is difficult to understand how Herr Falls could write so many pages about their wanderings in the desert in search of the shrine.[2]

Even so, fairness requires us to give credit where it is due, and it was the two Germans, Monsignor Kaufmann, then in his sixties, and his thirty-year-old cousin Ewald Falls, who definitively located the site and together excavated it without any outside help. Their adventures began from that moment when Monsignor Kaufmann lay in his tent, exhausted and so ill that his cousin thought he was dying, and a Bedouin boy brought in a perfect example of a Menas flask, complete with the inscription, 'Blessing of St. Menas'. The two Germans knew, then, that they had found the lost city, for when the boy took them to the hole in the ground where he had disinterred the flask, a few minutes' digging showed that the artefact came from a potter's workshop: the archaeologists were able to lift out from a burial kiln flasks, jugs, and lamps in mint condition, just as they had been fired 1,500 years before for sale as souvenirs to the pilgrims.

The story of the excavations at Karm Abum is told in its scholarly version by Monsignor Kaufmann in his various reports and in its popular version by his cousin, Ewald Falls.[3] The story is fascinating as belonging to the last days of the private archaeologists, men who worked alone (with a gang of local diggers) and not as members of a highly organised expedition; who laboured with understandable fanaticism under conditions of great difficulty and strain because the rewards were usually fantastically rich. Kaufmann was able to send more than 100 large packing cases crammed with marbles, statuettes, flasks, lamps, vases, coins, and the like to Frankfurt, in addition to the artefacts which were claimed by the museum at Alexandria. No one knows how many other treasures were smuggled to the Cairo dealers by the Bedouin labourers, but sixty years later the dealers in antiquities will still produce a genuine Menas flask for you if you are prepared to pay enough.

But in addition to the immense haul of museum exhibits archaeologists like Kaufmann could make on a virgin site, there was the indescribable thrill for the two Germans of finding the actual tomb of St. Menas himself. The sanctuary was finally reached after a trial dig which uncovered a subterranean passage. This passage was filled right up to the roof with rubble and sand. When this detritus was removed, the archaeologists found a marble staircase of thirty steps which led to the crypt and tomb of the saint, nearly thirty feet under the high altar of the original church built during the reign of the emperor Constantine and consecrated by St. Athanasius around A.D. 300. There was no mistaking that the excavators had reached the sacred shrine for here they found the portrait of Menas as the Arab geographer el Bekri had described it: a Roman officer standing between two kneeling camels.

The visitor to the City of St. Menas today feels some of the excitement of that find as he descends the marble staircase to the underground tomb of one of the most curious saints of the ancient world. For the surroundings hereabout are in keeping with the forgotten legend. On the occasion of my visit, there was nobody at the site except the priest who was showing me round and the usual Bedouin boy who turns up on these occasions with his handful of Roman coins and his Roman lamp. Yet these neglected ruins are among the most important in Egypt, for they symbolise the apex of Roman–Christian civilisation—Roman in the fact that a city of this size was built in the middle of the desert; and Christian in the sense of a city dedicated wholly to the glory of God. Obviously, the builders spared nothing, for they were patronised by the emperors Constantine and Arcadius, the latter of whom ordered the building of the great cathedral over the original crypt of the saint. Other patrons and benefactors paid for the building of a second basilica, a baptistry, extensive baths, a monastery, and a pilgrims' hostel. The needs of the community led to the cultivation of the surrounding hills, today bare of any shred of vegetation; the sinking of wells and building of water tunnels; and the establishment of kilns, factories, and shops. All this undertaking was typical of the faith and zeal of men who were prepared to devote their wealth and lives to the things of the spirit.

Though Menas is no longer included in the Catholic hierarchy of saints, he is still very much venerated by the Copts. The present Patriarch, Kyrillos VI, is particularly interested in resurrecting the ancient glory of the City by building on the site of the ruins a new monastery and cathedral. One must admit that the spectacle of this vast project out there in the desert arouses doubts as to the desirability, let alone the need, of such a religious centre. One wonders where the monks for the monastery are to come from, seeing that all the other Egyptian convents are more than half empty. And how are the worshippers to reach the huge church since there is no proper road to this remote place and no public transport whatsoever? Interesting speculations, and symptomatic, one must admit, of our own times, because if the Patriarch's project involved, say, the building of a city for oilmen, industrial workers, or even gamblers, we would probably not question its efficacy, as the early Christians did not question the rightness of building basilicas, hostels, baths, and monasteries for a saint and the pilgrims who came to venerate him.

At all events, the Copts are convinced that Menas is worthy of his cult, past, present, and future. Did not the previous Patriarch, Christopher II, issue an encyclical letter in 1943 ascribing the saving of Egypt from invasion at the battle of el Alamein to 'the prayers to God of the holy and glorious martyr Menas, the wonder-worker of Egypt'? Whether the present patriarch sees the restoration of the shrine as a memorial to the Allied Victory or not is unclear. I had the impression during my interview with His Blessedness that he was not concerned to that extent with such mundane affairs as warfare. His life had been passed in the ancient fashion of the Egyptian Church, as a monk in a desert monastery and a hermit. Yet the question does arise, not only in the minds of sceptics but also in those of theologians, as to whether Menas has not lost that spiritual authority which was once so considerable that legend ascribed to him the power of raising the dead. Indeed, the miracles of the saint, which led the Patriarch Christopher to call him 'the wonder-worker of Egypt' and which constituted the essence of his cult, have been called into question by the most authoritative hagiographers who have rejected them as either ludicrous, quasi-blasphemous, and even improper.

Let us look at some of these miracles, as they give us an insight into the medieval Egyptian mind. St. Menas, then, is accredited with thirteen miracles in all. His first achievement was to reassemble and restore to life a man who had been hacked to pieces by a bandit. Subsequently, he did the same thing for one unfortunate who had been drowned and another who had been chewed up by a crocodile. Modern theologians are not prepared to accept these prodigies at their face value. They are also inclined to have reservations concerning the fifth miracle which some maintain is a slander on the good name of the holy man, while others argue that, to the contrary, it is a practical proof of his insight into human nature. For, according to this miracle, a paralytic was taken to the shrine of the saint in the hope of a cure, and here he met a dumb woman on the same mission. Both implored the martyr's aid, but without success. Then, during the night, the paralytic had a vision of the saint who gave the following advice:

> Don't be afraid, but fasten your lips to the dumb woman's. Then get into bed with her and you will be cured.

The sick man was astonished at such a suggestion, and said so. But the saint insisted and, says the legend, 'the poor man allowed himself to be persuaded'.

> Thereupon, having found out where the dumb woman lodged, he waited until all those in the lodging house were asleep and then going up to her couch and gazing at her, bent down and fastened his mouth to hers and taking down her nightdress left her naked.

At this point the dumb lady awoke and, seeing the state she was in, yelled out at the top of her voice. The paralytic, alarmed at being caught, fled. And so the woman was cured of her dumbness and the man of his paralysis. Not a very edifying story, says the Bollandist Father Delehaye;[4] yet not untypical of St. Menas, who seemed to have had a special sympathy for his female devotees. For we find him in his third miracle rescuing a rich woman called Sophia who was about to be kidnapped by a soldier on horseback. Sophia appealed to St. Menas, who immediately came to the rescue, he, too, on horseback, tied the lustful soldier by the foot to his horse, and galloped off to his shrine, dragging the guardsman along the ground. 'One can be sure the soldier profited from the lesson', says the legend.

In fact, all the saint's miracles had a good moral: it was just the means by which the lesson was taught that troubled later commentators. Thus, admittedly, it was right and proper that a herdsman who cheated Menas out of one of three baby camels promised as a thanksgiving gift for the curing of a sterile she-camel should be punished by seeing all three offspring drawn back into the mother; but the phenomenon of the birth-process in reverse does not seem convincing in a scientific age.

Hence St. Menas, the warrior saint, he who always turned up on horseback to succour ladies in distress, has lost his appeal. His cult is dead for all but the most zealous Copts. His holy well with its curative waters has long since dried up. And his shrine at Karm Abum is too far off the beaten track for organised tours. In any case, religious spas like Lourdes are much better organised and much more discreet in their methods of curing paralytics and dumb females. Thus it is inevitable that the traveller to the City of St. Menas gets the impression that this once-famous shrine, lost in the twelfth century and discovered in the twentieth, is about to disappear again under the Libyan sands; for as far as I can gather nobody in the world, with the exception of Pope Kyrillos VI and his adherents, is in the least interested in an Egyptian soldier who suffered martyrdom in A.D. 296.

REFERENCES

1 *Relation d'un Voyage dans la Marmarique* (1827), p. 10.
2 Anthony de Cosson, *Mareotis* (1935), p. 136.
3 See *Die Ausgrabung der Menas-Heiligtümer in der Mareotiswüste* (1906–8); and *Three Years in the Libyan Desert* (1913).
4 *Analecta Bollandiana*, Tomus XXIX, pp. 117 ff.

12 The desert rediscovered

We can assume on the basis of what facts we have that the Egyptian deserts, after they had been more or less abandoned by the Roman administration during the troubles of the third century A.D., became the country first of Christian hermits and exiles, then of those who were inclined towards asceticism, mysticism, and monachism. But by A.D. 700 when the Arabs had completed their conquest of Egypt and the process of Islamisation was far advanced, the monasteries of both the Eastern and Western Deserts were already beginning to decay. They were in particular danger from the Bedouin Arabs who, following the withdrawal of the Roman legions, had returned to their traditional role of nomadic herdsmen roaming back and forth across the desert and making short shrift of any outsiders. The unarmed and pacifist monks in their caves and cells were now in great danger of periodic massacres and were, in fact, frequently murdered by the tribesmen who now had religious hatred and bigotry to spur them on. The only monasteries to survive were those which had fortified themselves like castles. Such are the four monasteries of the Western Desert, Baramous, Macarius, Surian, and Bischoi; the two of the Eastern Desert: St. Antony and St. Paul; several others in the desert contiguous to the Nile, among them St. Simeon at Aswan, and the Red and White Monasteries near Soohag; and St. Catherine's in Sinai. In short, a total of not more than ten monasteries survive out of the hundreds which once testified to the extent of the commonwealth of desert Christians.

Yet by A.D. 1000 the Christian religion in Egypt was in danger of complete extermination, as it had already been wiped out to all intents and purposes throughout the rest of

North Africa. This development was not due to the intolerance or bigotry of Mohammedanism as a whole: to the contrary, the Moslems had no particular quarrel with the Christians whose Saviour they accepted as one of their own prophets.

Hence, there was really no particular reason why the two religions should not have co-existed almost as two sects of the same basic belief. For example, the Egyptian Christians for their part were monophysites believing in a single godhead which approximated closely to the Moslem concept of Allah, which is one explanation of why the Egyptian church-politicians tacitly welcomed the invasion of the Arabs in A.D. 641: the Arabs, as 'monophysites' and enemies of Constantinople, were seen as allies in the cause of Egypt for the Egyptians. And in the beginning, Moslems and Christians lived together amicably, because the Arabs, being fervent admirers of learning and culture, were glad to avail themselves of the Egyptians' superior talents and skills; and the Egyptians shrewdly used their intellectual and technical superiority to lighten the usual penalties inflicted on a conquered people.

Writing in the twelfth century, Abu Salih the Armenian relates that many Moslem princes loved the Christian churches for their mosaic decorations, their ikons, and their good wine.[1] One has the suspicion that the last item was the chief attraction, especially as it was prohibited. However that may be, the more enlightened of the Arab rulers protected and even encouraged the Christian Church in Egypt and might have continued to do so if it had not been for the Crusades, which led to an open declaration of war between Christendom and Islam. For what, of course, the Crusaders omitted to take into their calculations was the presence of hundreds of thousands of their fellow-Christians living in tenuous security throughout the Moslem world. These survivors of early Christianity had obviously been forgotten, or written off, as expendable.

The ignorance of European Christians is well illustrated by the interview between St. Francis of Assisi and the sultan Kamil during the sixth Crusade which had begun in A.D. 1213. St. Francis with a small band of brothers eager for martyrdom had joined the Crusaders' army who were besieging Damietta at the mouth of the Nile. When the saint perceived that the Christians were unsuccessful against the infidel (despite the fact that God was on their side and their troops were led by a papal legate), he decided to confront the sultan and courageously crossed the enemy lines into the city and the palace. He informed the Moslem prince that he had come to convert him and his people to the religion of Jesus, a proposal which implied that he was totally unaware that Kamil, who was largely dependent upon his Coptic advisers, was fully familiar with the Christian faith and ritual. The difference between the two men is seen in the outcome of their meeting; for when St. Francis offered to enter a fiery furnace provided Kamil and his people would embrace Christianity should he, Francis, survive the test, Kamil declined on the grounds that gambling with one's life was not a valid proof of one's god; and he thereupon dismissed the Christian emissary with oriental courtesy and lavish gifts.

But meetings between Christians and Moslems were not always so chivalrous, and as the holy wars continued through the centuries (three centuries in all), the two worlds and the two religions they upheld became implacable enemies. In fact, the Crusades virtually ended all contacts between European and Oriental Christians; and, more than that, almost signed the death warrant of the latter. The sultans who reigned subsequent to the First Crusade of the eleventh century grew increasingly hostile and bloodthirsty towards their Christian subjects, the persecutions reaching their culmination during the sultanate of El-Hakim who destroyed 3,000 churches and reduced all Egyptian Christians to virtual slavery.

Indeed, until the late Renaissance knowledge of Egypt and of the existence of the Christian Church there was limited to ill-digested facts, tall stories, and quaint fantasies of the kind promulgated by Sir John Maundeville, that mysterious Englishman whose *Voyages and Travels* was a world best-seller during the fourteenth and fifteenth century. We cannot say with certainty whether Sir John was ever in Egypt until we can say, with certainty, that there was such an English knight who wrote the celebrated travel book, 'having passed through

Tartary, Persia, Armenia the Little and the Great; through Lybia, Chaldea, and a great part of Ethiopia; through Amazonia, India the Less and the Greater; and through many other isles that are about India'. However, in Maundeville's *Voyages* there are references to the Christian churches and monasteries of Egypt, and a fairly factual account of the great St. Catherine's Monastery on the Sinai Peninsula. But when Sir John declares:

> In that abbey [St. Catherine's] no flies, toads, or lizards, or such foul venimous beasts, nor lice nor fleas ever enter, by the miracle of God and of Our Lady.[2]

one can be quite sure that the knight never slept in that celebrated convent.

Out of contact with the rest of Christendom, a great deal of what was going on in the outside world passed the desert monasteries by. St. Antony's and St. Paul's were now fortress-convents, designed to hold out against the attacks of the nomads. The citadel or keep, so characteristic of these institutions, tells its own story. The monks crossed into this tower by a wooden drawbridge, drew up the bridge, and remained inside their citadel for as long as necessary. The keep was provided with food, a well, a chapel, and their most precious books and ikons, so that their monastic life of prayer and fasting continued much the same as before while the barbarians outside went about their usual practice of looting and destruction.

By the middle of the fifteenth century, however, the monasteries of Egypt were almost deserted and in ruins. Their fall was due to a number of causes: first, the constant attacks by the desert nomads—the monastery of Macarius in the Wadi Natrun, for instance, having been sacked five times by A.D. 817, then almost wholly destroyed in 1350; second, the persecution of the Christians by various Moslem governors and the consequent difficulty of recruiting new monks; third, the frequent outbreaks of the Black Death which during one epidemic decimated Egypt at the rate of 15,000 a day in Cairo alone. The Arab historian Makrisi who visited the Western Desert monasteries in 1430 reported that only a few monks were left in the ruins of their convents. It is incredible to think of men surviving under these conditions; whence it ill behoves the European travellers who finally reached these remote shrines of primitive Christianity to denigrate the old, sick, and ignorant men they found still guarding the heritage and treasures of the Desert Fathers.

St. Antony's and St. Paul's, being so far from the main centres of conflict in Alexandria and Cairo, managed to flourish until about 1490, when the Arab servants rose in the night and slaughtered all the monks. They did so because their monkish masters had prohibited them from marrying. Freed from the onerous rule of the abbot, the Arabs settled down to a prolonged binge during which they ate all the food stores, drank the sacramental wine, used the ancient manuscripts as fuel to light the bread ovens, and bivouacked in the church. When there was nothing left to eat in the monastery, the usurpers gradually drifted away, back to the desert whence they came.

In 1561 the monastery was rebuilt and a few monks, probably 'volunteers' from the monasteries of the Wadi Natrun, took up residence. But it is obvious that the original fervour, the genuine mysticism, of the first monks and hermits no longer animated these ancient shrines, so that when the first European travellers got through to them after a thousand years they found a colony of old, dirty, ignorant men described by one of the earliest travellers as '*si maigres, si abbatus, qu'ils ressemblent plutôt à des squelettes qu'à de véritables hommes*'.*

The first modern travellers to reach these almost forgotten outposts of Christendom were those seventeenth-century adventurers to whose accounts we owe practically all our knowledge of the history, culture, and geography of Africa before 1900. One of these intrepid explorers was Jean Coppin who reached St. Antony's in 1640.

An 'old soldier' at the age of twenty-three, Coppin managed to get himself appointed as French consul in Egypt, a post much more suited to a swordsman than a diplomat in 1638.

* 'So emaciated, so infirm that they are more like skeletons than real men.'

Indeed, these early European consuls in Moslem countries were a breed on their own, with little resemblance to the foreign officers of modern diplomacy. A quite ordinary occupational hazard in those lusty if not good old days was for a consul to be thrown periodically into jail—and occasionally into the sea. There is one recorded instance of a consul being fired by the Bey of Tunis from the barrel of a cannon. Jean Coppin makes the standard complaints about the ill treatment meted out to him by the Moslem authorities in Egypt where he had his spell in prison; and it was possibly his hatred of 'the Turk' that led him in later life to campaign for one more crusade to the Holy Land.

He expounds his proposals in a curious book called *The Shield of Europe; or, The Holy War*[3] in which he exhorts Louis XIV, the French war minister Louvois, and the pope to wage total war on the infidel. He even goes so far as to invent a number of 'secret weapons' for the purpose; and it is a commentary on the innocence of his age that he includes his blue prints for these engines in his book. Thus he has one machine 'for defending the cavalry from the infantry' and another 'for defending the infantry from the cavalry'. The general principles which should, perhaps, be studied by modern military men, was for the entire army, both cavalry and infantry battalions, to carry about with them pieces of wood, one section per man, which could be quickly assembled into a fortress in which they could live and fight as from a medieval castle. It follows, of course, that a modern army would need to use sheets of lead in order to protect itself from atomic radiation; but the principle undoubtedly still holds good as a guide for military thinking.

Quite often, Coppin says, while he was living in Cairo, he bethought himself of visiting the desert where St. Antony and St. Paul had their hermitages, but he could never find anybody among his Christian friends who shared his enthusiasm. The Turkish janissaries, moreover, were cool towards the project, with considerable reason, inasmuch as whenever they caught one of the Bedouin who inhabited the desert between the Nile and the Red Sea they flayed him alive and carried his carcass, stuffed with straw, back to Cairo on the end of a lance as a present to the Pacha. The Bedouin for their part, says Coppin, repaid the Turks for their cruelty by cutting slices off their prisoners and eating the flesh, though he does not say whether raw or cooked. At all events, one and all were chary of the Frenchman's proposed expedition.

Fortunately, however, just when he was about to abandon the project, two French friars agreed to accompany him; so assembling his caravan, Coppin set out to cross the desert between the Nile and Mount Colzoum. 'I was mounted on a she-camel,' he says, 'who was followed by her son, for whom she had such a deep affection that she never stopped turning her head to see if he was still there. I think camels more than any other animals fear to lose their babies. . . .'

And so, mounted on the affectionate *mehari*, Coppin reached the convent of St. Antony on the third day and was drawn up on the end of a rope twenty-seven feet to the top of the wall. The Frenchman was not keen on this method of entry until a monk demonstrated how it was done: namely, by being partially pulled and partially walking up the wall, taking care not to get into a spin on the end of the rope. Once inside the monastery Coppin and his companions were treated with the greatest kindness, even to having their feet washed by the superior '*avec beaucoup d'humilité*'. After this the guests were treated to hymns sung in Syriac, accompanied by drumming on long black stones tapped by wooden mallets—'a most lugubrious and austere sound', says Coppin, no doubt with reason. The service continued in the chapel: more hymns, more stone-tapping; then the reading of St. Antony's advice for the reception of pilgrims—a ceremony which causes these pious men to weep copiously 'in view of the perils which we had undergone in order to visit them'.

Coppin, who seems to have been something of a gourmet, and, as a Frenchman, regarded food and wine with respect, was appalled at the diet of the monks which consisted of beans, a few other vegetables, and water. He had, in fact, prepared a good dinner for the superior who came, however, with his own plate of lentils sprinkled with oil. This priest could neither be persuaded to eat the meat and eggs offered him or to take more than a few sips of wine. I found the monks just as abstinent today as they were in Coppin's time.

It is obvious from the Frenchman's account, the first that we have of the Egyptian monasteries, that the tremendous spiritual force which had once peopled the deserts with ascetics and mystics and had led to the establishment of the great European monastic orders had expended itself in this ruined fortress by the Red Sea. The French officer paints a very sad picture indeed—the washing of the pilgrims' feet, the weeping of the monks as they listen to the adjurations of their founder, the starvation diet, that terrible cacophony made by little mallets tapping on stones. Once there had been 300 monks at this desert monastery, each with his own cell (seven feet long by five wide by four high). By Coppin's time, there were only forty of whom twenty-two were priests and eighteen lay-brothers. Thirty years later, when the next traveller came through to St. Antony's, their numbers had been reduced to nineteen—two priests and seventeen lay-brothers. Today there are only five.

Coppin, who marched over the mountains by night to visit the monastery of St. Paul, the hermit of Thebes who spent sixty years in this corner of the desert, found the site abandoned and in ruins. 'Yet we had the great joy of celebrating mass in the chapel itself', Coppin adds—a joy indeed for a Christian who remembered that near this spot was the spring where the old hermit Paul and the younger hermit Antony first met and shared the bread brought to them by a raven. A modern student would have been more interested in the wall paintings which must have dated from the foundation of the monastery, still visible on the crumbling walls of the church but already seriously defaced by the Bedouins who camped inside the convent with their flocks and herds.

For a true eyewitness account of Christian Egypt, Europe had to wait until the 1660's when a Dominican missionary called Johann Michael Wansleben, known as Vansleb, travelled along the Nile and took the trouble to acquaint himself with the history of the National Church of Egypt. Vansleb was the first of a succession of intrepid German scholars who, with the equally intrepid but less scholarly British explorers, penetrated the *terra incognita* of Moslem Africa. Vansleb was also the first of the emissaries of the European courts and libraries to be commissioned to bring back manuscripts from the Egyptian monasteries. He brought back a number, which are now treasures of the Bibliothèque Nationale and wrote the first competent account of the Copts and their ritual. Like all travellers in North Africa until the beginning of this century, he underwent many trials and tribulations, not the least of which was his dislike of the Egyptian people themselves.

> Their ordinary vices are idleness and cowardice, which is so natural to them, whether they be Moors or Copts . . . The common people are thieves, liars, treacherous and so greedy of gain that for the love of a *meidin* [a small copper coin] they would kill their own fathers . . . The women of the country are usually of a low stature, of a brown complexion. All their beauty consists in a lively eye. Their discourses are troublesome, and their clothing is not handsome.[4]

It can be seen from this statement that Father Vansleb, a Protestant soldier who found it expedient to turn Catholic priest, had strong views about Egypt, but at least they were based on his personal observation. He shows himself in this respect to be an extremely valuable reporter, for very little factual knowledge of Egypt was available in seventeenth-century Europe since Pliny wrote on the subject. The Roman historian for his part presents us with a hodge-podge of fact and fancy, and Vansleb is the first man to correct Pliny's far-fetched yarns about the crocodile. Vansleb says he kept two baby crocodiles for some time, one in his closet, the other in his cellar. 'I cautioned the latter to be tied with a great cord about the jaws that it might not offend such as came to see it.' But despite his laboratory observations of these captive reptiles, he falls back on Arab authors for a description of certain characteristics:

> The Arabian authors say that it casts out its excrements by the throat, because it hath no hole under the tail, and its

> stones have the smell of musk. But as I have had no experience neither of one nor t'other, I refer myself to their relation.
>
> And because the crocodile cannot well turn itself when it lies upon the back and that it is needful that the female be in that posture when the male covers her, the male takes care when he hath laid upon her and performed his duty to turn her again upon her belly, for fear of the hunters.[5]

A later traveller, the French officer Charles Sonnini de Manoncourt, states that the female had another reason to fear being left stranded on her back; for he asserts that the fellahin, on discovering a crocodile in this position, united themselves with it in unnatural intercourse.

> Will it be believed that there are in Upper Egypt men who, hurried on by an excess of unexampled depravation and brutality, take advantage of the helpless situation of the female, drive off the male and supplant him in this frightful intercourse? Horrible embraces, hideous enjoyment, the knowledge of which was yet wanting to complete the disgusting pages of human perversity.[6]

One's impression is that Sonnini reports this yarn perhaps to shock, perhaps to amuse, his readers at the court of Louis XIV, a rather irresponsible attitude for a man who was made a doctor of philosophy at the age of sixteen by the Jesuits.

Vansleb fully intended to visit the monasteries of the Nitrian desert, but was apprised at the village of Feranch that the local chieftain intended to murder him *en route* because of a box of money he was supposed to have with him. The box was actually the priest's wine-chest, but he was loath to reveal this fact on account of the Moslem prohibition against wine. His report on these famous monasteries, therefore, is based on what he was able to learn in Cairo and Alexandria, which was not very much. He did, however, see a number of Coptic churches in old Cairo and also several monasteries—one for women. His description of the latter is brief: 'It is a place so filthy and stinking that I could not stay there any time.'

Wherever Vansleb travelled, he acquired manuscripts and claims that he 'emptied Egypt of such kind of books'. The

Coptic priests were usually ready to sell the treasures of their libraries for a few piastres at this time, for by the middle of the seventeenth century when Vansleb was travelling through Egypt, the persecution of the Christians had reached its ultimate stage. The Dominican gives the reason as follows:

> I must confess that there is no nation in Egypt so much afflicted as are the Copts *because they have nobody among them who deserves to be honoured for his knowledge,* or feared for his power and authority; for all that were rich and wealthy are destroyed by the cruelty of the Mahommedans: therefore the rest are now looked upon as the scum of the world and worse than the Jews. The Turks abuse them at their pleasure; they shut up their churches and the doors of their houses when they please to draw from them some sums of money.[7]

It is not surprising that the unhappy Patriarch whom Vansleb calls one of his best friends had not been out of his house for a year and was obliged to refuse the visitor's invitation to dine with him. The rank and file of the Christians were no better off than their priests, for the Turkish policy at this time seemed to be to tax them literally to death. The only Egyptian Christians who had some respite from direct persecution were those in the ancient monasteries whither Vansleb set out in his search on behalf of the French king's library. In September 1672 he began his journey to the monastery of St. Antony and his account of this experience is a little classic of early Egyptian travel.

He says that his caravan consisted of five camels, five Copts, and Idris, 'my blackamour'. The journey of sixty miles took four days. On arrival at the monastery, which he found in a very dilapidated condition, he was hauled up over the ramparts by a pulley and found himself in a walled town consisting of three churches, a keep, the monks' cells, and a small garden. Each monk had his own cell which was a mud-brick hovel just high enough for the occupant to sit but not stand up in. It was lit by holes knocked in the wall. Herein the monks slept on a mat in all their clothes, including their girdle, which they were not allowed to loosen. Before they went to sleep, they were required to prostrate themselves 150 times, spreading out their arms with their fists clenched and touching the ground with their forehead. On rising from each genuflection, they made the sign of the cross. Father Vansleb's comment on this ritual is apt. 'These prostrations,' he says, 'together with the poor nourishment that their bodies take, renders them very lean and cast down, so that they appear like so many skeletons rather than men.'

The population of the monastery numbered one vicar, one priest, and seventeen lay brothers, 'almost all of them with one eye, deaf, lame, and halt, or worn out with old age'. This pathetic little company of Christians were alone in the desert in constant danger of attack from any passing Bedouin or band of robbers. Their only defence were the walls of the monastery and the keep to which they retired as a last resort. This keep was a square tower three storeys high and built of stone, which in itself gives some idea of the dangers to which the monks were exposed, and had been exposed since the conquest of Christian Egypt by the Arabs in A.D. 640. This keep was entered by a drawbridge which was drawn up once all the monks were inside. The method of surviving a siege was to beat off their attackers by dropping boulders or hurling stones from the roof of the tower. Otherwise they cowered inside their stone walls until the raiders outside had looted what they could from the churches and the garden, had grown tired of waiting, and had gone on their way. Thus Christian monks in many monasteries throughout Egypt saved themselves, their libraries, their most prized relics, and their stock of grain which was kept permanently locked up in the keep.

It is difficult to imagine a more pathetic outpost of Christianity than this convent dedicated to the founder of Western monasticism. Father Vansleb, though a priest himself, obviously could see neither purpose nor justification in this collection of cripples slowly and inexorably dying of malnutrition in the middle of the desert. As a north European, a former military man, and very much of a realist, he could not be expected to understand or sympathise with the rule of the Egyptian monks. He accepts, of course, the vows of chastity and poverty which he had taken himself, but the rest is beyond his comprehension. For the Coptic monks were obliged to dwell in the wilderness; to be clothed only in woollen garments which they never took off; to be girt with a thick leather belt which they never loosened; to eat no flesh nor drink wine all their lifetime; to shorten their dinner; and to deny themselves all the nourishments without which the body is able to live. It commanded them, in addition, to employ all their time in fasting and prayer and worship, and always to have their mind on God by applying themselves to the reading of the Bible.

Such was the life and rule of these nineteen old and sick men imprisoned in their dilapidated fortress. During the day, they tottered about on their curious T-shaped crutches, on which they leant during the interminable prayers or the readings from devotional books; worked in the garden; ground the corn in the mill; or, if too feeble to do anything else, wove mats from the palm fronds. One brother was required to keep constant vigil on the wall, for, as in the case of the Nitrian monasteries, the Christians were obliged both by custom and necessity to feed any passer-by who demanded food, whether he was a friend or enemy. Friends—in point of fact, the only visitors who ever qualified as friends were foreign Christians—were admitted to the convent and housed as well as fed. What Vansleb calls 'the roguish Arabians' were kept outside the walls and given supplies lowered to them in baskets—for reasons of expediency as well as charity. It appears that the donors were never thanked by those they fed. To the contrary, they were abused and threatened and despised.

Vansleb, though an ex-soldier and undoubtedly a brave and intrepid traveller, was thoroughly alarmed by dangers which the poor monks evidently took as everyday occurrences of desert life. It came about that a party of Bedouin arrived at the monastery of St. Antony determined to rob the foreign visitor. 'The monks had much ado to pacify them by giving them shirts, cloths, caps, girdles, in a word, all that they wanted.' Indeed, in order to protect their guest, they gave away every useful possession they had, so that they were unable to bury one of their brethren in any kind of covering at all; whence

Above Hermits' cells in the cliffs of Feiran, the Sinai oasis
Below Feiran was an important monastic centre in the fifth century

Above The Road of the Inscriptions along which pilgrims passed *en route* to St. Catherine's
Below A Coptic monk of a desert monastery

they entreated Father Vansleb for a shirt and gown to clothe the dead man. Still the Arabs insisted on interviewing the German priest, for the more the monks tried to keep them out and the more Vansleb hid away, the more curious were the tribesmen, until the abbot was unable to restrain them any longer. 'My privacy made them believe that I was some great person that was afraid of them. They resolved, therefore, to give me a visit to know who I was.'

The monks now had to take still further precautions to protect their guest. His possessions were accordingly taken into the tower; he was dressed in the habit of a monk; and the Arabs were received in his guest room, completely empty except for the mat on which he sat. Vansleb kept his head during the subsequent interview and showed neither fear nor servility; and when his dinner was brought (consisting of a wooden bowl of lentils, a piece of bread, and an onion—a meal arranged beforehand), he invited his guests to share it with him. The upshot was that they parted the best of friends and 'by this one may understand that there is no nation in the world so barbarous but is to be won by fair means'. What Vansleb had discovered, to his astonishment, was the first and simplest law of the desert: namely, if an outsider offers hospitality and friendship, he will be accepted and treated as a kinsman. It is astonishing how few of the African explorers who followed Vansleb during the next two centuries knew of this law. Those who did and who practised it survived, unless 'the fever' carried them off. Those who did not were almost invariably murdered.[8]

During all these vicissitudes, the Dominican had not lost sight of the object of his visit to the monastery of St. Antony, especially when he found what he was looking for—the ancient manuscripts which he had been commissioned to bring back for the collection of Louis XIV. He reports that he saw several chests of old books both in Arabic and Coptic. One of these manuscripts was a priceless treasure at that time, for it was Coptic grammar and dictionary in Arabic—'one of the exactest and largest I ever saw . . . I dare say that with this dictionary and grammar it is possible to re-establish the Coptic language, which is now lost.' The 're-establishment' of the Coptic language might, in fact, have advanced the decipherment of Ancient Egyptian by over a century, though when Vansleb spoke of Coptic being 'lost', he meant as a living language. It still survived as a hierarchical language and was still spoken, or read rather, during church services. But it was certainly an unknown language to Europeans, so that one could, perhaps, compare the existence of this Coptic-Arab dictionary to the Etruscan-Latin grammer and word-book said to have been compiled by the emperor Claudius.

The monks, however, were chary of parting with their books on account of their fear of excommunication. (Most of the manuscript volumes had this anathema inscribed as a frontispiece.) On the other hand, they tentatively put a price on their treasures, and, as we know from later travellers, they were easily persuaded to sell under the influence of alcohol. The monks suggested thirty crowns foı the Coptic-Arabic dictionary. The French crown or *ecu* was worth five English shillings at this period, so that the price of the manuscript was 130 shillings—in today's money, say, £30. Vansleb was very tempted to buy this particular book, but he was, with reason, afraid to reveal how much money he had with him, especially in view of the fact that the desert he had to cross was notorious for robbers and bandits. If he had acquired this book, the world of scholarship would have been incalculably enriched and the Bibliothèque Nationale richer by several million francs. But 'for fear of the thieves', he says, 'I was not very earnest to buy'.

He must, however, have bought many books, for he claims to have 'emptied Egypt' of manuscripts, though where he obtained his treasures he does not tell us. It was, after all, his private source, and he had had to undergo a great many privations and considerable danger to acquire his books. Apparently he found nothing in either the White or the Red convents, once the most beautiful of all the Egyptian monasteries, though later travellers made quite a haul at both places, which Vansleb describes as 'altogether ruinated'. Other monasteries in the once famous and populous Thebaid, the region of saints, martyrs, and hermits, the headquarters, in fact, of Schenoudi who, with St. Antony, laid down the first principles of the monastic life—the explorer found 'so woeful that I shall not mention them any more'.

Almost exactly a hundred years later, a very different sort of traveller visited St. Antony's and gave his eyewitness account of the monastery. He was the rather mysterious M. Tourtechot* who, for reasons unknown, changed his name to Granger, a doctor and naturalist who regarded even the weird world of eighteenth-century Egypt through the judicious eye of a man of science. Granger saw the great pharaonic temples before they had been looted by the collectors and amateur archaeologists, when the colours of the wall paintings were as bright as the day they had been painted. He does not, however, enthuse over what he saw, but contents himself with giving the measurements of temples, tombs, statues, and obelisks. His main interest was biological and he gives us more information about a sacred snake 'about two feet long and an inch thick' which was allowed to creep into a woman's bosom and thence under her shift than he does about the ruins of Luxor.

Granger took twelve days from Akmin on the Nile to cross the desert to St. Antony's, but he was in no hurry. We can imagine him wandering off by himself always in search of plants and animals, very few of which he found in this arid country. Yet he seems to have been supremely happy trudging along, noting rare patches of vegetation and entering the names of species like mugwort, wild sorrel, and broom in his notebook—the classic botanist. He has nothing at all to say about the two Bedouin and the two camels who accompanied him! From this, one can be sure that men and animals were in perfect accord as they travelled slowly and wearily across the wasteland, sustained in the case of the Bedouin by that fatalistic acceptance of silence and solitude and in that of the Frenchman by the dedication of the true naturalist.

Granger's account of his arrival at the monastery is a classic example of a scientist's dry, factual report. This is what he says:

* He sometimes gets confused with the botanist Tournefort (1656–1708), who also travelled in the Levant.

> Having rested a little before the convent, I perceived a monk in the window, and I informed him of the reasons that had brought me hither. After the superior was acquainted with this, they called to me from a trap door at the top of the convent, and I saw them letting down a rope for me to fasten round my middle. I was by this means drawn up and taken into the monastery, had a cell assigned to me, and was treated like a monk: that is, I received a portion of lentils and bad bread every morning and evening.[9]

Still no complaints unless for the criticism of the bread, a criticism every Frenchman is surely permitted to make abroad.

M. Granger then gives his usual matter-of-fact description of the famous monastery, with the customary measurements of all the buildings. But it now becomes obvious that the eighteenth-century rationalist had no sympathy for either physical or spiritual disorder and was appalled by what he saw. He describes the two churches within the monastery, one consecrated to St. Peter and Paul, the other to St. Antony as 'very filthy, little, and dark . . . with some bad paintings on the walls, now quite black from the fumes of incense'.

The garden (measurements: 160 yards long; 120 broad!) he approves of. In it the monks cultivated 'dates, olives, St. John's bread, peaches, apricots, and vines, besides many kitchen herbs'. But the monks themselves—twelve priests and thirteen lay-brothers—excite neither his admiration nor his pity. He had a very modern view of the value of asceticism which these strange men were still practising almost unchanged thirteen hundred years after the death of their founder. He beheld them prostrating themselves 150 times on the ground, with arms extended while making the sign of the cross between each prostration. Six of the twelve priests were wearing a hair shirt—the 'angelic dress' as it was once significantly called; and these ascetics prostrated themselves *300 times* before they lay down on their straw mats in their narrow cells. No! The rationalist could neither understand nor approve of such behaviour. Besides, he says, 'they waste their time in search of the philosopher's stone, or writing bills which they pretend will cure the sick'.

'At noon', M. Granger writes, 'I took leave of these friars. I had but little pleasure from what I saw of them, there being nothing that could attract the curious and inspire the devout. . . .'

Seventy years later, an English explorer travelled through Egypt and sent back to Europe more details concerning the Coptic monasteries and their fabulous libraries. This was Richard Pococke (1704–1765), an indefatigable traveller in an age when the whole world outside Europe was almost *terra incognita*. For that matter, Pococke discovered in his tours in England, Scotland, and Ireland that the British Isles were almost as unknown to the educated urban dwellers as Upper Egypt, which he reached in 1738. His contemporary explorer, Frederick Lewis Norden, was also in Egypt at this time and the two men, in fact, passed each other on the Nile during the night. Norden as an artist was able to illustrate his findings in a series of 200 splendid engravings published posthumously in 1792; Pococke wrote the customary stately travel book of his period, *A Description of the East*. It is from this book that we catch another glimpse of the Egyptian monasteries.

How different a guide and companion from the German Vansleb and the English Pococke—both clericals by disposition—is the lively young Frenchman Charles Nicolas Sigisbert Sonnini de Manoncourt, the raconteur of the tribulations of the female crocodile. Imagine today prefacing one's travel book with an attack on those relatives who 'overwhelmed me with disputes and contestations; and, like barefaced plunderers, found means to divide among themselves considerable portions of my fortune, which they pulled to pieces. . . .'[10] Imagine, too, the boldness of attacking a fellow-author in these words:

> Savary himself, who published two volumes on Upper Egypt, never set his foot in it; and the tone of assurance in which he speaks of it and the details he gives of his journey, as if it had been really performed, are a stain upon the reputation of that elegant writer. . . .[11]

Sonnini, the son of a Roman who had settled in France, was a brilliant youth who, in addition to brains and good looks, was endowed by nature with gifts of courage and that special fortitude which distinguished the eighteenth- and nineteenth-century travellers. Sent to the French South American colony Guiana in 1772, Sonnini, though only twenty-one years old, crossed the unknown continent from Guiana to Peru; then, as was customary, fell ill with 'the fever' and had to return to France. He brought back with him a precious collection of rare birds which interested the great French naturalist Buffon, with whom the young Sonnini now had the honour to be associated. He was next sent as a member of a royal commission to make a study of Egypt which had been marked down at the end of the eighteenth century as a French sphere of influence.

In those days the annexation of foreign territory by a European power went hand in hand with scientific expeditions—the historians, geographers, and naturalists preceding the soldiers into what was usually still unexplored and dangerous country. Such an explorer was Sonnini who returned to France in 1780 to write his valuable *Travels in Upper and Lower Egypt*, from which European scholars first learnt of the condition of the Coptic monasteries.

Characteristic of this remarkable age of reason and enlightenment is the young Frenchman's curiosity on every aspect of human behaviour and social custom—a curiosity unfettered by the squeamishness which marks the observations of Victorian travellers, with the notable exception of Richard Burton who wrote about biological phenomena in plain language. Thus Sonnini examines at first hand the custom of circumcision among the Egyptians on the grounds that 'the natural history of man is too important to be passed over in silence'. He was particularly interested in reports that this operation was, from ancient times, also practised on women, but was not satisfied with the facts and explanations of earlier travellers.

> At length I resolved to leave no doubt upon this subject and formed the design, which must appear sufficiently bold to any person acquainted with the inhabitants of Egypt, not of having a drawing made of a circumcised girl, but of having one circumcised in my own apartments; and by the mediation of a Turk, who served as a broker to the French merchants

> at Rosetta, I succeeded in getting to my room a woman whose profession it was to perform circumcision and two young girls, one of whom had been circumcised two years before and the other who was now to undergo that operation.[12]

As a result of this practical demonstration, Sonnini felt that he had made another useful addition to anthropology, as he had certainly drawn the attention of the academic world, at least, to the barbarity of this ancient custom. For we see in this, as in other anecdotes, that he was a fervent humanist as well as a naturalist, a combination which seems to differentiate the men of science of his age from the scientists of ours. And so he can write of clitoridectomy:

> A barbarous refinement of tyranny and the lowest degree of debasement of the one half of the human species which, by cruel means, the other half moulds to its pleasures at the will of its jealous despotism!

Turning his attention next to religious matters, Sonnini set out from Alexandria to visit the monasteries of the natron lakes. He relates how his caravan arrived at the first of the convents, Baramous.

> I do not believe that there is upon earth a situation so horrible or forbidding as this sort of monastery. Built in the middle of the desert, its walls, though very high, when they are seen at any considerable distance cannot be distinguished from the sands, having the same reddish colour and naked aspect. There is no apparent entrance. Not a tree, not a plant of any size surrounds it; no road leads to it; no trace of men is to be observed near it; or if some footsteps are imprinted, they are soon covered by the sands, or effaced by the feet of wild and ferocious animals, the proper inhabitants of these frightful solitudes. Such is the harsh and repulsive appearance of this retreat of men, as useless as their habitation.

It is not surprising that the Frenchman felt bitter towards the monastery of Baramous, for immediately on his arrival his party was attacked by Bedouin and he himself robbed and stripped down to his long under-waistcoat and his breeches. He had also lost his turban and was obliged to try and protect his head 'which was bare and shaved' with his hands—though he also informs us he was biting bis nails 'with a look of anger and indignation', while his colleague wept loudly and when asked if he had been hurt, replied, 'No, sir. But what can we now get to eat?'

As Sonnini tells this story it becomes an almost perfect sample of the romantic Victorian episodes concerning bandits—as used, for instance, by Bernard Shaw in *Man and Superman*. For the robbers, far from being thugs and murderers as the French explorer assumed, turned out to be very gentlemanly highwaymen indeed, actually restoring all the clothes, goods, and even ammunition they had taken—all this done with the greatest cordiality, the robber chief actually dressing Sonnini himself. The explanation of this change in the bandits' conduct was again practically right out of a fairy-tale book, for we are given the speech that the Frenchman's dragoman made. It must be the grandfather of hundreds of examples of such histrionics and is reported as follows:

> Arabs, you have stripped a man entrusted to my protection and for whose safety I will stake my life; a man with whom I have eaten, who has slept in my tent, and has become my brother! Never again can I enter that tent; never again dare I return to my camp; I must henceforth renounce all hopes of the pleasure of embracing my wife and children. . . .'

Et cetera. It reads like pure Hollywood and is undoubtedly true—even the ridiculous sequel in which, after the whole band had been fed by the monks under the walls of the monastery, the leader of the bandits demanded that a scribe be lowered down in a basket to write out a 'certificate of good conduct' which Sonnini signed with the name *La Déroute* ('Disorder'). Next followed an altercation with the monks who had observed the day's events from the ramparts of the monastery as to whether Sonnini and his French companions were Europeans, a fact which the priests required to be demonstrated to one of their examiners. The test consisted of an examination of the soldier to see if Monsieur Sonnini was circumcised. 'This obstacle being removed,' says the Frenchman, 'the monks invited our party into the monastery by the usual means; viz. a bucket drawn up on a pulley.'

At this stage of his adventure, the explorer behaved, for the first time, in a churlish manner, refusing to comply with the ancient custom of entering the monastery via a basket, a rope, and a pulley. The monks patiently explained that they never opened the gate, which was sealed up, when there were Arabs in the neighbourhood; and they demonstrated the safety of the pulley by sending an old monk up and down on the rope. Sonnini still refused to use this means of entry, still demanded that the gate be opened, and allowed his dragoman to threaten the defenceless priests unless this was done. The monks, who had, after all, endured fifteen centuries of bullying, finally complied and opened up their gate. They seem to have had their revenge on the arrogant Frenchman who, as a guest of the convent, was obliged to attend a very long service before he was given a bowl of rice for his supper.

Sonnini, whose *Travels* were first published during the French Revolution, a fact which may explain his anti-clericalism, reports that the half a dozen monks lived in low-vaulted cells, or 'dens suitable to the slothful and ignorant wretches by whom they are inhabited'. He frequently jeers at their pathetic services, their singing, their postures whereby they leant on their crutches or *tau* sticks, their murals of the saints (since destroyed), their ritual, and even their mistreatment at the hands of the Arabs. The fact that they fed every passer-by on demand, including the surly Bedouin, whether robbers or not, is sneered at as an example of their poverty of spirit, as are their black vestments which 'render them the most ugly of mankind and, at the same time, the most filthy and disgusting'. In short, Sonnini was so hostile to the 'hideous anchorites' that he missed altogether the priceless manuscript treasures which later and more sympathetic visitors like Curzon, Tattam, and Tischendorff were able to inveigle from the monks for a few pounds. His last act on leaving the monastery of Baramous was to threaten to knock down the abbot, an old and emaciated friar called Michael. It was the Moslem Bedouin who intervened to protect the old Christian from the young one—an episode which needs no comment except to say that it is typical of the history of the Coptic Church.

Count Antoine-François Andréossi, French general and diplomatist (1761–1828), accompanied Napoleon to Egypt in 1798 as one of the soldier-scientists who set themselves to explore and describe Egypt in that now curious fashion, no longer even possible among nations at war, whereby science and learning were considered over and above national aggrandisement. Thus, the findings of Napoleon's Egyptian Mission were available to scholars throughout Europe, as those of the British expeditions sponsored by the old African Society were circulated to libraries and academies throughout the civilised world.

Andréossi, together with Citizens Berthollet and Fourier, left Ferranch at 2 a.m. on the 4th of the month *Pluviose* (i.e. January 1798). After fourteen hours' march they reached the Wadi Natrun and noted the extreme aridity and desolation of the terrain. Having made a scientific exploration of the famous lakes, only one of which was at that time being worked for the natron, the team visited the four monasteries and gave the outside world the first specific details of their size and construction. As regards the monks themselves, Andréossi has this to say:

> The monks are for the most part one-eyed or blind. They have a haggard, sad, and discontented appearance. They live on a few revenues and mostly gifts. Their food consists of lentils and beans cooked in oil. They spend their lives in prayer: incense burns in these retreats surrounded by a sea of sand.
>
> There are 9 monks in the convent of Baramous
18 ,, ,, ,, ,, ,, the Syrians
12 ,, ,, ,, ,, ,, Amba Bischoi
20 ,, ,, ,, ,, ,, Macarius
>
> We do not know what can be the pleasures of these holy men: we saw nothing which indicated that they occupied themselves either with spiritual or manual labours. Their books are merely religious manuscripts written on parchment or paper, some in Arabic, others in Copt with an Arab translation in the margin. We brought away several of the

> latter which seem to be 600 years old. We inspected the interior of these monasteries in great detail. The monks accepted our presence complacently and, indeed, appeared to be flattered by our visit and gave us their communion bread before we left.[13]

Andréossi goes on to describe the manner in which the monks were obliged to feed every passing Bedouin, both from fear and charity, and how the gifts of bread, vegetables, and grain were let down via the pulley. Living constantly in a state of dread and suppression, they longed for the downfall of their ancient enemies and persecutors and frequently asked the visiting Frenchmen in pious tones, 'When will you kill off all the Musselmans?' Such information, however, could have been of little interest to Napoleon and his general staff; and it was doubtful whether anybody else in Europe, churchmen or laymen, was particularly concerned about these forty-nine half-blind or wholly blind Christians out there in 'these retreats surrounded by sand.' But Count Andréossi's reference to manuscripts 'written on parchment', though he dismisses them as 'merely religious', was not missed by bibliophiles and collectors. Some of these book-lovers were young, adventurous, and rich. They were to set out on a sort of treasure hunt; and what some of them came back with in their campaign chests was worth many times its weight in gold.

REFERENCES

1 Abu Salih, *The Churches and Monasteries of Egypt*. Edited and translated by B. T. A. Evetts (1895).
2 *The Voyages and Travels*. Cassell's National Library (New Series), Vol. 85, p. 44.
3 *Le Bouclier de l'Europe, ou La Guerre Sainte*, 1686.
4 J. M. Wansleben, *The Present State of Egypt*, 1678, pp. 26–7. The spelling and punctuation have been modernised.
5 op. cit., p. 49.
6 C. S. Sonnini, *Travels in Upper and Lower Egypt*, 1800, p. 663.
7 op. cit., p. 174.
8 See the account of eighteenth- and nineteenth-century exploration in my *The Great Sahara* (1965), Chapters 8 and 9.

9 M. Granger, *A Journey through Egypt*. Translated by John Reinhold Forster, F.R.S. (1773), p. 297.

10 C. S. Sonnini, op. cit., p. 4.

11 op. cit., p. 7.

12 op. cit., pp. 265 ff.

13 Count Antoine-François Andréossi, *Memoires sur la Vallée des lacs de Natron et celle du fleuve sans eau* (1800), p. 58. Andréossi's book (unlike Sonnini's *Travels*) was never translated and published in English.

13 The treasures of the desert monasteries

Organised scientific exploration of Egypt—its deserts, oases, pharaonic monuments, and Christian monasteries—could only really begin in the nineteenth century after the Moslem world had been opened by European military, commercial, and diplomatic penetration. Even so, during the first half of that century, it was still not safe to travel in parts of the Middle East or, for that matter, anywhere in Africa; but this was because the Great Powers, notably Britain and France, had not yet had time to consolidate their newly acquired territories or 'spheres of influence'. Explorers and travellers to these lands which had been for so long cut off from the Christian world underwent immense hardships in their journeyings, and not all returned to their homes to sit down and write an account of what they saw. Those who survived the hazards wrote excellent travel books, the like of which can never, of course, be written again, for the world they described—a world in which even the deserts were teeming with animals—has vanished. All these books are now out of print.

We find that those adventurers who first penetrated into what were still unknown lands were usually young, well born, broadly educated with an emphasis on classical learning, not specialists on any particular subject, yet searchers animated by a genuine love of knowledge as well as of adventure. At the same time, the majority of them were collectors—usually for some rich patron; and so apparently inexhaustible was the treasure-house of Egypt that every museum in Europe and thousands of private collections were enriched with the loot of palaces, tombs, mummy-holes, and the sites of once-glorious cities. The chief purveyors of these priceless artefacts were the Egyptians themselves who had never ceased their ancient profession of tomb-robbing. In 1881 Emil Brugsch, Assistant Keeper of the Cairo Museum, found a contemporary tomb-robber's cache of artefacts from the tombs of some *forty* pharaohs. These objects were sold in the bazaars to the small collectors. The real hauls, of course, were made by excavators like the Italo-Englishman Belzoni ('the Patagonian Samson') who sent shiploads of treasure to England, including the famous alabaster sarcophagus of Seti; and the German Lepsius who despatched some 15,000 artefacts to Berlin.

During the last decades of the nineteenth century the scholars were hot on the track of papyrus manuscripts, the source material of pre-classical history, a field of scholarship which was being scientifically worked for the first time. Thus, in 1888, Wallis Budge bought the Ani Papyrus (known as 'The Book of the Dead') for the British Museum, though this kind of transaction was becoming hazardous as the Egyptian authorities sought to put an end to the dispersal of their national treasures. Wallis Budge himself was actually arrested while trying to buy the Amarna tablets from peasants who had dug them up in the fields and were selling them for a few shillings apiece. (It was on the evidence of these clay tablets written in the cuneiform script that the true history of the ancient Near East was eventually written.) The agent of the British Museum writes:

> I asked to see the warrants for the arrests . . . and he told me that he was acting on instructions from the Chief of Police at Luxor to take possession of all the houses of all the dealers and to arrest us. He then told Muhammed and myself that we were arrested . . .
>
> I then tried to make arrangements to get the remainder of the tablets from Tell al-'Armanah into my possession, but they told me they belonged to dealers who were in treaty with an agent of the Berlin Museum in Cairo. Among the tablets was a very large one, about 20 inches long and broad in proportion. We now know that it contained a list of the dowry of a Mesopotamian princess who was going to marry a king of Egypt. The man who was taking this to Cairo hid it

> between his inner garments and covered himself with his great cloak. As he stepped up into the railway coach this tablet slipped from his clothes and fell on the bed of the railway and broke in pieces. . . .[1]

In the meantime, while the Egyptologists, both amateurs and professionals, were acquiring whatever they could lay their hands on in the form of mummies, sarcophagi, statues, plaques, papyri, jewelry, and so forth, the smaller and less publicised group of bibliophiles were ransacking the Coptic monasteries in search of ancient manuscripts as priceless for the history of culture as the Amarna tablets and the mortuary papyri of the tombs. Vansleb's boast, made in the 1660's, that he had 'emptied Egypt of such kind of books' was, of course, ridiculous. A number of travellers since his time had come away with quite a haul of manuscripts, notably the Maronite priest Joseph Assemani who had been sent into Egypt by the Vatican in 1717 to acquire manuscripts. Assemani came back with 150 choice and beautiful volumes in the Coptic, Ethiopian, Persian, Turkish, Syrian, and Arabic languages. Forty of these books came from the Nitrian monasteries and formed part of the library accumulated in the tenth century by Moses of Nitibis. In 1735 Assemani was sent off again to Egypt and returned with still earlier books. Travellers after Assemani continued to visit the Coptic monasteries and to note the libraries and store rooms still crammed with beautiful manuscripts.

But it was left to the English bibliophiles of the mid-nineteenth century really to ransack the monks' libraries, even though hundreds of manuscripts had already been acquired by the French and Italian libraries, or had been burnt by the monks in the bread ovens of the convents.

The first and most successful of these audacious and colourful bibliophiles was Rubert Curzon, fourteenth Baron Zouche, in many respects the typical British explorer of the early Victorian period.

He was born in 1810, educated at Charterhouse and Oxford, which he left without taking his degree in 1831. At the age of twenty-one, in fact, he was actually returned by his borough to the House of Commons. A year later, the borough was disenfranchised and that was the end of Curzon's parliamentary career. At twenty-three he left for the Levant where, he says in the Preface to his book,[2] 'the difficulties to a traveller were as great as they would be now in China or the most distant lands'. His interest was in old manuscripts, some of which he had found in the library of the family home at Parham in Sussex. He was not so much interested in the contents of ancient manuscripts as in the handwriting, upon which subject he intended to write an exhaustive history. So it was in search of manuscripts that he set off for Egypt, for like most amateurs of the time, he believed that many of the lost Greek classics might be found in the monastic libraries of the Near East. Such manuscripts were undoubtedly once on the shelves of either the monastery collections or in the lumber rooms of Turkish soldiers who plundered the convents during the Greek Revolt. It was the dream of European bibliophiles to have the luck of Edward Clarke, traveller and antiquary, who brought back an early manuscript of Plato from Patmos, in addition to other precious books, notably an *Arabian Nights* procured in Cairo.

The first half of the nineteenth century, then, was the golden age for rich collectors who had the time, means, and fortitude to roam through the Near Eastern countries looking for statues, coins, vases, mummies, manuscripts, and the treasures of the ancient world. Thus, the same Dr. Clarke who carried off the Plato from Patmos also removed from Eleusis in Greece a colossal Greek statue of the fourth century B.C. weighing nearly two tons. Clarke's problems involved not only bribing the Turkish authorities to allow him to carry off this monument, but appeasing the local peasants who had been accustomed for generations to burn a lamp before it on festive days—perhaps from classical times themselves, since the statue was thought to be of Demeter, the Earth Mother. When the peasants objected to losing their divinity, Clarke brought in a priest to exorcise the image by striking the first blow with a pickaxe at the rubbish in which the statue was partially buried. All two tons of it were loaded aboard an Italian merchant ship which proceeded with dozens of cases of classical loot collected by

One of the priceless early ikons in the collection of St. Catherine's monastery, now in Israeli-occupied Sinai and difficult to reach

Above View from Mount Sinai at dawn. This whole region is sacred to Moslems as well as Christians
Below The famous convent of St. Catherine

Clarke to England where the freighter was wrecked off Beachy Head. The statue of Demeter, however, was saved.

All of this gives us some idea of the treasures which were available to the more intrepid travellers of the nineteenth century, explaining, in fact, the fantastically rich and varied collections now owned by the national (and even local) museums of the Western world. And Robert Curzon, at twenty-three, already a keen antiquary and bibliophile, decided to take part in the hunt. His connections as the grandson of a viscount and the son of a baroness were especially good among the contemporary aristocracy who held diplomatic posts in the capitals of the Ottoman empire; and the young Curzon probably heard from these well-informed observers of the treasures in the libraries of the Egyptian monasteries. In fact, Lord Prudhoe, afterwards fourth Duke of Northumberland, may have tipped him off about the Nitrian monasteries where he, Prudhoe, had actually seen an oil cellar littered two feet deep with ancient manuscripts, none of which the monks would part with, despite the presence of Linant de Bellefonds Bey, friend and adviser of the viceroy Mohammed Ali. Lord Prudhoe was too much of the old-fashioned English gentleman either to browbeat the monks or to bribe them, and he came away with nothing except his memories of the treasures in the oil cellar. Curzon was determined to see that particular cellar at all costs, and how he made his way to the desert monastery of the Syrians and what befell him there is one of the best stories in the travel literature of the nineteenth century.

He was certainly an 'original' and describes his own appearance himself in his usual drily witty vein.

> My personal appearance must have been remarkable: I had a long beard and so thin a face that my nose was translucent, if not transparent. I had a Persian cap upon my head, and over other garments a toilette of my own invention, which vested me with a dignity peculiar to myself: this was a large eiderdown quilt, of bright green silk, in the middle of which I had caused a hole to be made through which I put my head, the two ends of the quilt hung down before and behind like a chasuble or a poncho; round it I tied a girdle.

My general appearance must have been rather striking to the beholder. . . .[3]

But Curzon was more robust than he gives us to understand here when he first visited Egypt in 1837 at the age of twenty-seven. He was that most felicitous type of traveller, a young man with a very keen eye and an even keener sense of humour. Naturally, like all young gentlemen of his generation, he feels obliged to express his indignation at the institution of the harem; at the same time he implies his interest in the occupants of the proscribed quarters in his report of the following letter from a lady of the harem to her Armenian agent. He gives it in the original:

Constantinople, 1884.

My Noble Friend,

Here are the featherses sent. My soul, my noble friend, are there no other featherses leaved in the shop besides these featherses? And these featherses remains, and these featherses are ukly. They are very dear. Who buyses dheses? Whatever bees, I only want beautiful featherses. I want featherses of every desolation, to-morrow.

Signed,
You know who.[4]

And what better picture of the relationship between oriental master and servant could be drawn than the young English aristocrat's account of his interview with Mohammed Ali, the Egyptian viceroy.

The Pasha wanted his pocket handkerchief and looked about and felt in his pocket for it, but could not find it, making various exclamations during his search, which at last were answered by an attendant from the lower end of the room—'Feel in the other pocket,' said the servant. 'Well, it's not there,' said the Pasha. 'Look in the other then.' 'I have not got a handkerchief', or words to that effect, were replied to immediately 'Oh yes you have.'—'No, I have not.'—'Yes, you have.' Eventually this attendant, advancing up to the Pasha, felt in the pocket of his jacket, but the handkerchief was not to be found; then he poked all round the Pasha's waist, to see whether it was not tucked into his shawl: that would not do. So he took hold of his Sovereign and pushed him half over on the divan and looked under him to see whether he was sitting on the handkerchief; then he pushed him over on the other side. During all these manoeuvres the Pasha sat as quietly and passively as possible. The servant then, thrusting his arm up to the elbow in one of the pockets of His Highness's voluminous trousers, pulled out a snuff-box, a rosary, and several other things, which he laid upon the divan. That would not do either; so he came over to the other pocket and diving to a prodigious depth, he produced the missing handkerchief from the recesses thereof. . . .[5]

Curzon's search for manuscripts led him first to the monastery of Baramous which was inhabited, he says, 'by two or three poor-looking monks'. He went at once to the keep of the monastery where he saw forty or fifty Coptic manuscripts on cotton paper, 'lying on the floor to which several of them adhered'. There was only one leaf of vellum, which he took possession of. Baramous contained nothing else, he reports, except some curious lamps of very ancient glass and 'a multitude of ravenous fleas' who drove him out of the half-ruined cells where he was trying to sleep.

He next visited Souriani where one of the typical and famous (or, according to some, infamous) incidents common to book-collecting in the nineteenth century took place. The Syrian monastery at the time of Curzon's visit in 1837 was inhabited by some fifteen monks, including an 'old blind abbot'. In the keep of the convent, Curzon found manuscripts lying about on the floor and in niches in the walls. One of these was a 'superb manuscript of the Gospels with commentaries by the early Fathers of the Church; two others were doing duty as coverings to a couple of large open pots or jars which had contained preserves, long since evaporated. I was allowed to purchase these vellum manuscripts, principally, I believe, because there were no more preserves in the jars.'

But Curzon was after other manuscripts which he had heard about in Cairo; and though the 'old blind abbot' denied their existence, the young visitor resorted to what he calls 'the opener of the heart'—namely, a bottle of rosoglio (a spirit distilled from raisins, sugar, et cetera) which soon had the abbot 'bland and confiding'. 'Take another cup of rosoglio,' Curzon said, leading the conversation round to the monastery's books. The ruse worked. The old monk, now inebriated, took his visitor to a small room which was filled with manuscripts two feet deep. Curzon was able to help himself to armloads of manuscripts which now form one of the chief treasures of the British Museum's Oriental collection. He describes the scene vividly:

> First there was the old blind grey-bearded abbot, leaning on his staff, surrounded with three or four dark-robed Coptic monks, holding in their hands the lighted candles with which we had explored the secret recesses of the oil-cellar; there was I, dressed in the long robes of a merchant of the East, with a small book in the breast of my gown and a big one under each arm; and there were my servants armed to the teeth and laden with old books. . . .[6]

In fact, Curzon had so many books that he could not get them all into the camels' saddle-bags. He had to leave one large volume which was later acquired by Archdeacon Tattam. The volume Curzon left behind was an edition of a number of lost works of Eusebius and was dated 411, one of the most precious manuscripts discovered in Egypt. The Eusebius, together with some 1,000 Coptic and Syriac manuscripts acquired by Curzon, Tattam, and other British bibliophiles, is now in the British Museum.

Curzon continued his search for precious manuscripts in other monasteries further up the Nile, arriving eventually at the Convent of the Pulley (sometimes called the Convent of the Virgin) in Middle Egypt. He was welcomed here by the monks wading out to his boat stark naked and carrying him ashore on their backs.

To reach the monastery, which was built on a pinnacle on the banks of the river, he had to climb up a rock-chimney, the way being led by the abbot who held up his robe in his teeth to permit him to find a foothold inside the chimney. He, says Curzon, 'appeared like a spread eagle above my head'. Under the Englishman came the captain of the vessel, naked except for his immense turban, and under the captain some twenty nude sailors with their clothes tied in a bundle on their heads. Having climbed up inside the rock for about 120 feet, Curzon found himself on a narrow slippery ledge overlooking a precipice. From here he had to shin up an overhang to reach the rock path that led to the monastery itself. His party, the whole lot of them naked, arrived, entered the monastery, and 'frightened the ladies who lived there terribly, except that the younger ones took more time in adjusting their veils before fleeing'. It is unlikely that they had ever seen some twenty or more naked men emerge from inside the rock ever before; and nor had the mongrel dog who greeted Curzon's arrival with a growl, 'only to be assiled with a volley of stones and invectives by the ladies whom he had intended to protect'.

Despite all his efforts to reach the Convent of the Pulley, where he had been told 'there was a great chest full of ancient books on vellum', Curzon was unable to acquire any MSS here, so he pushed on to Thebes where, he tells us, he took up residence in a cave made habitable by another Englishman, one Hay: whence the name of the cave 'Mr. Hay's tomb'. One of Curzon's visitors at this time was a Copt 'whose poverty was such that his costume consisted of nothing but a short shirt, or tunic, made of a homespun fabric of goat's hair, or wool, and a common felt skull-cap, with some rags twisted round it for a turban. This Copt was none the less a well-educated man who wrote and read both Arabic and Coptic and knew the history of the nearby monastery which had only recently fallen into ruins and been abandoned by the last of the monks. The Copt also revealed that the monastery library was still in existence, concealed in one of the ancient subterranean temples. He agreed to take Curzon late at night to avoid spies and led the Englishman into a great sepulchral hall covered with hieroglyphics and full of statues of the ancient gods. Obviously this temple had been converted at a very early time by the Egyptian Christians into a church where they could meet secretly, perhaps at the time of the persecution of Diocletian and Decius.

At all events there was a stone altar at the end of the hall and here Curzon began to examine the manuscripts of the monastery library by the light of three candles. In the middle of his perusal of an ancient volume, the subterranean temple was filled with 'a fearful howling, like the roar of a hundred wild beasts . . . as if legions of infernal spirits were let loose upon us'. This was too much for Curzon, his guide, and the guide's little son, all three of whom rushed out of the temple pursued by—a donkey. Curzon obviously loved a good story so much that one wonders about that 'ancient volume' and the existence of the monastery library. On the other hand, a donkey's hee-hawing in a subterranean temple at midnight might have genuinely sounded like 'the roar of a hundred wild beasts'! Who knows . . .?

Curzon next visited the White Monastery. The year was 1838, yet his description of the convent and his reception there could apply to my visit 130 years afterwards. Now as then, the priests and their families live in houses inside the great ruined basilica, the women peer out from the windows of hovels built up in corners among the ancient ruins, and children toddle about between the fallen columns, thirty of which once lined the central aisle. Now as then, the visitor gazes up at the half-domes of the apsis with the original frescoes, trying to make out the portraits in the poor light, but recognising the splendid Christ Pancrator over the altar. The decay and neglect of this oldest and finest Roman church in Egypt continue; and only the fact that it was built by Roman, or Roman-trained, masons of a fine white dressed stone ensures that it will last perhaps for some other traveller 130 years hence.

Three monks resided in this great monastery, once the headquarters of Schenoudi. They told Curzon that 100 manuscript volumes of their library written on vellum and gazelle skins had been destroyed a few years previously by the Mamelukes. If this was true, and there is not the slightest reason to doubt the story, then the world probably lost some of the most precious manuscripts ever written, as gazelle skin was used only for the earliest Christian literature; and since the White Monastery was once the largest and richest of the Egyptian monasteries, it undoubtedly housed a large library of the gospels, including those works like *The Gospel According to the Egyptians* now lost in whole or in part. Certainly the monastery archives would have contained a bible at least as old as the *Codex Sinaiticus*, but all such manuscripts, particularly if written on vellum and gazelle skin, would have been looted by the Mameluke soldiers and made into ornaments for their women, saddle-bags, purses, and so on.

Yet Curzon brought back from Egypt some 127 manuscripts which were eventually deposited in the British Museum's Oriental collection. He has, of course, been criticised for robbing the wretched monks of the Nitrian monasteries where he acquired most of his treasures; and his account of how he plied the abbot of the Syrian convent with rosoglio has been quoted (by the Germans) as an example of British perfidy. In actual fact, of course, he saved many precious books from going into the bread ovens or from rotting to pieces on the floor of the cellars; and he pioneered the way for professional orientalists like Henry Tattam, Archdeacon of Bedford, to rescue the last remnants of the literature of early Christianity.

The difference between these two bibliophiles—the young and gay aristocrat and the elderly, sober archdeacon—is a fascinating aspect of the story of desert travel. Henry Tattam, incidentally, did not write his own account of his 1838–9 expedition in the Wadi Natrun, but left this job to his travelling companion, a Miss Platt who 'very reluctantly' printed (for private circulation only) what she calls 'a few notes hastily penned on the spot'. One gets the impression that this fretful and prejudiced old maid should never have left her English village to face the world across the English Channel, for she continually scolds about the transport, accommodations, and food in the countries she passed through on her way with Dr. Tattam to Egypt. She describes her bout of seasickness sailing along the west coast of Italy as though the Italians were to blame and her opinion of a French doctor who prescribed *potage* for her 'exhaustion by fasting and illness' as 'a remedy worthy of a Frenchman'. So she remained in her cabin 'with no other amusement than feasting on thoughts of home: the smallest circumstance connected therewith is inexpressibly sweet when two thousand miles away'. [Miss Platt wrote this off Sicily, 1,000 miles as the crow flies from England.] 'My mother's face is ever before me; and I cannot but feel thankful that she is not sharing with me the misery of this week.'

At all events, Dr. Tattam and Miss Platt safely crossed the Mediterranean, landed at Alexandria, where 'a sudden and violent cramp seized me, which increased to such a degree that I was removed to my bed in agony'. However, Miss Platt managed to be present that evening at the dinner table, though only able to eat small portions of the four-course meal. The party was off next day on donkeys, from which the ladies frequently fell to the ground to be picked up by the donkey-boys. After wandering about for a few leisurely weeks visiting monasteries up and down the Nile (all of them in an extreme state of dilapidation and none with any MSS which excited much interest), Dr. Tattam and Miss Platt with a fairly large caravan of camels, donkeys, and armed Bedouin crossed the Libyan Desert to the monasteries of the Natrun Lakes. It seems to have been during the crossing of the desert (inhabited at that time by flocks of ibis, cranes, wild geese, ostriches, herons, and other large birds—all having been exterminated in the last fifty years) that Miss Platt suddenly felt a stirring in her sensible British soul and surrendered herself a little to a world which had not been shaped in the image of a middle-class Victorian God. She fell in love with the desert.

Dr. Tattam, in the meantime, was eagerly waiting his opportunity to examine the libraries of the four Nitrian monasteries and to obtain as many rare MSS as he could. Curzon, of course, had passed through only a year or so previously, but the rumours of the treasures he had had to leave behind must have reached the English clergyman. Miss Platt, in fact, makes a haughty reference to 'the European who visited the convent and made such strenuous efforts to obtain possession of it [i.e. a very beautiful Coptic-Arabian dictionary] that they were almost afraid to show it to travellers'. The European was, of course, Robert Curzon, equipped with his bottles of rosoglio.

Tattam began his researches at the Syrian monastery. Miss Platt comments: 'There is no doubt as to their possessing a great quantity of MSS; but the principal difficulty is to discover the most likely method of getting possession of them. . . . Their avarice is so excessive that the most distant idea that they were of any value to Europeans would be sufficient to induce them to fix an exorbitant price on them, or withhold them altogether.' Despite the unwillingness of the monks to part with the only objects of any value left to them, Tattam managed to obtain a splendid haul of ancient scriptures written on vellum, the books today being worth several hundred thousand pounds. Among his finds was the hitherto unknown treatise by Eusebius of Caesaria, the big volume which Curzon had been unable to find room for in his saddle-bags.

From the Western Desert, the archdeacon and his companion journeyed to the Eastern, or Arabian, Desert, in order to visit the monasteries of Antony and Paul. Poor Miss Platt was not allowed inside the former convent and so had to camp outside the walls where she watched the Bedouin reject the food lowered in baskets on the grounds that the monks had not crumbled the bread sufficiently in the broth. 'A terrible uproar ensued', she says, as the soup went up and down in the basket, until the monks, who had learnt from centuries of experience how to deal with these mendicants, finally gave way and crumbled up the bread as ordered. In the meantime, of course, the broth had got cold, but this did not bother the sturdy beggars down below half as much as not having their bread served to them in the traditional manner. One rather admires the spirit of men who place their dignity above their hunger.

Archdeacon Tattam, in the meantime, was examining the library, but found no manuscripts which he had not already obtained from the Nitrian convents. What he did find was a young monk who begged to be freed from his unendurable imprisonment in this desert fortress, giving as his excuse his longing to make the pilgrimage to Jerusalem whither the Tattam caravan was bound. The other monks refused this novitiate permission to leave the monastery, no doubt for the very good reason that he was the only young and active member of the convent. The archdeacon upheld their decision.

> He [i.e. the novitiate] was almost frantic when he found that his entreaties were in vain; and the brotherhood suspecting he would attempt to follow us, locked him in his cell, where he sobbed and howled in the most piteous manner . . . It was really affecting to see the poor dejected prisoner leaning over the little balcony from which he was permitted to take a last look at our caravan as it moved off, while the tears streamed down his pale and haggard face.[7]

Miss Platt was not a very vivid or even an interesting writer; but her account of this young monk's anguish is perhaps the most significant of all the stories told by travellers who visited the Egyptian monasteries from the fourteenth to the end of the nineteenth century.

After leaving St. Antony's, Archdeacon Tattam and Miss Platt visited St. Catherine's on Mount Sinai, and while she wrote the expected purple passages about the awesome scene of the Ten Commandments, her companion examined the library of the convent. In fact, the archdeacon knew that the monastery had in its possession what is probably the most precious book in the Christian world: namely, the fourth-century manuscript of the Bible, in other words, the *Codex Sinaiticus.* No doubt Dr. Tattam had some hope of purchasing this beautiful and venerable book; and failing that, of collating the text of the gospels with other manuscripts, none of which were as old and therefore as authentic as the *Sinaiticus.* But the English scholar, though he had travelled so far, was disappointed: the old abbot evaded his request and even refused to show him the manuscript at all, until Dr. Tattam was leaving when he was allowed a quick peek. Evidently the abbot regretted to seem discourteous, but he explained that a certain Englishman 'visiting the convent some time since, had offered the sum of £300 for it; upon which he [the abbot] immediately wrote to the Greek patriarch in Cairo respecting the proposal, and, in reply, received orders that as it was so valuable not to part with it on any account whatever'.

When we read the subsequent history of this famous bible, Miss Platt's comment is quite incredible: she actually states that £300 was an 'imprudently high price for things of this kind and gives to the Oriental an impression that they must be of immense value'. Miss Platt would have been shocked to hear that 100 years later the British Museum paid the Soviet Government £100,000 for the *Codex Sinaiticus* and that, immediately afterwards, the Americans offered twice that sum for the manuscript.

It would appear that the 'certain Englishman' who had tried to buy the manuscript was Lord Prudhoe who nearly acquired it in 1828 for £250 (worth, of course, at least five times that amount today) and might even have succeeded if the patriarch in Alexandria and the abbot in Sinai had not fallen out over the division of the proceeds. This, at any rate, was the account as given by Lobegott Friedrich Constantine Tischendorf who was also in the field in search of ancient manuscripts, more particularly the *Codex Sinaiticus*. The great German scholar is an engaging person, for he was both a wily as well as a humorous man and enlivens his *Travels* with many a light-hearted story. While not as young and gay as Curzon, or as old and serious as Tattam, he was one of those nineteenth-century Germans who combined immense erudition with a life of adventure. He belongs, therefore, with those German scholar-explorers who travelled so extensively in the deserts a hundred years ago—Heinrich Barth, Gustav Nachtigal, Oskar Lenz. Tischendorf's achievements were correspondingly brilliant, among them the acquisition of many precious manuscripts from the desert monasteries, including eventually the greatest MS of all, the Sinai Bible.

He first saw the manuscript in the form of a basketful of tattered parchment leaves with which the monks were about to light their bread oven. Such was their custom. Who knows how many manuscripts had been burnt in this manner? At any rate, Tischendorf made the mistake of acquainting the monks with the value of the 'rubbish' they were burning, with the result that instead of acquiring all 129 leaves of the Old Testament which were in the basket, they gave him only forty-three which he presented to Frederick Augustus II, King of Saxony.

There now began among the scholars, bibliophiles, and museum directors of Europe a race to win the greatest prize of biblical literature. Tischendorf, now that the three English contestants, Lord Prudhoe, Robert Curzon, and Henry Tattam, had failed, was in the lead. He was apparently the only man who knew the full facts about the manuscript. He kept the knowledge to himself, however, and waited until he was able to visit the monastery again, which he did nine years after his first visit. But his search seemed in vain. The monks denied all knowledge of the *Codex*. They were evidently telling the truth for when Tischendorf finally discovered the manuscript, it was by a piece of good luck. A young monk had it in his cell where he kept it with other old books and the coffee cups. The monk obviously had no knowledge of the value or significance of the book which was unbound and wrapped in an old red cloth.

> I unrolled the cover and discovered to my great surprise not only those very fragments which fifteen years before I had taken out of the basket, but also other parts of the Old Testament, the New Testament complete, and, in addition, the Epistle of Barnabas and a part of the Pastor of Hermas. Full of joy, which this time I had the self-command to conceal from the steward and the rest of the community, I asked, as if in a careless way, for permission to take the manuscript into my sleeping chamber to look over it more at leisure. There by myself I could give way to the transport of joy I felt. I knew that I held in my hand the most precious Biblical treasure in existence—a document whose age and importance exceeded all that of all the manuscripts which I had ever examined during twenty years' study of the subject.[8]

The scholar now proceeded to transcribe the *Epistle of Barnabas* even though, as he says, his lamp was dim and the night was cold. It is this devotion of the German, alone in his cell in January 1859, that one recalls on visiting St. Catherine's today and groping one's way into a guest room which is provided with a broken-springed bed, a washbowl, and enamel jug, and an electric light which goes out about nine o'clock at night. It is difficult to appreciate or imagine the conditions in which Constantine Tischendorf copied the *Epistle of Barnabas* which excited him so greatly since scholars had been searching for the original Greek version for centuries. The *Epistle* was stated to have been held as 'sacred writing' by the first Christians, though it had been suppressed as heretical by the Gelasian Decree of A.D. 494, and consequently was only known through a faulty Latin translation.

Tischendorf worked all through that and subsequent nights copying the *Epistle* and another 'heretical' book called the *Pastor of Hermas*, and then tried to get permission to take the precious volume to Cairo to copy all 110,000 lines of it—'of which a great number were difficult to read, either on account of later corrections, or through the ink having faded, and that in a climate where the thermometer during March, April, and May is never below 77° of Fahrenheit in the shade. No one can say what this cost in fatigue and exhaustion'.[9]

Now comes the curious and controversial part of the *Codex Sinaiticus* story, for Tischendorf having got the abbot's permission to have the manuscript sent from Sinai to Cairo (a special camel rider did the return journey of 500 miles in nine days), next inveigled the archbishop and monks into allowing the document to be taken to St. Petersburg '*under the form of a loan*, to have it copied as accurately as possible'. I underline the phrase 'under the form of a loan', because the statement proves that the *Codex* was, in the last analysis, stolen from the monastery by the connivance of Tischendorf, aided and abetted by the Grand Duke of Russia, Prince Lobanow, Russian ambassador to Turkey, and eventually the Czar, Alexander II. Tischendorf could hardly deny that he tricked the monks since his original letter to the head of the monastery promising to return the manuscript was carefully kept by the archivist and is now pointed out, with obvious rancour, to every visitor to the library.

The *Codex* was presented as a gift to the Czar at the Winter Palace of Tsarskoe-Selo in November 1859, while St. Catherine's received as compensation just over £1,000 and a number of Russian decorations for the Patriarch and the abbot of the monastery.

But in fairness to Tischendorf one must admit he was strongly influenced not only by the ignorance of the monks, who had not the slightest interest in the *Codex*, but by the real danger to the manuscript if it remained in their hands. The monks, of course, were at the time not in the least indignant about losing their book to the Czar of Russia, as imperial head of the Greek Orthodox Church; they only became indignant some eighty years later when they learned that the old book which had laid for years in a cupboard was worth £100,000.

The whole controversy is curious, for one might ask what difference does the actual *possession* of this manuscript make to anybody. It has been published in facsimile and is available therefore for scholars anywhere in the world to consult. The original, of course, is an object of great beauty to bibliophiles; but judging from the number of visitors who come expressly to see the exhibit case in the manuscript gallery of the British Museum, the *Sinaiticus* does not excite anything like the interest of the Rosetta Stone or the Egyptian mummies. Yet, according to Tischendorf,

> 'I would rather,' said an old man, himself of the highest distinction of learning, on the occasion of the conferring of a doctorate on me by the Universities of Oxford and Cambridge, 'I would rather have discovered this Sinaitic manuscript than the Koh-i-noor of the Queen of England.'[10]

One assumes that this academician had never gone very far from his study and so had never had the opportunity of discovering either manuscripts or diamonds. But what he meant, no doubt, was that scholarship gave him greater satisfaction than jewels. And certainly the Bible which Tischendorf had discovered and, in particular, the manuscripts of the two heretical books, the *Epistle of Barnabas* and the *Pastor of Hermas*, enriched the world much more than another large diamond. For, at about the time that the German scholar appeared with the two 'lost' books, historians were beginning to re-examine the facts about Christ, the primitive Christians, and their suppressed books. A direct result of their inquiry was, of course, the great wave of scepticism, agnosticism, and atheism which swept the late Victorian world and washed up on to the shores of the twentieth century. The force of this upheaval is still being felt, if anything more strongly than ever. The old academician was right: the discovery of the *Codex Sinaiticus* was far more important and exciting than the acquisition by Queen Victoria of the Koh-i-noor diamond. The book was to help change men's beliefs and to help change society itself. The reason was that men were now asking, 'Who wrote the Bible? and when?' And, 'Why was the *Epistle of Barnabas* and the *Pastor* suppressed if they were both considered part of holy scripture in the fourth century when the *Codex Sinaiticus* was copied out?' And again, 'What books did the primitive Christians read in addition to the Old Testament and the synoptic gospels?' And, 'What were their basic beliefs?'

For two reasons, we have to go to Egypt and the Egyptian monasteries to get the answers, however incomplete, to these questions: first, because the Egyptian climate preserved the early manuscripts, even when they were buried in the graves of monks; and secondly, the monasteries where the earliest scriptures were chiefly copied and stored in the libraries were out of reach of the Church of Rome and its censors. It was for these reasons that the Greek original of the *Epistle* and the *Pastor* survived, though both had been condemned as heretical by the Western Church.

REFERENCES

1 Sir Ernest A. T. W. Budge, *By Nile and Tigris* (1920), p. 87.
2 Robert Curzon, *Visits to Monasteries in the Levant* (1916).
3 'Notice of Lord Zouche.' From the Miscellanies of the *Philobiblon Society* (1874), pp. 14 ff.
4 *Visits to Monasteries in the Levant* (1955), p. 79.
5 op. cit., pp. 81–2.
6 op. cit., p. 112.
7 op. cit., Vol. II, p. 94.
8 *Codex Sinaiticus* . . . Tischendorf's story as related by himself (1934), pp. 27–8.
9 op. cit., p. 29.
10 op. cit., p. 193.

Epilogue

The Egyptian nun placed in my hands an object like a Japanese bolster. It was oval and apparently made of wood.

'The arm of St. George,' she said. 'For those who truly believe, it will perform miracles.'

She took back the relic which despite its sanctity she handled as if it were a rolling-pin, meantime explaining that the saint's severed limb was efficacious even for Moslems, whose women often sought the aid of the relic in cases of barrenness.

The nun was watching my face as I examined the object, obviously more concerned about my response to this particular treasure than she had been when I was shown the iron collar and chain with which the saint had been bound and shackled in prison. In fact, she had shown me these fetters with a certain scepticism, though why the pieces of old iron were less impressive to her than this arm in a green canvas bag was one of the mysteries of her faith. I have no idea of what will happen to these prized relics now that St. George has been 'liquidated', as it were, by the Vatican. One recalls, however, that numerous saints of both the Coptic and Orthodox Churches which have always been regarded as bogus in the West have been revered as national heroes in the East.

Yet for all the disdain or scepticism intellectual or sophisticated people may feel, St. George's arm helps to explain why Christianity survived in Egypt for over 1,500 years of intensive persecution. Laugh at these sacred relics as we will, they have outlived the signs and symbols of the pagans. Every Egyptian Christian is entitled to ask, would a political movement have been able to withstand the continual murder of its leaders, the harassment of its followers, the destruction of its meeting-places, and the pillaging of its treasures as we have done? What body of men and women could have endured such treatment apart from those who had our sort of faith?

So this nun with her bolster and her convictions is, in a sense, the living proof that the monks and mystics of the Egyptian deserts were right, and the politicians, warlords, and pagan philosophers were wrong.

And yet . . . all one's travels through the deserts where this faith was born, one's visits to the ancient shrines of Christianity, one's view of the birthplace of Christian mysticism, and one's conversations with the contemporary representatives of the Egyptian Church, all lead to the conclusion that what one has seen is a world as antique and remote as the ruins of Troy. This, of course, is true of most of Africa, with the exception of a few pockets of desert in which commercial interests have not yet found anything profitable to exploit. The real desert, in other words, whether we are speaking of the Algerian sand seas or the Libyan or the Arabian Desert, is a sort of museum-cum-zoo. In the museum section one can see the ruins of certain ancient civilisations. (What could be more intriguing than the empire of the Garamantes in the Fezzan or the occupation of the Central Sahara by the Tuareg?) In the zoological enclaves, the tourist in his Land Rover will see quite a few camels, an occasional small herd of gazelle, and possibly even ostrich in the wild.

But what has actually gone from the desert is a way of life and an attitude that perforce went with it. The way of life was the outcome of a struggle for survival which needed resources of physical and mental endurance that Western man can scarcely conceive of; the attitude was an ability, indeed a readiness not only to believe but to trust in God. This, in fact, was the special attribute of the Desert.

From what I have seen in my wanderings, I am forced to conclude that just as the old way of life has almost been destroyed, so the spiritual attitude that went with it was bound to change. True, the outward manifestations continue both among Christians and Moslems, so that religion is actually an operative force in African life. But one is more conscious of the ritual than of the religion. So while Christianity is still the creed of 1,500,000 Egyptians, it is now more of a tradition proudly maintained than a vitalising way of life. It has thus lost nearly all resemblance to the faith of these Desert Fathers and hermits who surrendered their lives to God by (in the language of mysticism) beating against the cloud of unknowing. Even though the Christians of Egypt have suffered longer and more severely from persecution and oppression than any other nationality (including the Armenians), they seemed to have retained until today the fundamental fervour and willingness to suffer that distinguishes the true religionist from the lip-server. What seems to have finally extinguished this light is not the oppressions or the sufferings they were subjected to by the Roman emperors Diocletian and Decius or the Arab caliphs Assama ibn Zeid and El-Hakim, for these attacks on their lives, property, churches and conduct were so terrible that they stimulated a comparative courage and endurance on the part of the persecuted—a familiar law of cause and effect in human behaviour. What seems to have crushed the Copts was two things: first, the incompatibility of their mystical concept of the Christian doctrine with the shape and demands of the modern world; and secondly, the petty vexations of the hostile Moslem society in which they must live as outsiders.

Consider the former of these two issues: the conflict between materialism and mysticism. Since no compromise is possible between these two outlooks, and since the former with the aid of its powerful allies, science and industrialisation, has in the Western world certainly almost completely wiped out even the vestiges of the latter, it follows that the longing for God instead of for money is a potentially 'subversive' doctrine. This is seen in the hostility of organised groups to the nonconforming individual—not that the nonconformist today is usually seeking God in any shape or form. But if he were and went to the lengths of the primitive Christians to find him, society would very quickly condemn him as an eccentric or even a madman. The argument would be that society must protect itself against those who will not accept, or work for, its declared values; and the declared values of all modern societies are the increase of wealth, the efficiency of industry, and the raising of the standard of living. These aims are now so obvious and accepted that no one appears to think there is any alternative, not even the obvious alternative of the Christian ethic. Some say, of course, that socialism or communism are alternatives to capitalism, others fascism, and so on. They are not alternatives. They are simply variants of the same materialistic philosophy.

It is true that society does permit what might be called the 'peripheral mystics' to voice their opinions—that is, the writers and artists—some of whom predict the horrors of a world ultimately based on purely commercial values. But the true mystic who goes beyond this stage of 'viewing with alarm' and rejects everything the materialist strives for would not be tolerated outside a monastic cell. Not that our rulers today have any problem in ridding society of such visionaries. The right-minded citizen would do it for them, since he would conventionally regard a practising mystic as something of a menace to himself, his family, and his neighbours: in other words, socially suspect. But even to talk of a practising mystic is, to a great extent, purely academic, unless one is referring to those visionaries safely confined within a convent and hence physically and spiritually isolated from the outside world. Other than entering such a place of refuge, the contemplative has nowhere to go to escape either the distractions or the hostility of everyday life as we are told we must live it.

There is no need, then, to re-examine the arguments of the Age of Reason regarding the alleged absurdities of primitive Christian mysticism. In any case, we have gone beyond the pure intellectual scorn of Gibbon and Voltaire to the clichés of the nineteenth-century political philosophers who defined all religion as the 'opiate of the masses'. And even these nineteenth-century critics sound old-fashioned in the light of the twentieth-century psychologists who label the ecstasies of the visionaries as manifestations of sexual frustration, masochism, hysteria, the Oedipus complex, and so forth. And, of course, it is quite easy to prove what one likes in the case of men so extraordinary as the Desert Fathers—whose lives were the antithesis of, for instance, those of the twentieth-century suburban businessmen.

It is not surprising, therefore, to find the unknown author of *The Cloud of Unknowing*, perhaps the greatest of all the 'textbooks' on the mystical life, defending himself and his fellow-contemplatives against the attacks of the fourteenth-century 'world outside'.

> For wherever a man or woman, whether religious or secular, feels himself stirred through grace to surrender all his outer affairs in order to devote himself fully to living the contemplative life, all his brothers and sisters, his close friends, and many others besides who do not experience these urgings, will immediately rise up against him in a spirit of grievance. They will speak sharply to him, saying that he is doing nothing of any use. They will tell many false tales (and many true ones, too) of the fall of men and women who gave themselves in the past to this life. But they do not tell the good tales of those who did not fall.[1]

How has this 'spirit of grievance', this opposition to the 'stirrings of grace', affected Christian Egypt, the first centre of the contemplative life and of the monastic institutions which remained, up to the end of the seventeenth century at least, the wellsprings of our faith?

The effects are, of course, obvious in the dilapidated state of the primitive shrines themselves. But more than that, the observer cannot escape the suspicion that the spiritual as well as the physical attributes of this original Christian culture are rapidly being submerged beneath the flood tide of modernism, so that the monasteries themselves no longer fulfil any significant religious function apart from perpetuating in a picturesque fashion the venerable Coptic ritual. Some of them—the four in the Wadi Natrun, for instance—are still served by a dozen or so of monks, delightful old gentlemen like Father David of Baramous, retired schoolmasters or civil servants, all men who struck me as having given up the struggle against this world rather than longing to discover the next. Confined within the walls of these desert outposts, they *seem* to have attained to that state of inner beatitude, the mark of the true religious, and one seldom seen outside a convent. In point of fact, they are really a group of elderly bachelors who have retired to a not uncomfortable old people's home, where they have no responsibilities and nothing to do apart from the routine. Not having to fight and push and worry, they become very gentle and sweet, even childlike; and, like children, love a visitor from the outside world, because it means a little party, such as I had with Father David and Father Ibrahim on the ramparts of the Deir Baramous where we ate dates and smoked and chatted about the outside world. But I felt that the significance of this place was not religious at all; it was, if anything, social: we were three people who were happy to be as far away as it is possible to get from the bright lights of Cairo and the Hilton Hotel.

Even so, Abuna Abd el-Masih was actually living his religious life out there in his cave, so that one could argue from his example that the old mystical fervour so typical of the desert was not wholly extinguished. But el-Masih, let us admit it, is as strange and remote to us as Simeon Stylites, because we have absolutely no means of comprehending him. If only one could have found out whether he had attained to the final mystical state of union with the Absolute of which all the Christian contemplatives speak with such conviction! It is quite possible that he had. On the other hand, the doubt constantly creeps back into the mind that this Ethiopian solitary has actually become mentally deranged by his terrifying ordeal. Logic and common sense add their voice to our doubting. What does his self-abnegation prove? And what do his sufferings contribute to the common good? That we ask these questions at all indicates conclusively that we no longer have much patience with the mystics. We do not necessarily rise up against them in a spirit of grievance. We are much more inclined to dismiss them, with Gibbon, as 'maniacs, spending their lives in a long routine of useless and atrocious tortures'.

Some might go farther and see in the austere life of Abd el-Masih, as in the apparently useless lives of his fellow-monks inside the monasteries, the signs of the disorientation of the Christian Church in Egypt. Certainly the other monasteries I visited gave this melancholy impression of decay. Admittedly some, like St. Simeon at Aswan, have been abandoned altogether since the thirteenth century, though this enormous fortress-convent with its twenty-five-foot-high wall and round towers at each of the four corners contained cells for 300 resident monks, pilgrims' quarters, churches, and all the necessary workshops of a self-contained community. Others like the Red and White Monasteries near Soohag are still occupied by a few priests and their families, but are in a state of advanced dilapidation which is a disgraceful comment on the Egyptians themselves and even more on the foreign Christians. To allow the physical and spiritual home of Schenoudi, second abbot of the White Monastery, eighty-three years its ruler, co-founder with St. Antony and Pachomius of the Christian monastic rule, and Father of the Egyptian Church—to allow such a shrine to go to ruin shows a monstrous indifference not only to our religious faith but to our cultural heritage. To such a stage has materialism brought us.

One other monastery struck me in particular as typifying the decline of the Egyptian Church, though this convent, the newest of all and still, for that matter, a-building, would seem to demonstrate the exact opposite. I am referring to the new Coptic cathedral and monastery being built on the outskirts of the ancient City of St. Menas. This project, I was told, was dear to the heart of the present patriarch, Kyrillos VI, and is to be his monument for all time. It will certainly be an enormous cenotaph, but who, one wonders, will visit it, who needs it? It is too far away from the populated centres of Alexandria and Cairo to be reached by commuting worshippers; and, in any case, the Copts of these two cities already have many churches, schools, and convents easily available.

Where the money comes from to build such a costly edifice is not, of course, our business. Let us hope that not too much of it came out of the earnings of the poorest Copts or, for that matter, from the salaries of those middle-class professional men who find such difficulty in making ends meet. For these Christians, I discovered, were more interested in leaving their unhappy country altogether than in building another great cathedral in the middle of nowhere. Who, then, is to fill the cells and cloisters of this new convent when the ancient sites are almost empty, and would be empty if it were not for a few old men who regard them as places of retirement?

How does all this relate to the Egyptian deserts? First, because the Desert Fathers, beginning with St. Antony, demonstrated to the Western world that the first and most important step along the mystical road which leads to union with God is self-purification, or the rejection of evil, imperfection, and illusions: in brief, the suppression of the 'old Adam'. Secondly, because the Egyptian deserts were the ideal proving-grounds for this experiment: they enforced the necessary physical restraints of solitude, quiescence, and frugality. In such surroundings the long training was much more practicable than it was in the home, the Church, or even the monastery. For the central idea of mysticism is this: that the world the normal person inhabits in his day-to-day existence is false and unreal—false in its desires, thoughts, ambitions, and values; unreal in its acceptance of the shadow for the substance. To grasp this idea, the would-be mystic must make a break with the sham world which governs every aspect of his being and withdraw himself to some 'desert', even if the location itself is not a place of rock and sand as 'the place called Scete' described by Palladius. For obviously the physical conditions must be right before even a start can be made, since the training for what the old writers called the 'athletes of Christ' is far, far more severe than that of the modern Olympic competitor.

What was that training? It was a long course of physical, mental, and spiritual control which could be described as the diametrical opposite of today's 'permissiveness'. The basic rules were demonstrated in their lives by the Desert Fathers, then refined and passed down to us in the writings of the medieval visionaries. These rules are based on the gradations of prayer: vocal prayer by which appeals for God's grace are made aloud as in church; mental prayer in which the mood is one of quiet contemplation; meditation in which the mind is emptied of mundane thoughts and distractions; mystical prayer in which the mind begins to be stripped of everything that obtrudes between it and the contemplation of God. This stage is sometimes referred to as 'the night of the senses' and is followed by 'the night of the spirit' for these are periods in the training when the ascetic is liable to suffer most, for all may seem hopeless and dark. But about now, with God's grace, the aspirant may begin to experience 'the touch of God', or in non-mystical language 'moments of vision', though the writers on the subject are adamant that such experiences cannot be described by words which are themselves chained to mundane emotions.

In fact, as these 'touches of God' come to the mystic during his moments of quiescence, he may attain to the ecstatic stage of full union with the Absolute, an indescribable experience which can only be comprehended by non-mystics in certain outward manifestations of this union: that is, in the expression of rapture and, in some cases, the actual trance. Such physical signs of union are not uncommon, distinguishing, in fact, the mystic from his unspiritual fellow-man; and there have been far too many examples of such ecstasies and trances for sceptics to dismiss these phenomena as mere psycho-physical aberrations. One notes that Socrates was subject to trances, which sometimes lasted for hours and on one occasion for a whole day and night. During these seizures, he would stand motionless, unconscious of the world around him.

The fact that Socrates underwent this particular exaltation, this elevation of mind over matter, is significant to those of us who cannot understand the nature of Christian mysticism and are unsympathetic or sceptical towards it, usually on the grounds that such phenomena as trances, ecstasy, and the like are either unnatural, irrational, or even psychopathic. Certainly the lives and behaviour of those early Christian ascetics like the stylites Simeon the Elder and the Younger, Daniel, Alypius, Luke, and so forth incline us to the view that the conduct of these solitaries was depraved and their claims to holiness so much exhibitionism. It is not so easy to dismiss Socrates and his abnormalities. He was in most respects a model Athenian, a brave soldier, a good citizen faithfully performing his civic and tribal duties, and the friend and teacher of men like Alcibiades, Xenophon, Crito, Plato, and so on. Yet there were two aspects of his personality which set him apart as a potential mystic—his austerity and his 'divine sign', the δαιμόνιον σημεῖον which prosaic commentators have found so puzzling, usually explaining it away as 'conscience'. It was nothing of the sort, of course, since all civilised men possess a 'conscience' of some sort, even if they disregard its voice. But Socrates heard this voice as clearly as he heard his fellow-men, and he was certain that he was in personal communication with some supernatural force when his 'divine sign' spoke to him. Whether we wish to believe this or not, it is quite clear that, like the Christian mystics, he had no difficulty in disciplining his will to do whatever his divine sign told him it was right to do, even to facing death in what is, perhaps, the noblest episode in human history.

And so we find that Socrates, though no mystic in the Christian sense, set about mastering his bodily desires and demands, going bare-footed summer and winter, as a symbol of his indifference to creature comforts. The Christian mystics, of course, went farther—to the point where the rationalist finds their behaviour not uplifting, but sordid. Indeed, the tortures which the visionaries inflicted upon themselves are utterly beyond our comprehension, since a very great part of our time is spent in avoiding not only any prick of pain, but even any threat of discomfort. What are we to think, then, of those saints, male and female, who deliberately burnt their genitals in order to conquer their sexual desire; the saints who embraced lepers or washed these unclean people and then drank the water? It is no use telling the practical-minded men that those things were done not as masochistic acts but as acts of love. He can only see life in terms of self-interest, whereas the mystic sees it in the exactly opposite way. Selfhood has to be destroyed at all costs. Sometimes the cost was appalling, as it was for the nun the Blessed Angela of Foligno.

> Innumerable are the torments of my body [she writes]. There remaineth in me not one of my members that doth not suffer horribly. Never am I without pain, without languor . . . I am always weak and so full of pain in all my members that it is a great punishment for me to move; and yet I am tired with lying and I am also unable to take sufficient food. . . .

Brother Arnold of the Friars Minor, Angela's confessor, who 'took down from her own lips' her Visions and Instructions, adds a significant footnote here.

> And I the brother who have written these things beheld the aforesaid faithful one of Christ at the above-mentioned sixth step, in a far more horrible state than can be described . . . She was full of pain, and all the members and joints of her body were swollen so that it was a torment for her to move or walk, or even sit; yet all these sufferings of body she accounted for very little.[2]

What were the rewards for these indescribable torments of Angela's mind and body? She describes them herself in a beautiful passage of her *Visions*:

> On the Purification of the Blessed Virgin, early in the morning, while I was in the church of the Friars Minor at Foligno, a voice spake unto me and said: 'This is the hour in which our Lady the Virgin Mary came with her Son into the Temple.' Then was my soul lifted up and went to meet her with great reverence and love . . . And our Lady herself held out to me her Son Jesus and said: 'O Lover of my Son, take Him!' and she delivered her Son into my arms. . . .
>
> While then I thus stood, of a sudden, the Child, all naked in my arms, opened and shut its eyes and then gazed at me again; and straightway in that look of those eyes of His I felt and had such love that it wholly overcame me.
>
> Then my soul in a marvellous and indescribable manner offered itself unto Him. And my soul understood that God graciously accepted that offering and received it with great readiness. But of the cheerfulness and ineffable joy and delight indescribable which I had when I understood that God received and accepted my offering with such great benignity, I can say nothing at all, for it is impossible for me to make it known.

The fact is that we hear very little of the 'cheerfulness and ineffable joy and delight indescribable' of the mystics, first because they themselves found their ultimate 'absorption into the Uncreated Light' or, in plainer terms, their 'union with God' exceedingly difficult, if not impossible, to describe; and secondly, because their critics either disbelieve these ecstatic experiences or hasten to interpret them according to the current psychiatric jargon. In short, we refuse to concede that such indefinable rewards are worth all the hard work, the severe discipline of both mind and body, that the mystic undergoes.

Perhaps the nearest we come to accepting total self-abnegation is in our admiration of those achievements which involve man's conquest of physical obstacles—climbing formidable mountains, sailing single-handed across oceans, and even swimming particular strips of water. We applaud such triumphs of the human will, even though they are as valueless in utilitarian terms as the stylites' perching on pillars, while comparable spiritual triumphs seldom arouse in us the same enthusiasm. For there has been a shift through the centuries as to what constitutes useful and what ridiculous achievements of this sort. No doubt zealous Christians of the fifth century would regard swimming the Straits of Dover as a foolish waste of time and energy. They saw nothing funny in the spectacle of a man retiring to the desert to train himself by self-denial to become an athlete of Christ. Moreover, to the victims of a system created and controlled by soldiers and politicians, the lives of the contemplatives were proof that men did not need to kill and hurt and exploit each other in order to survive, but could actually live together in peace and love. Because when the early Christians fled to the Egyptian deserts, they were not only escaping from their persecutors, but even more from society itself. It was a society in which religion, morals, piety, respect for law and order—in fact all the virtues which once constituted the old civic conscience—seemed to have been abandoned. To the Christians this materialistic civilisation was already rotten at the core, which partially explains the obsession men had in those days with the literal end of the world.

Some of the fugitives fled to the desert, then, out of fear, others out of desperation, a few out of religious conviction. The original Desert Fathers belonged to the last group, though we should not think of them as seeking silence and solitude in order to become conscious mystics. They went rather in order to find God who, we must remember, was for them a personal deity, a real person, and not, as in modern theology, a sort of primeval force that pervades the universe. Obviously one cannot have any meaningful relationship with primeval forces, but a God conceived as a Father (which is how Christ conceived of him, of course) can be loved, sought after, and, according to a host of witnesses, actually entered into —the union with the Absolute. The Desert Fathers discovered these first principles of mysticism by accident, as it were; for they were neither philosophers nor theologians, but practising Christians, striving to see 'who could be more merciful than his brother, kinder, humbler, more patient. Some of them have been so purged of all thought or suspicion of malice that they no more remembered that evil was still wrought upon the earth.' So Rufinus of Aquileia described them; and he knew, because he had himself lived both on Mount Nitria and in Scete and had conversed with Macarius, the disciple of Antony. Indeed, Rufinus's description of the innocence of the hermits is echoed in the St. Antony's own childlike question to a foreign visitor. 'Tell me, I pray thee,' the old man said, 'how fares the human race; if new roofs be risen in the ancient cities: whose empire is it that now sways the world?'

Yet even if we admit the kindness, patience, and humility of the solitaries, we still find ourselves asking of what use was their self-sacrifice? What practical benefit did they bestow upon the rest of mankind?

The answer depends, of course, on one's sense of values and, even more, on one's concept of reality. Reality for the philosopher is one thing, for the scientist another, for the mystic another, and for the 'plain man' something else again. For the plain man it depends on what he calls 'facts' which are actually a set of practical or utilitarian opinions which convention or convenience make acceptable. To such a realist, the lives and examples of the Desert Fathers have no value whatsoever. Their self-sacrifice was merely a waste of opportunity and their innocence a lack of ambition. In short, their lives, however saintly, had no effect on the world outside the desert wastelands they inhabited any more than did those later recluses who followed the mystical road in the convents of Europe during the early Middle Ages.

Yet history itself contradicts this point of view, for what

would have happened to civilisation with the collapse of the Roman *imperium* if it had not been for the descendants of the Desert Fathers, Athanasius, Jerome, Augustine, and Dionysius the Areopagite? What would have happened to society during the Dark Ages if it had not been for the spiritual light shed across Europe by a continuous line of saintly men and women? For that matter, what has happened to civilisation since the passing of William Blake, the last of the European visionaries, who warned us of the 'dark Satanic mills'—industrialisation, commercialism, and economic tyranny?

Like the Victorians, we today in the last decades of the twentieth century seek all kinds of substitutes for the lost vision. The Victorians had their aesthetics, their poetry, their oratorios, spiritualism, and table-rapping. We have even more bizarre remedies for our spiritual malaise. Perhaps that is because we feel that we have nothing in common with our fellow-men of the fourth and fifth centuries—certainly not their passionate conviction that a man could only save his life by losing it. But we certainly have wars, tyrannies, injustice, cruelty, and despair in common with them. It is interesting, therefore, to see what the braver and nobler spirits among them did about it. As we have seen, they withdrew to a far country to create a new society based on mercy, pity, truth, and love—the Christian commonwealth which spread across the civilised world, lasted for 1,000 years, and was finally destroyed by the triumph of materialism.

To see the birthplace of this experiment in a theocentric society which put the communal good above personal gain and the love of God above the love of oneself brought me to the Egyptian deserts where Christian mysticism was born. And even though all but a handful of the thousands of hermits and monks who once peopled these places have gone, and even though their names and achievements have been forgotten, I felt that my pilgrimage was worth while as the completion of many years' wandering across the sands of Africa.

REFERENCES

1 *The Cloud of Unknowing*, Chapter 18.

2 *The Book of Visions and Instructions of Blessed Angela of Foligno* (1871), pp. 40–4.

Bibliography

I. HISTORY, GENERAL

ABU DAKN (Abudacnius, Josephus), *The True History of the Jacobites . . . and Their Origin* (1693)

ABU SALIH AL-ARMANI (Edited by A. T. Butler), *The Churches and Monasteries of Egypt* (1895)

ATTWATER, DONALD, *The Christian Churches of the East* (1948)

BAEDEKER, C., *Egypt* (1914)
Lower Egypt (1895)
Upper Egypt (1892)

CAUWENBERGH, P. VAN, *Étude sur les moins d'Égypte depuis Chalcédoine jusqu'à l'invasion arabe* (1914)

CHAULEUR, S., *Histoire des Copts* (1960)

COPPIN, JEAN, *Bouclier de l'Europe, ou la Guerre Sainte* (1686)

DAVIES, NORMAN DE G., *The Rock Tombs of Deir el Gebrawi* (1902)

DIEHL, M. C., *L'Égypte chrétienne jusqu'à la conquête arabe* (1933)

DIONISIUS THE MONK, *Manuel d'iconographie Chrétienne* (1851)

EUSEBIUS, BISHOP OF CAESAREA, *Ecclesiastical History* (Penguin Classics, No. 138)

FARAG, RAFAIL, *Sociological and Moral Studies in the Field of Coptic Monasteries* (1964)

FORSTER, E. M., *Pharos and Pharillon* (1923)

Geographical Survey Report, Topography and Geology of Egypt (1902)

HARDY, E. R., *Christian Egypt: Church and People* (1952)

JULIEN, M., 'À travers les ruines de la Haute-Égypte', *Études*, 1901, vol. lxxxix

KEES, HERMANN, *Ancient Egypt: a Cultural Topography* (1961)

KINGSLEY, CHARLES, *The Hermits* (1891)

LITTLE, TOM, *Modern Egypt* (1967)

LUDWIG, EMIL, *The Nile* (1936)

MACKEAN, W. H., *Christian Monasticism in Egypt* (1920)

MARIETTE, F. A. F., *The Monuments of Upper Egypt* (1877)
Murray's Handbook for Egypt (1907)
RESCH, PETER ANTHONY, *La doctrine ascétique des premiers maîtres égyptiens du quatrième siècle* (1931)
RUFINUS OF AQUILEIA, *Historia Monachorum* (Catholic University of Medieval History. New Series. Vol. 6)
RUSSELL, DOROTHEA, *Mediaeval Cairo and the Monasteries of the Wadi Natrun* (1962)
SCOTT-MONCRIEFF, P. D., *Paganism and Christianity in Egypt* (1913)
WILKINSON, SIR JOHN GARDNER, *Modern Egypt and Thebes* (1843)
WORRELL, W. H., *A Short Account of the Copts* (1945)
WRIGHT, T., *Early Christianity in Arabia* (1855)

2 GEOGRAPHY

ALFORD, C. J., *Ancient and Prospective Gold Mining in Egypt* (Public Works Ministry, Geological Survey Report, Cairo, 1900)
BAGNOLD, R. A., *Libyan Sands* (1935)
BALL, JOHN, *The Kharga Oasis* (1900)
DE COSSON, A., *Mareotis* (1902)
DIODORUS SICULUS, *Works*, vols 7, 8, 9 (1933)
FORBES, JOAN ROSITA, *The Secret of the Sahara* (1921)
HASANAIN, AHMED MUHAMMAD, BEY, *The Lost Oases* (1925)
JARVIS, CLAUD SCUDAMORE, *Desert and Delta* (1938)
Three Deserts (1936)
KING, HARDING, 'The Libyan Desert from Native Information', *The Geographical Journal*, vol 42 (1913)
KING, W. J. H., *Mysteries of the Libyan Desert* (1925)
MEREDITH, D., *Mons Porphyrites* (1950)
Proceedings of the Royal Geographical Society, vol ix (1887)
QUATREMÈRE, ETIENNE MARC, *Memoires géographiques et historique* (1811)
SONNINI DE MANONCOURT, CHARLES, N. S., *Travels in Upper and Lower Egypt* (1800)
Transactions of the Royal Institute of British Archaeology (1887)
WEIGALL, A., *Travels* (1909)

3 SINAI

AMMON OF RAITHU, *The Forty Martyrs of the Sinai Desert* (Horae Semiticae, No. 9, 1912)
BAEDEKER, C., *Palestine and Syria* (1912)

BROOKE, DOROTHY, *Pilgrims Were They All* (1937)
COSMAS INDICOPLEUSTES, *Christian Topography* (Haklyut Society, No. 98)
ECKENSTEIN, LINA, *A History of Sinai* (1921)
ETHERIA, ST., *Pilgrimage* (1919)
GLUEK, N., *Rivers in the Desert: A History of the Negev* (1959)
JARVIS, C. S., *Yesterday and To-day in Sinai* (1931)
LABORDE, L. E. S., *Journey Through Arabia Petrea to Mount Sinai* (1838)
PALMER, E. H., *The Desert of Exodus* (1871)
The Desert of Tih (1881)
PALMER, H. S., *Ancient History: Sinai* (1892)
PETRIE, SIR W. M. F., *Researches in Sinai* (1906)
PROCOPIUS, *Of the Buildings of Justinian* (1887)
ROTHENBERG, BENO, *God's Wilderness: Discoveries in Sinai* (1961)
TISCHENDORF, L. F. C., *Codex Sinaiticus* (Trustees of the British Museum, 1963)
Travels in the East (1847)
WILSON AND PALMER, *Ordnance Survey of Egypt* (1869)
WOOLLEY, SIR C. L. AND LAWRENCE, T. E., *The Wilderness of Zin* (1936)

4 MONASTERIES

ABBOTT, NABIA, *The Monasteries of the Fayyum* (1936)
BRACCIA, EVARISTO, *Dans le desert de Nitrée* (1932)
COTÊT, 'Un grand pélérinage chrétien de l'ancienne Égypte. La ville de St. Menas', *Bessarione*, No. 22 (1907)
CRUM, WALTER EWING, *A Nubian Prince in an Egyptian Monastery* (1932)
EMERY, WALTER B., *Nubian Treasure* (1948)
FEDDER, HENRY ROMILLY, *A Study of the Monastery of St. Antony in the Eastern Desert* (1937)
GRIFFITH, F. L., *Christian Documents from Nubia* (1928)
HYVERNAT, H., 'The Monastic Libraries', *Revue Biblique Trimestuelle*, X, December, 1911
MONNERET DE VILLARD, UGO, *Il monastere de S. Simeone presso Aswan* (1927)
MURRAY, MARGARET ALICE, *St Menas of Alexandria* (1907)
SAWYER, E. H., 'The First Monasteries', *Antiquity* 4, 1930
SIMAIKA, MARCUS H., *A Brief Guide to the Coptic Museum and the*

Christian churches of Cairo (1938)
TUSUN, PRINCE UMAR, *Notes sur le desert Lybique: Cellia et ses couvents* (1935)
WHITE, HUGH G. E., *The Monasteries of the Wadi 'n Natrun* (1923)

5 TRAVELLERS

ANDRÉOSSI, COUNT ANTOINE-FRANÇOIS, *Memoires sur la vallée des lacs de natron et celle du fleuve sans eau* (1800)
BAGNOLD, R. A., *Libyan Sands* (1935)
BAYLE, ST JOHN, *Adventures in the Libyan Desert* (1849)
BEECHEY, F. W. AND H. W., *Proceedings . . . in 1821, 1822* (1828)
BEVAN, SAMUEL, *Sand and Canvas* (1849)
BREYDENBACH, BERNARD VON, *Descriptio Terrae Sanctae* (1486)
BROWN, WILLIAM GEORGE, *Travels in Africa, Egypt, and Syria* (1806)
BRUCE, JAMES, *Travels in Nubia and Abyssinia* (1816)
Travels to discover the source of the Nile (1790)
CURZON, ROBERT, *Monasteries of the Levant* (1916)
Notice of Lord Zouche (1873)
EDMONSTONE, SIR ARCHIBALD, *Journey to Two of the Oases of Upper Egypt* (1822)
EDWARDS, AMELIA BLANDFORD, *A Thousand miles up the Nile* (1877)
ELWOOD, MRS. 'COLONEL', *Narrative of a Journey Overland from England by the Continent of Europe, Egypt, and the Red Sea* (1830)
FALLS, J. C. EWALD, *Three Years in the Libyan Desert* (1913)
FORBES, JOAN ROSITA, *Appointment in the Sun* (1949)
From Red Sea to Blue Nile (1925)
GRANGER, M., *Relation d'un voyage en Égypte* (1773)
HOSKINS, GEORGE A., *Visit to the Great Oasis* (1837)
KENNEY, C. L., *The Gates of the East* (1857)
KINNEAR, JOHN G., *Cairo, Petra, and Damascus in 1839* (1841)
LINANT DE BELLEFONDS, LOUIS M. A., BEY, *Journal d'un voyage à Merué dans les années 1821 et 1822*, Sudanese Antiquities Service, Occasional Papers, No. 4 (1958)
MANDEVILLE, SIR JOHN, *The Voyages and Travels*, Cassell's National Library (new series) vol. 85 (1903)
NIEBUHR, CARSTEN, *Description de l'Arabie* (1792)
NORDEN, FREDERICK LEWIS, *Travels in Egypt and Nubia* (1742)
PACHO, J. R., *Relation d'un Voyage dans la Marmarique* (1827)

POCOCKE, RICHARD, *A Description of the East* (1743–5)
SANKEY, MARJORIE, *Care of Mr. Waghorn* (1949)
SONNINI DE MANCOURT, CHARLES N. S., *Voyage dans la Haute et la Basse Égypte* (1810)
SUCHEM, LUDOPH VON, *De Itinere Terrae Sanctae* (1350)
TATTAM, HENRY, *Journal of a Tour through Egypt, the Peninsula of Sinai, and the Holy Land, 1838, 1839* (1841)
TISCHENDORF, L. F. C., *Travels in the East* (1847)
VILLIERS DU TERRAGE, E. DE, *Journal et souvenirs de l'Expédition en Égypte, 1798–1801* (1899)
WAGHORN, THOMAS, *Particulars of an Overland Journey from London to Bombay* (1836)
WANSLEBEN, JOHANN MICHAEL, *The Present State of Egypt* (1678)
WILLIAMS, R. S. G., *In the Hands of the Senoussi* (1916)

6 MYSTICS AND MYSTICISM

ANSON, P. F., *The Quest for Solitude* (1932)
ATHANASIUS, ST., *The Life of St. Antony* (1950)
BRÉMOND, M. J. F. R. I. H., *Les Pères du Desert* (1930)
CASSIAN, ST., *The Works*. Translated by E. C. S. Gibson (1894)
DELEHAYE, P. H., *Les Saints Stylites* (1923)
The Legend of the Saints (1907)
HODGSON, P. (Editor) *The Cloud of Unknowing* (1958)
HUXLEY, ALDOUS, *Grey Eminence* (1956)
MENZIES, LUCY (Translator). *The Revelations of Mechthild of Magdeburg* (1953)
OMAN, J. C., *The Mystics, Ascetics, and Saints of India* (1903)
ROSAN, LAWRENCE J., *The Philosophy of Proclus* (1949)
UNDERHILL, EVELYN, *Mysticism* (1930)
WADDELL, HELEN, *The Desert Fathers* (1936)
WENSINCK, A. J., *Legends of Eastern Saints* (1913)
WILSON, R. MC., *The Gnostic Problem* (1958)

Index

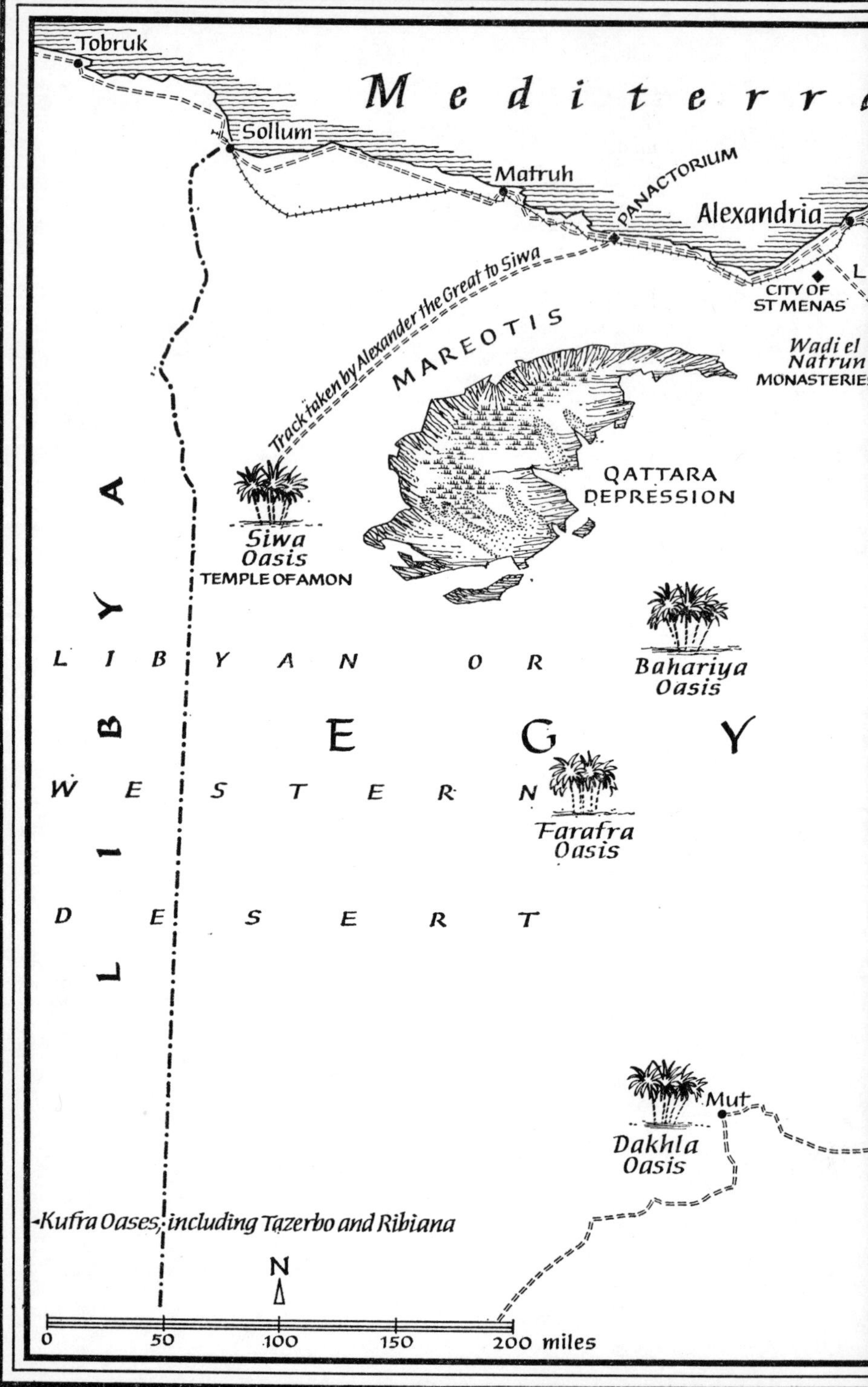
Tobruk
Mediterra
Sollum
Matruh
PANACTORIUM
Alexandria
Track taken by Alexander the Great to Siwa
CITY OF ST MENAS
MAREOTIS
Wadi el Natrun MONASTERIES
QATTARA DEPRESSION
Siwa Oasis
TEMPLE OF AMON
LIBYA
LIBYAN OR
Bahariya Oasis
E G Y
WESTERN
Farafra Oasis
DESERT
Mut
Dakhla Oasis
Kufra Oases, including Tazerbo and Ribiana
N
0 50 100 150 200 miles